Joseph C. Martindale

A History of the Townships of Byberry and Moreland, in

Philadelphia, Pa.

Joseph C. Martindale

A History of the Townships of Byberry and Moreland, in Philadelphia, Pa.

ISBN/EAN: 9783337419417

Printed in Europe, USA, Canada, Australia, Japan

Cover: Foto ©ninafisch / pixelio.de

More available books at **www.hansebooks.com**

A HISTORY

OF THE

TOWNSHIPS

OF

BYBERRY AND MORELAND,

IN

PHILADELPHIA, PA.,

From their Earliest Settlement by the Whites to the Present Time.

BY

JOSEPH C. MARTINDALE, M.D.,

PRINCIPAL OF THE FOREST GRAMMAR SCHOOL, PHILADELPHIA; A MEMBER OF THE
ACADEMY OF NATURAL SCIENCES, PHILADELPHIA: OF THE HISTORICAL
SOCIETY OF PENNSYLVANIA; CORRESPONDING MEMBER
OF THE BUFFALO SOCIETY OF NATURAL HISTORY; AUTHOR OF A HISTORY
OF THE UNITED STATES, ETC.

PHILADELPHIA:

T. ELLWOOD ZELL,

17 & 19 S. SIXTH ST.

1867.

SHERMAN & CO., PRINTERS.

TO MY UNCLE,

WATSON COMLY,

AS A MARK OF RESPECT FOR HIS MANY EXCELLENT

.

QUALITIES OF HEAD AND HEART,

AS WELL AS FOR HIS EARNEST ENDEAVORS TO PRESERVE THE

HISTORY OF HIS NATIVE PLACE,

THIS VOLUME

IS AFFECTIONATELY DEDICATED BY

THE AUTHOR.

1*

PREFACE.

In presenting this History of the townships of Byberry and Moreland to the public, a few words in reference to it will not be out of place here. The late Isaac Comly, of Byberry, was exceedingly fond of local history, and spent a great portion of his time in collecting and arranging all matters of local interest that came to his notice. He kept a regular account of all the more important events which transpired in these and the adjoining townships, from about 1810 to the time of his decease, in 1847. Some years previous to his death, with the material then on hand, he wrote a history of Byberry, which, however, was never published. After his death, the manuscript passed into the hands of his executors, Watson Comly, Charles B. Comly, and Dr. Isaac Comly. It was, however, far from being complete, and after some consultation we concluded to collect such additional matter as could be obtained and have it published. We therefore commenced the work in earnest, and after much labor and not a little trouble, on account of the indifference manifested by many persons, we have so far succeeded as now to be able to present a connected history of these townships from their earliest settlement by the whites to the present time.

In writing this history we have been influenced entirely by a desire to preserve many valuable historical records and interesting reminiscences connected with olden times, and have not "set down aught in malice" to any one.

The work embraces not only a history of the townships but also a sketch of their topography, geology, and mineralogy, a few biographical sketches of prominent individuals who resided in them, and a genealogical account of the Bolton, Carver, Comly, Duffield, Gilbert, Knight, Martindale, Saurman, Thornton, Tomlinson, Walmsley, Shearer, and Worthington families.

I cannot close this, however, without expressing my obligations to Watson Comly and Isaac C. Martindale, both of Byberry, for the interest they have manifested in this history; to the former I am indebted for such information and assistance as could nowhere else have been obtained, and which has added much to the interest of these pages; to the latter, who first engaged in preparing this history, and who has spent much time and labor in hunting up old manuscripts, &c., too much credit cannot be given for the valuable assistance he has thus rendered.

We are well aware that this history is incomplete, and that mistakes in it have undoubtedly been made, but, as it is, we give it to the public, hoping that they may find much pleasure in perusing its records and reminiscences of bygone times.

CONTENTS.

xii   CONTENTS.

THE HISTORY

OF

BYBERRY AND MORELAND.

PART I.

FROM THE EARLIEST SETTLEMENTS TO THE CLOSE OF THE REVOLUTION.

ALTHOUGH North America was discovered by the Cabots in the year 1497, and the whole coast was explored by contemporary navigators, yet the Delaware River was unknown to the civilized world until Henry Hudson, in 1607, made a visit to the coast and revealed its existence. This distinguished navigator spent several months in carefully exploring every bay and inlet along the coast, and was amply rewarded for his toil in the discovery of the two noble streams—the Delaware and the Hudson—between the thirty-sixth and forty-second degrees of north latitude, and the bay which bears his name further to the north. These discoveries made him justly celebrated as a navigator, and will serve as lasting monuments of his glory.

2

The Hudson River was named the North, and the Delaware the South River. The name of the latter, however, was changed to Delaware, in honor of Lord Delaware, who sailed into the bay in the year 1610. At what time the first European entered the river is not now known, but in Rogger-veen's map of New Netherlands, printed at Amsterdam in 1676, the course of the Delaware River, with most of its tributaries, among which is the Poquessing, is delineated with considerable accuracy.

The settlement of Pennsylvania is generally considered as having been commenced in 1681 by William Penn, but the Dutch and Swedes had made settlements on the western bank of the Delaware previous to that time, and had given to the country now embraced in Delaware, Chester, Philadelphia and Bucks Counties, the name of "Upland County." William Penn changed this name to that of Chester soon after his arrival, and some time in the same year, the exact date of which is not known, he divided it into three counties,—Chester, Philadelphia, and Bucks. We find no account of any Swedish settlements having been made in the vicinity of Byberry, but it is quite probable that some such settlements were made, as we find in the list of "overseers for the highways nominated and elected by the Court, March 14th, 1682, for one year next ensuing, which is to be done within their respective precincts before the last day of May 'ut sequitur,' the name of Erick Mullikay, as over-seer for the district extending from Tawrony (Ta-

cony) Creek to Poynessink (Poquessing) Creek."
That there was a settlement made in Byberry previous to the arrival of Penn there can be but little
doubt; and we learn from a communication made
by Benjamin Kite to Roberts Vaux, that the Walton family settled within the limits of Byberry in
the year 1675, seven years before Penn arrived in
America. This family consisted of four brothers,
Nathaniel, Thomas, Daniel, and William, who were
all young and single men. They gave to the place
the name of Byberry, in honor of their native
town, near Bristol, in England. They arrived at
New Castle, from England, early in 1675, provided
with axes, hoes, &c., ready for making a settlement
in the wilderness. From New Castle they proceeded
along the Delaware in search of a place for a settlement, and carried their whole stock of utensils,
provisions, &c., on their backs. After some time
spent in examining the country, they arrived at
the Poquessing Creek, and were so highly pleased
with the level lands in that vicinity, the abundance
of good water, and the beautiful appearance of the
country, that they determined upon making a settlement near the banks of that stream.

Having neither the time nor the means for erecting a dwelling, they dug a cave in the earth and
covered it with bark and dirt, in which they resided for several months, while they proceeded to
prepare the land for their crops. Not having any
wheat with which to sow their lands, two of the
brothers, in the latter part of the same summer,
walked to New Castle to procure a bushel of wheat

for seed; and, shouldering a half a bushel each, they carried it all the way home, a distance of nearly fifty miles. The land, for want of other utensils, was prepared with hoes, and the bushel of wheat sown, from which it is said they reaped sixty bushels at the next harvest. This was probably the first wheat ever raised in the townships.

In 1678 we find there was surveyed to Peter Rambo, Jr., a tract called "Ramsdorp," extending from the Pennypack northeastwardly along the Delaware, and which contained three hundred acres. In the preceding year (1677), warrants were issued to Ephraim Herman, Pelle Rambo, and Captain Hans Moens, for three hundred acres each (making nine hundred acres); and, in 1678, to Ephraim Herman (who, in the following year, relinquished his right to Laers Laersen), for the remainder of the land between the Pennypack and Poquessing Creeks. Poquessing is mentioned by Campanius as an Indian village, in which presided a chief or sachem. Its precise location has been lost, but was probably near the Byberry Creek, not far from Reuben Parry's meadow, as several Indian utensils and implements have been found in that vicinity.

How many had settled in Byberry previous to 1682, is not now known, but in November, 1677, the whole number of taxables north of the Schuylkill, including every male inhabitant of twenty-one years of age, amounted to sixty-five, and these were scattered over the whole country between that river and the Neshaminy Creek. Among

these we find the names of Lansey Bore, Hans
Liken, and Andrew Benksen, probably persons of
some note. Our accounts of these settlements are
indeed meagre, yet there can be no doubt that such
settlements were made, and that they continued
until William Penn, on account of services rendered the crown of England by his father, Admiral
Penn, received the grant of Pennsylvania in letters-
patent from King Charles II, dated the 4th of
March (May), 1681. In this grant the townships
of Byberry and Moreland were included. Penn
did not consider the grant of these lands from the
king a sufficient title ; therefore he purchased them
from the Indians, in whose possession they were at
that time, and they accordingly gave him a release
from their claims. Those having reference to the
tracts of land of which Byberry and Moreland
formed a part were as follows :

We, Essepanaike, Swanpees, Okettarico, and
Wessapoet, this 23d day of 4 month, called June,
in ye year according to ye English account, 1683,
for us and o'r heirs and assigns, do grant and dispose of all our lands lying betwixt Pemmapecka
and Nesheminck Creeks, and all along Nesheminck
Creek, and backward of same, and to run two days
journey with a horse up into ye country as ye said
river doth goe, To William Penn, Propriet'r and
Govern'r of ye Province of Pensilvania, &c., His
Heirs and Assigns for ever, for ye consideration of
so much Wampum, and so many Guns, shoes, stockings, Looking-glasses, Blankets and other goods, as

ye said William Penn shall be pleased to give unto
us, hereby, for us, o'r heirs and assigns, Removing
all claims or Demands of anything in or for ye
Premise for ye future, from him, His heirs and assigns.   In Witness whereof we have hereunto sett
o'r hands and seals, ye day and year first above
written.   Sealed and delivered in presence of

LASSE COCK,   MENANE,
PHILIP TH. LEHNMAN,   HITTOKEN,
PIETER COCK,   RICHARD,
JOS. CURTEIS,   SHOCKHANNO.

The mark of X ESSEPENAIKE,
The mark of X SWANPEES,
The mark of X OKETTARICKOW,
The mark of X WESSAPOAT.

I, Tamanen, 23 day of 4 month, called June in ye
year according to ye English account, 1683, for
me, my heirs and assigns, do grant and dispose of
all my lands lying betwixt Pemmapecka and Neshamincks Creeks, and all along Neshamincks Creek,
to William Penn, Propriet'r and Govern'r of Pensilvania, &c., his heirs and Assigns for Ever, for ye
Consideration of so much Wampum, so many guns,
shoes, stockings, Looking-glasses, Blanketts, and
other goods, as he, ye said William Penn, shall
please to give unto me : and my Parcell being much
smaller than Ossepenaikes and Swanpees, Hereby
for me, my heirs and Assigns, renouncing all claims
or demands, of or in, and for ye future, from Him,
his heirs and Assigns.   In Witness whereof I have

hereunto sett my hand and seal, ye day and year
first above written.

TAMMANENS, X his mark.

Received, moreover, all matchcoats, stockings,
shirts and blankets, besides several guilders in silver, and I acknowledge I have sold all my lands as
above.

LASSE COCK, JOHN BLUNSTON, JOS. CURTEIS.

Indians present.

RICHARD,   SHOCKHUPIO,   MESSAMEQUON.

The mark of X TAMMANENS.

Witness—CRILBERT HILLEELER.

23 of *ye 4 month,* 1683.

We, Tammanen and Metamequan, do hereby
acknowledge to have received of William Penn,
Propriet'r and Govern'r of Pensilvania, &c., these
following goods, being the consideration for our
tract of land Betwixt and about Pemmapecka and
Neshaminck Creeks, and all along Neshaminck
Creek, sold and granted unto ye said William Penn,
Propriet'r and Govern'r, &c., as by a deed dated ye
23 of ye 4 month, in ye year 1683, doth more plain
appear, bearing ye date hereof, with w'h we doe
hereby hold o'selves fully contented and satisfied.

5 p. Stockings, 16 knives, 10 Glasses, 20 fish-
hooks, 20 Barrs Lead, 100 Needles, 5 Capps, 10
Tobacco Tongs, 10 Tobacco Boxes, 15 Combs, 5
Hoes, 10 pr. Sissers, 6 Coats, 2 Guns, 9 Gimbletts,
7 half Gills, 8 Shirts, 2 Kettles, 6 Axes, 2 Blan-

ketts, 4 Handsfull Bells, 12 awles, 5 Hatts, 20
Handsfull of Wampum, 25 lbs. powder, 4 gal.
Strong Water, 38 yds. Duffills, and 1 peck Pipes.

In Witness whereof we have hereunto sett o'r
Hands.

TAMMANEN, X his mark.
METAMEQUAN, X his mark.

Among the settlers who came over in the ship
"Welcome," which left England 8 mo. 30, 1682,
and arrived at New Castle on the Delaware, two
months afterwards, and who settled in Byberry,
were Giles Knight, from Gloucestershire, Mary, his
wife, and their son Joseph, and John Carver, maltster, from Hertfordshire, Mary, his wife, and their
daughter, Mary, who was born near Philadelphia
four days after landing at New Castle. About the
same time John Hart, his wife Susannah, and several children, arrived from Oxfordshire; Richard
Collett, with his wife Elizabeth, and Josiah Ellis,
also arrived, and all located within the present limits of Byberry. Some time during the next year
(1683) John Rush, an elderly Friend from Oxfordshire, arrived with his family, consisting of five
sons and one daughter. One son, William, brought
his wife Aurelia and three children. Soon after
this we find the name of Nicholas Moore mentioned as having taken up a tract of land containing 10,000 acres, and which embraced the manor of
Mooreland, which has since been divided into
Upper and Lower Mooreland. We also find the
names of Thomas Knight, half brother to Giles,

Samuel Ellis, Thomas Groome, Henry English, Joseph English, William Hibbs, Walter Forrest, William Nichols and wife, and John Gilbert, Florence, his wife, and their son Joseph. Most of these settled in Byberry at once; but a few of them settled in the adjacent parts of Bensalem, and afterwards moved over the creek. Their names frequently occur in the records of the Society of Friends previous to 1685. Most of these early settlers took up large tracts of land, which were laid off in the form of parallelograms, from forty to eighty perches wide, and extending in a north-westerly direction from the Poquessing, across Byberry to near the road now the Byberry turnpike. They were subject to innumerable hardships in their attempts to settle the new country, some of them dwelling in caves or excavations* in the earth, which the Indians taught them how to construct: and Giles Knight, it is said, lived about six weeks by the side of an old log, near the present location of Knight's mill-dam, without any shelter except the blue canopy of heaven. The Indians afterwards taught him how to construct a wigwam, which was erected in a meadow now belonging to Jacob Eckfeldt, where he resided several months, and until he built a log house near the location of

---

* These caves were dug in the ground to the depth of about three feet, the roofs were formed of timber, limbs of trees, &c., and were usually covered with sod or bark, and the chimneys were built of stone, mortared with clay, &c. They were damp and gloomy abodes, yet served to protect their inmates from the weather.

the present mansion. The intercourse between the early settlers and the Indians was of the most friendly kind, and they lived together like brothers, assisting each other in times of distress, and each trying to outvie the other in their endeavors to promote the comfort and happiness of all. The Indians seem to have been fully sensible of the honorable motives of the settlers, and to have acted accordingly by welcoming them to the lands they had purchased. They taught our forefathers how to construct their wigwams, build canoes, cultivate corn, beans, pumpkins, and other vegetables; and in return, the colonists paid the Indians for all they obtained, and uniformly treated them with kindness. Game was indeed plenty; but the whites knew not how to capture it; and the streams abounded with the most excellent fish, which required only the trouble of catching. The food of the settlers was plain; and often the only dish they could offer was fish and pumpkins—a dish which would not be very palatable to the people of this epicurean age.

At certain seasons, however, provisions were plenty. Wild pigeons were in such great abundance that they could be knocked down with poles; and as the settlers became more accustomed to hunting, they procured plenty of wild turkeys, some of which weighed from thirty-five to forty pounds, and sold as low as one shilling each. Deer were killed in such numbers that they were sold for 2s. apiece.

With all these natural surroundings, it is not

surprising that such a beautiful place as the banks
of the romantic Poquessing should have been selected for a settlement—

"Where homes of humble form and structure rude,
  Raised sweet society in Nature's solitude."

Although the rude cabin of the white settler dotted
the course of the streams, and the land was gradually being reclaimed from its uncultivated state,
yet the wild animals of the forest still lingered
around the settlements, and the fox's bark, the panther's cry, or wolf's lugubrious howl, often broke
the stillness of the night, and Nature reigned here
in all her pristine grandeur. In the magnificent
beauties of these surrounding solitudes, doubtless,
our forefathers saw much to draw them still closer
to the Author of their own existences, and make
them feel their utter dependence upon His protect-
ing arm.

In those early times the settlers labored under
all the inconveniences of an unsettled country.
They had no flour-mills to grind their corn or
wheat, but had to pound it in wooden or stone mor-
tars, after the manner of the aborigines. They at
first dwelt in damp and gloomy caves, but these
were soon given up for the greater comforts of rude
cabins; and these, again, were in time replaced by
log-houses covered with bark or thatched with
straw, and which made very comfortable dwellings, yet would contrast strangely with the edifices
of modern times.

The men were at first dressed in the skins of the

wild animals; but in a short time the women, who
were noted for their industry, by means of spin-
ning and weaving, furnished them with garments
more in accordance with their tastes. Cattle were
soon introduced, and mush and milk became a favorite dish. To this was added honey from the
wild bees, and molasses and sugar from the sugar
maple trees. Horses were introduced soon after
the settlement, and the comforts and conveniences
of civilized life were thus one by one added to their
wilderness homes.

In those early days, however, women were by
no means numerous, and many of our forefathers
had, for years after they first arrived, to do without "heaven's last, best gift"—a lovely wife, to be
the partner of all their toils, to comfort them in
their desolate homes, to prepare for them their
humble fare, and welcome them with untold affection to their rude domestic hearths. The sufferings and hardships attendant upon the settlement
of a new country were too great for her delicate
constitution; and the absence of all the domestic
comforts, as found in her British home, effectually
precluded her leaving her kindred for this bleak
clime; but as the country became more settled,
and comfort after comfort was added to the condition of those early settlers, she tore herself from
kindred and loving friends, braved the storms of
the billowy deep, and took up her residence in the
wilds of Pennsylvania. Oh, how joyfully must she
have been welcomed by those hardy sons of toil,
the early pioneers!

During the scarcity of females, few were left unmarried, and it was indeed rare to find one still
single who had attained to the age of twenty years.
Those that were here must have been happy, although deprived of so many comforts, for "wives
were then never jealous of their husbands," and
all dwelt together in the greatest harmony. The
children were generally healthy; the active life
which they led, and the plainness of their fare,
made their cheeks glow with the roseate hue of
health, and their frames became as strong and
robust as those of their neighbors and companions, the hardy sons of the forest. Then nearly
every cabin was filled with a lusty race of those
who were soon to reclaim the uncultivated soil,
convert it into fine fertile farms, and help to rear
a settlement, where the persecuted of every clime
might find a happy refuge, and where all might
dwell together in unity and peace.

The Indians welcomed the early settlers of Byberry, and were ever ready and willing to lend
their white neighbors a helping hand when in distress. On one occasion, John Carver made a journey to Chester, and left his family with provisions
which he thought sufficient to last them during
his absence; but, from some unforeseen circumstances, he was detained longer than was expected,
and his wife, with their two children, was reduced
to great distress for want of food. Under these
circumstances she applied to a party of neighboring Indians for assistance. They treated her with
much kindness, furnished her with some provisions

to relieve her immediate wants, and, taking off the
little boys' trowsers, tied up the legs and filled
them with corn, to be carried home for a further
supply. At another time, Giles Knight and Josiah
Ellis went among them to procure some beans and
other vegetables; these were kindly furnished,
along with instructions for cultivating them. For
these many acts of kindness they neither asked
nor received any recompense; they were satisfied
with having relieved the wants of their friends,
and their reward was the sweet consolation of
having performed a charitable act. Many other
things, equally honorable to the Indian character,
might be narrated, for the friendly intercourse between the whites and their red neighbors was
never so far broken as to cause one act of violence
to be committed by either party, until after the
peaceful principles of the early settlers were forgotten.

Before the first settlers left England, Penn had
decided upon founding a city on the banks of the
noble Delaware. Accordingly, soon after their
arrival, the commissioners went on a tour up that
beautiful stream in order to fix upon the site for
the future city. Several places seem to have attracted their attention, and, among others, that
in the southern part of Byberry, at the mouth
of the Poquessing.* They were much pleased
with the bold shore at this spot, and had nearly

* The land along the Poquessing clear to the river, is believed to
have been included in Byberry at the time of the first settlement.

concluded to found here the city of Brotherly
Love, when, having in their minds the future
greatness of the city they were about to found,
they wisely concluded that a greater depth of
water in the channel was advisable, so as to admit
the passage of larger ships, and this alone determined them to fix it where it now stands.

At the time of the first settlement, the townships of Byberry and Moreland were noted hunting grounds of the Indians; and in order to facili-
tate securing the game, they were in the habit of
setting fire to the rank grass that grew indigen-
ously in all parts of the townships, and thus destroyed all the young timber. We find, as proof
of this, that at the time of the first settlement
there were but few large trees, scarcely enough to
furnish firewood for the settlers, and that the division lines between the tracts were made by means
of embankments and ditches—some of which are
still visible. Some portions in the southern part
were under cultivation by the Indians, but the
northern parts of Byberry and the whole of Moreland, were covered with the tall grass. The settlers did not burn this off, as the Indians had done,
and in a few years the whole surface, except where
cultivated, was covered with a growth of fine timber. Two large trees are mentioned as having
stood, one on the lower end of the place now belonging to Watson Comly, and the other about
Samuel Smedley's, and these served as way-marks
for the people. It is said that Joseph Knight,
who was brought from England in 1682, at the age

of two years, was afterwards frequently sent, while a boy, in search of the cows, which, for want of fences, often strayed away, and that when he lost his way he would ascend some eminence and look out for these two trees, which served as guides to direct him home again.

The first houses were generally erected near springs or running streams, to save the expense and trouble of digging wells. We find no account of the latter having been dug for several years after the first settlement, and when first introduced they occasioned much conversation among the settlers.

Penn, in his conditions for the settlement of Pennsylvania, said that those who bought shares in the province could have five thousand acres for £100 sterling, but would be annually subject to a quit-rent of one shilling sterling, for each one hundred acres—the quit-rent not to begin until 1684. On this account the land of the whole country became subject to a quit-rent, which was to be paid to the Proprietor, or his legal heirs, and which continued to be paid until 1775, when the Commonwealth of Pennsylvania purchased the claims for 580,000 dollars, and all quit-rents ceased.

[1682.] During this year provisions were scarce in the colony, and the best dish that could be set before visitors was fish and pumpkins,—a dish to most of us rather unpalatable. In the summer a good supply of horses, cows, sheep, and hogs arrived from England, which were soon followed by others, so that in a few years enough had arrived to stock all the farms and furnish food for the colonists.

As we have already seen, a number of persons arrived during this year and settled in Byberry, the land there having been taken up in small tracts of from one hundred to five hundred acres each. In the manor of Moreland the plan was different, for the whole of it was taken up by Nicholas Moore,* a prominent attorney of London, and being held by him until his death in 1689, we find no mention of any other persons settling in that township previous to that time. Moore was president of a company called "The Free Society of Traders in Pennsylvania," the object of which was "to purchase lands to make an agricultural settlement, to establish manufactures, and carry on the lumber trade, and whale fisheries." He came over with Penn, in 1682, and was chairman or speaker of the first Provisional Assembly, held at Chester, on the 4th of December of that year. He was a man of superior abilities; and from having the confidence of William Penn, who placed him in the most responsible positions in the colony, his name is identified with much of our early history, and will be remembered while Moreland, with its fine fertile fields and happy people, continues to exist.

[1683.] Nearly all the early settlers of Byberry

---

* William Penn, on the 7th of Sixth month, 1684, conveyed to Nicholas Moore a tract of land in Philadelphia, containing ten thousand acres. This embraced what is now Moreland in Philadelphia and Montgomery Counties.

were members of the Society of Friends; and one
of their first objects, after settling, was to have a
place where they could meet together in love and
unity, and worship the God of their fathers in spirit
and in truth.   Tradition says that Friends built a
log meeting-house on the flat lands belonging to
John Hart, near the present residence of Wilmer
Canelle, about one hundred yards northward from
the junction of Poquessing and Byberry Creeks,
in the southern part of the township.   It stood on
the west side of the road now leading to the Red
Lion.   It is said that a lot adjoining the meeting-
house was fenced off during this year, to be used
as a burying ground by Friends, but every vestige
of both has long since passed away.   Previous to
this two of Giles Knight's children died, and were
buried on his own land near the Poquessing Creek,
not far from the present location of Knight's mill-
dam.

    In the Fifth month of this year, at a Quarterly
Meeting of Friends in Philadelphia, "It was then
and there agreed and concluded that there be established a First-day meeting of Friends at Took-
any and Poetquessink, and that these two make
one Monthly Meeting, men and women, for ye or-
dering of ye affairs of ye church."   The Monthly
Meeting was accordingly held alternately at the
house of Sarah Seary, at Oxford, and at John
Hart's house, on the Poquessing.   Soon after this
meeting commenced, a lot of about one acre, a few
yards northward of Hart's house, on the rising
ground, was set apart as a place of interment for

Friends and others.* This was used as a burying place for all the settlers until the separation, after which it was used only by the followers of Keith. Among those buried in this ancient cemetery were Aurelia, wife of William Rush, in 1683; Thomas Young, 1684; Mary Borman, 1685; Joseph English, 1686; Christopher Growden, Bensalem, 1687; and William Rush, 1688.

[1684.] One of the first papers issued by Byberry Monthly Meeting, on the Poquessing, was a marriage certificate granted to James Morris and Elizabeth Buzby, who formerly belonged to Byberry, but who had lately removed to the Falls of Delaware. It is preserved for its antiquity, and is as follows:

To Friends of ye Monthly Meeting about ye Falls of Delaware, in ye County of Bucks:

Whereas, James Morris and Elizabeth Buzby, who formerly belonged to our meeting, did, in the Seventh month, appear at our monthly meeting and declare their intentions of marriage, and they did produce certificates and testimony sufficient to satisfy us of their clearness; and after deliberation

---

* John Hart, grandson of the ancient John Hart, in 1786, bequeathed this ancient cemetery to the township of Byberry in the following words: "I give and devise to the overseers of the poor in the township of Byberry, in the county of Philadelphia, who shall be such at the time of my decease, and to their successors, forever, a certain burying ground lot of one acre of land, which was conveyed to me by my late grandfather, deceased, the same to be occupied as a burying ground forever."

and inquiry, we did permit them to proceed to accomplish their marriage. But so yt they have been
from us absent, we are informed yt they belong to
your meeting, and now they desire a certificate
from us.

These are to certify that thus far they have proceeded, and we have not anything against ym to
obstruct ym to your meeting, in order to ye accom-
plishing their marriage, and we remain your
Friends and Brethren.

At our Monthly Meeting at John Hart's house,
Poetquessink creek, in ye county of Philadelphia,
ye 2d of ye 4th mo., 1684.

JOHN CARVER,	SAM'L HART,
RICHARD TOWNSEND,	JOSEPH ENGLISH,
HENRY WADDY,	ANN TOWNSEND,
THO. KITCHEN,	GILES KNIGHT,
RICH'D DUNGWORTH,	WILL'M PRESTON,
WALTER FORREST,	SAM'L ELLIS,
JOHN HART,	ANN SESSIONS,

DOROTHY DUNGWORTH.

The early Friends seem to have felt their iso-
lated condition, living, as they did, in the wilds of
Pennsylvania, with but few persons near enough
to be called neighbors, and to have been fully sensible of their dependence upon each other, which
acted like a chain to bind them more firmly together in the pure bonds of love. When a mis-
fortune befell one of their neighbors, all were ready
with their services or their means to relieve their
wants, or with them shed the sympathetic tear.

The records of the meeting show the benevolence of those early settlers, whom, although living a life of penury and toil themselves, we find entering into an agreement to pay four shillings per week for the support of William Nichols, " on account of his penury."

[1685.] It would seem that some were desirous of having a larger lot of ground for a cemetery than the one at John Hart's, for in this year a minute of the Monthly Meeting, dated 5th mo. 28th, says: " Friends did freely accept of ten acres of land given by Walter Forrest, for a burying place for the service of Friends, near Poetquessink creek, and it is left to the trust and care of Joseph Fisher, John Hart, Samuel Ellis and Giles Knight, to get the ground conveyed, the deed of conveyance to be made from Walter Forrest to themselves, for the only use and behoof of Friends forever, and that from henceforth it shall be made use of for the service aforesaid." As no further mention of this donation has been found, it is doubtful whether it was ever applied to the purpose intended, and its location cannot now with certainty be known. It is, however, probable that it was on the Poquessing, not far from Thomas's mill, which was at that time owned by Forrest. In his last will and testament, dated 1st mo. 18th, 1691-2, Forrest bequeathed a mill and lands situated in the township of Byberry, one-half to his wife, and the other half to three persons named Albertson, but in it we find no mention made of the ten acres.

Although the Monthly Meeting of Friends at

Byberry had been held at John Hart's since 1683,
yet the weekly meetings for worship continued to
be held at the house of Giles Knight, until the 4th
month of this year, when the Monthly Meeting
ordered it to be removed to the house of John
Hart. No reason is assigned for this change; and
as the location was not by any means so central as
when held at Knight's, it is probable that it was
through the influence of Hart, who was then the
leading Friend in Byberry. It, however, shows
that Friends would then rather suffer inconveni-
ence, than disturb the peace and harmony of the
Society.

Some time during the summer of this year,
Nicholas Moore commenced the erection of a mansion in the manor of Moreland, at a place he called
Green Spring, about half a mile west of the present
village of Somerton. This mansion is said to have
been far superior to those in the surrounding country, and to have been built in correspondence with
his official dignity as speaker of the first Assembly
of Pennsylvania. The house was near a spring of
excellent water, which, as it trickled away, kept
the grass green along its banks, hence the origin
of its name. It was the first house erected within
the present limits of Moreland. One account says,
"While he was Chief Justice, he erected a court-
house and jail near his residence at Green Spring,
where those who disregarded the laws were tried,
and the guilty culprits punished; but owing to the
general good morals of the inhabitants the jail
seldom had any inmates."

[1686.] After the meetings for public worship were removed to John Hart's house, the distance proved too great for many Friends living in the northern parts of the township, and, in order to accommodate them, it was decreed that a meeting be held once a month, on First days, at the house of Henry English,* so that two meetings for worship were, for a time, held in Byberry. The localities of these meetings appear to have been unsatisfactory, and frequent changes were the result. In this year, at a Quarterly Meeting of Friends, it was agreed that a Monthly Meeting should be held at Byberry, Oxford and Cheltenham, "in course," the last week in each month, and on the days of the respective weekly meetings, that at Byberry coming on Fourth day. The time and place for this meeting were not satisfactory, and it was agreed, during the First month of the next year, [1687.] to hold the monthly meetings at the house of Richard Worrel, Jr., and the time of meeting was changed to the last Second day of each and every month, to which place it was accordingly soon after removed.

From this time until 1691 the accounts preserved are very meagre. A few new settlers arrived from England, and the condition of those who were already here was gradually improving. There appears to have been a reciprocal exercise of friendly feelings and good understanding among them, and

* This house is thought to have stood near a spring of water on lands now owned by Silas Vanarsdalen.

through the blessings of Divine Providence upon
their industry and prudent management, their
temporal affairs were daily improving, and cheer-
ing prospects of untold wealth were opening
around them. The young men who came over in a
state of single blessedness had taken to themselves
affectionate partners, and settled on the fine lands
in the township, and large families of loving children were growing up around them, so that but
little was wanted to fill up their measure of happiness, and make their condition as desirable as
could reasonably be expected to fall to the lot of
mortals; but earthly enjoyments, like all other
earthly things, must find an end, and we learn that
difficulties and dissensions began to spring up in
the colony, and, by the year 1691, had increased to
such an extent as to involve nearly the whole of
the inhabitants in a bitter discussion of religious
principles. This was not confined to Byberry, but
spread all over Pennsylvania, and involved the
Society of Friends in much trouble. These dissensions appear to have originated through the
agency of George Keith, who then resided in
[1691.] Philadelphia. He had been an eminent
minister and writer, and being a man of
extensive learning, had gained many followers. He
desired to make some radical changes in the discipline and the doctrines held by the Society, which
they were not willing to adopt. He was, therefore, warned of his conduct by some Friends,
which was not well received, and he finally withdrew from the Society. After this, a declaration

was issued by his supporters in his favor, who then
proceeded to disown those who testified against
him. Such was the influence exerted, that they
gained the ascendency in sixteen out of thirty-two
meetings. In Byberry, the leading advocate of
Keith and his doctrines was John Hart, who owned
a tract of land containing four hundred and eighty-
four acres in the southern part of Byberry, and was
in respectable circumstances. He had been several
times elected a member of the Assembly, and is
described as having been a man of rank, character, and reputation, and to have been an eminent
preacher. He early embraced the views held by
Keith, and from his influence and connections, drew
the Rushes, Colletts, and the most of those living
in the southern part of Byberry to his support.
The burial ground was on his farm, and the house
for worship near his residence, so that, on account
of these difficulties, Friends were induced to withdraw from the Meeting, and afterwards assembled
at the house of Henry English.

Those who remained at the old meeting were
John Hart, John Rush, Nathaniel Walton, and
Richard Collett, with their families, and some
others by the name of Johnson, Jackson, and Fos-
ter. Those who seceded are mentioned as Giles
Knight, John Carver, Daniel Walton, Thomas
Walton, William Walton, Henry English, Thomas
Knight, John Gilbert, William Hibbs, John Brock,
Thomas Groome, and others.

The Keithian meeting appears to have been unsuccessful, and after two or three years it was

broken up—the adherents joining other religious persuasions. Some became Episcopalians, and assisted in founding a church called "All Saints'," in Lower Dublin; while others, becoming Baptists, but retaining the dress and language of the Quakers, were called Quaker Baptists. Some of these again changed into Seventh-day Baptists, and were the originators of that sect.

Notwithstanding the long term of controversy and discord through which the infant Meeting had just passed, it still continued to survive, and soon outgrew all its troubles. As Friends had seen fit to withdraw from Hart's meeting, they did not feel willing to bury their deceased Friends in the cemetery on his farm; therefore, we find that Henry English, one of the most prominent members remaining with the Society, did, on the 2d of the 1st month, give one acre of land to John Carver and Daniel Walton, in trust for Friends.

[1694.] The deed specifies that " the said one acre is for the use of the people of God, called Quakers, who are and shall be and continue in unity and religious fellowship with Friends of Truth, and shall belong to the Monthly Meeting of said people, for whose use the said piece of ground is intended to be employed as a burying-place, and to no other use or service whatsoever; provided always, that it is the true intent and meaning of the parties hereunto, that no person or persons who shall be declared by the members of the Monthly or Quarterly Meeting, whereunto he or she shall belong, to be out of unity with

them, shall have any right or interest in said piece
of ground hereby granted, while he or she shall
remain out of unity and church fellowship with
those people to whom he or they did so belong."
It seems quite singular that this instrument should
confine the use of said piece of land to a "burying-
place," as a meeting-house was badly needed at
that time; and shortly afterward, with the full
consent of the donor, a meeting-house was erected
thereon. It was built of logs, ridged and notched
at the corners, chinked with mud, and according
to the custom of the times, covered with bark.
It stood in the northern corner of the present site
of the old graveyard, and was the origin of the
present Friends' Meeting. Here, in this humble
structure, scarcely sufficient to shield its inmates
from the weather, did our forefathers meet to manifest their devotion and gratitude to a bountiful
Providence for the many favors which they were
daily receiving. It was a rude structure, but served
as the only place for worship during the next
twenty years.

The most noted members of the Meeting at this
time were John Duncan, John Brock, William
Beale, Thomas Scott, and Abel Hingstone, in Byberry or adjoining part of Bensalem. About the
same time, we find the name of Thomas Groome,
as having settled near Somerton; and the names
of John Cross, John Tibby, John Hybert, Nicholas
Williams, Nicholas Tucker, Nathan Watamore, and
William Carver, as residents of the township.

[1695.] The Meeting seems to have been on a

firmer basis than at any previous time, and the
members were much concerned, not only for the
welfare of each other, but that the youth might be
preserved in the Truth. The Yearly Meeting, held
at Burlington, N. J., in 1694, recommended that
four Friends be appointed to have charge of the
youth belonging to the Society, and in 2d mo. of
this year, John Carver, of Byberry, was appointed
one of the four for that purpose. It appears that
some Friends in those days did not observe the
golden rule, and the Meeting, feeling the necessity
of having a closer observance of the principles and
customs of the Society, appointed in the 12th mo.,
John Carver and John Brock, "to admonish those
that profess God's truth and do not walk answer-
ably thereto." This was the origin of the appoint-
ment of overseers* in Byberry Meeting, a custom
continued to the present time. The great concern
of Friends seems to have been "to watch over each
other for good, and to build each other up in that
most holy faith which works by love to the purify-
ing of the heart."

In the early part of this year some of the Gilberts settled in Byberry. In the 4th mo., 1685,
Thomas Holmes, the surveyor-general, obtained a
patent for six hundred acres of land in Byberry,

---

* Those appointed to act in this capacity from this time to 1740,
were John Brock, Abel Hingstone, William Beale, Thomas Groome,
John Carver, Everard Bolton, John Duncan, Henry Comly, John
Carver, 2d, Thomas Knight, son of Giles, Edmond Dunkin, Thomas
Walton, William Dunkin, George James, Jonathan Knight, Joseph
Gilbert, and Evan Thomas.

bounded on the east by the Poquessing, and in the same year sold it to Nicholas Rideout. On the 19th of 12th mo., 1695, John Gilbert purchased the said tract of land of Rideout, and having sold about one-half of it to John Carver, divided the remainder between his two sons, Samuel and Joseph, who settled on it. These were the first of that name we have met with residing in Byberry.

Affairs in Moreland began to assume a different aspect about this time. Nicholas Moore, who had been in delicate health almost from his arrival in America, died at his mansion, in Moreland, in 1689. During his life he retained possession of all his property, but it was much incumbered at the time of his decease. His creditors, among whom was John Holmes, on 23d of April, 1695, presented a petition to Council to have the accounts of the said Nicholas Moore examined, when it was found that the estate was indebted to different individuals to the sum of upwards of £270 sterling. The Council, therefore, empowered John Holmes to sell the plantation and manor house at Green Spring, and such lands and improvements in other parts of Moreland as might be sufficient to pay all his just debts, educate his surviving children, and provide for the improvement of the remainder of the estate. Soon after this, in the same year, the mansion house, together with six hundred acres of land, was accordingly sold at public sale. It was purchased by Henry Comly, of Middletown, Bucks County, who, in 1704, erected a mansion thereon, which is yet standing, and is the oldest house* in Moreland. In the year 1701 or '2, portions of this estate were sold in lots to suit purchasers, and the population soon began to increase. No account of these sales has been met with.

[1701.] It was agreed in the Monthly Meeting, "that a Preparative Meeting be established at Byberry, to be held on the weekly meeting day that happeneth next before the Monthly Meeting, and that those Friends that are appointed as overseers to attend that service." This was the origin of the Preparative Meeting at Byberry, and it commenced soon afterwards, although no records of its proceedings have been found previous to 1721.

In the fore part of the eighteenth century, the children of the early settlers were entering upon the stage of active life. They were noted for their strength, activity, and vigor; and had been brought up accustomed to many hardships, and inured to a life of toil. They were expert at hunting wild turkeys, bears, and raccoons, and many of them had acquired considerable reputation in that business. They could use the axe, the grubbing-hoe, the spade, and the sickle, and prided themselves in so doing. Then all the grain was reaped with

---

* This house has, at different times since, had additions and alterations made to it, which have entirely changed its appearance. It has remained in the possession, and been the residence of descendants of the family of that name ever since, until the death of the late occupant, Franklin Comly, Esq., in 1860, when it passed into the hands of his son-in-law, Moses Knight.

sickles, and there was frequently some strife among them as to who was the best reaper. In all trials of this kind Joseph Gilbert is said to have carried off the palm, and was acknowledged the best reaper in the whole country. Upon one occasion a man came from New Jersey to try him, but yielded the contest long before night. The women, also, frequently engaged in outdoor work, and some of them were excellent hands. In those days the grain was generally stacked and all the threshing was done with flails. But few barns were then to be found, and these few were made of logs, and thatched with straw. They were generally small, without any floors, and sufficed only for a shelter for some of the stock. Wagons had not yet been introduced, and sleds were used for hauling grain to the stacks and barns. When it was threshed and ready for market, if the ground was not covered with snow, it was carried on the backs of horses to the mills on the Pennypack or Poquessing Creeks. This was the custom until the introduction of carts, several years afterwards. The harness was all of home manufacture, the collars being made of straw or calamus tops, and the traces and lines of hemp or flax.

Some thirty-five or forty years had already passed away, and the land so destitute of timber, at first, was now covered with a growth of thrifty chestnut, oak, hickory, maple, ash, &c. As timber became more plenty, the settlers began to divide their farms by means of fences instead of ditches. Many of the young men became expert at chop-

ping wood and splitting rails; and it is said, on
one occasion, that Job Walton split three thousand
six hundred rails in one week, the logs being cut
off for him. This was a large week's work, and
few of our rail-splitters of this day can beat it.
Fencing, however, was not universal at that time,
and some preferred to dig ditches and plant privet
(Ligustrum vulgare) hedges, in order to inclose
their farms. These hedges answered the purpose
very well, and presented an effectual barrier
against the encroachments of cattle and wild
beasts. They gave the farms a pleasing appearance, particularly when in blossom; and when the
berries were ripe they afforded food for multitudes
of wild pigeons, thousands of which were killed
by the settlers. It is said these hedges from some
unknown cause, nearly all died a few years previous to the Revolution, and have never been in
general use since.

We have met with no accounts of any schools
previous to 1710. The children of the first settlers were brought up with a very limited chance
of obtaining an education, and many of them were
unable to read or even to write their own names.
In this year it appears that Richard Brockdon
[1710.] commenced a school at Byberry, but did
not continue there more than a year, as
the Meeting records, in 1711, mention the application of Richard Brockdon, late schoolmaster at
Byberry, for a certificate to return to England.
He was succeeded by William Davis, who remained until 1717, and then removed to New Jer-

sey. After this we find mention of John Wat-
more, Roger Bragg, John Pear, and Walter Moore,
as teachers in Byberry previous to 1753. The
school was poorly conducted, and a want of interest in the great cause of education, in those having charge of the schools, seems to have been
the great fault.

[1712.] Some time during this year, Giles Knight
erected a bolting mill on the small stream of water
passing through his meadow, lately owned by
Nancy Walton. No flour was made at this mill,
but the people took their grain to Pennepack or
Poquessing mills, and, when it was ground, hauled
it to Giles Knight's to have it bolted.

About this time we find among the early settlers of Moreland the name of William Roberts,
Albertson Walton, William Tillyer, Henry Comly,
Nicholas Moore, Jr., John Blackford, Joseph Mitchell, Jonathan Comly, Richard Marple, and Der-
rick Krewson.

[1714.] The old log meeting-house in Byberry,
being no longer tenable, in this year a new house
was erected on the acre given by English. It was
a few feet to the east of the old one, was built of
stone, thirty-five by fifty feet, two stories high,
with arched ceilings, and double doors in front. It
had large windows, with small lights of glass set
in a leaden sash attached to a wooden frame, which
was hung on hinges so as to open and close, and
was without shutters. The gable ends of this
house were not carried to a point, but from about
midway of the rafters, another roof from each

end was carried up to meet the main one. This
was the style of building at that early day. The
plan for warming this building was not by any
means as complete as that now in use, for it is
stated that the only means devised for warming it
was by a fireplace in the west end, on the outside
of the building and communicating with an artifi-
cial stove, formed of cast iron plates, through
which the heat was communicated to the room.
The men warmed themselves before going in, and
the women occupied the end next to the fire. In
order to complete this house, Friends borrowed
£50 of James Cooper, which was paid off by sub-
scription, in 1723.

[1720.] About this time such things as fortune-
telling, astrology, &c., were in considerable repute,
and many of the settlers, even the most respectable, frequently resorted to them. Most Friends
seem to have been in advance of the age in which
they lived, for they not only bore testimony against
these things as great evils, but dealt with some of
their members for "meddling in predicting by astrology," &c. During this age of superstition many
Friends were awakened to a just sense of the value
and importance of properly educating their youth,
and the Meeting was soon impressed with the necessity of erecting a suitable building for school
purposes. Accordingly, in this year, we find a
school-house was erected near the meeting-house.
It was a log building about eighteen feet square.
Here in this humble structure many of our early
ancestors were educated; and it is probable that

the opportunities for acquiring an education were much better after the erection of the building than they had been before, as those who were educated about this time were generally spoken of as possessing considerable literary qualifications, and their autographs, as found in some of the old papers, certainly would not suffer any disparagement if compared with many of the present day. No further account of this school-house has been found. Some time previous to this a few houses had been built near each other in the eastern part of Moreland; and as the place began to assume more the appearance of a village, it was called Smithfield, the name of which has since been discarded for that of Somerton. About this time it contained ten buildings, among which were a store, a tavern, and a blacksmith shop, about half of which was situated in Byberry. This is the first account we have found of this village, and the time of its foundation cannot now with any certainty be known.

The houses, and indeed all the buildings erected by the settlers previous to this time, were with but few exceptions formed of logs. They were rudely constructed tenements, being scarcely sufficient to shield their inmates from the rigors of the climate; but in them our forefathers dwelt in peace and contentment, and seemed to enjoy life quite as much as most of us in this more progressive age. The houses were but one story high, with hipped roofs; and the room used for cooking contained a large fireplace, in which a fine blazing fire was kept during the cold weather of winter.

In these large quantities of wood were consumed, often as much as ten to fifteen cords in one season, but as timber was plenty, and required only the trouble of cutting, but little economy was exhibited in its use. These fireplaces were large enough to allow a person to sit on each side of the blazing fire, and those favored spots were generally occupied by the heads of the family, while the children hovered around in front in order to keep warm.

Farming was carried on in a rude and slovenly manner; the implements were but poorly suited to their designed uses, and much of the fertility of the soil had been exhausted by continued farming, no pains being taken to make or apply manure so as to produce better crops. The dress of both male and female was of homespun, which was manufactured by the "busy housewife" of that day. During the summer it was customary for all classes to go barefoot, except on First days, when going to meeting; the shoes, however, were taken off as soon as they arrived at home, and put away for a similar occasion. In going to market the men seldom wore shoes, and even the women did not think it necessary to hide their feet and ankles, and were not troubled with such scandal as would be showered upon them for so doing at the present day.

Game had annually been growing more scarce; and most of the wild animals, such as deer, wild turkeys, panthers, and wolves, had become scarce. Previous to this time (1720) the latter animals had been troublesome to the settlers by destroying their sheep and hogs, so that they had to be carefully secured in strong pens every night, or in the morning some would surely be missing.

Smaller animals, such as wild-cats, foxes, raccoons, &c., were still plenty, and the flocks of poultry often suffered from their depredations. Squirrels, partridges, pheasants, &c., were very abundant, notwithstanding the severity of the winters, and thousands of them were annually killed to furnish food for the settlers. Deer and bears were sometimes killed and furnished food for the family of the fortunate hunter, but at this time such things were not common.

[1721.] The earliest records of the Byberry Preparative Meeting, which have escaped the destructive hand of time, bear the date of 2d month 18th. These are made up almost entirely of the pecuniary matters of the Society, being accounts of subscriptions for raising money for the necessary expenses of the Meeting, and for maintaining the poor. The charge for tending the meeting-house was only twenty shillings per annum, and this continued to be the price paid for several years thereafter. John Carver is mentioned as the clerk at that time. He appears to have given good satisfaction, as he was continued until 1740, when he requested the Meeting to appoint some one in his place. About this time African slavery was first introduced into Byberry by the more opulent settlers, as help for the rougher parts of the work indoors and out. They were mostly brought directly from Africa to Philadelphia, but some were brought from Long Island. In 1727, in an inventory of the property of a de-

5

ceased Friend, the following items occur: "One
negro girl, £20; one negro boy, £30;" and again,
in 1743, are these: "A negro woman, Phillis, £20;
and one negro boy, Wallis, £14." These give us
an idea of the value of slaves at that time.

The following list of names are found in the records of 1721, as subscribers for maintaining the
poor belonging to Byberry Preparative Meeting:

JOHN DONKON,	THOS. WALTON,
JOSEPH GILBERT,	GILES KNIGHT,
WM. CARVER,	EDM'D DONKON,
GEORGE JAMES,	ABEL HINGSTONE,
THOMAS KNIGHT,	THOMAS WALTON,
JOHN CARVER,	SAM. SCOTT,
THOS. KNIGHT, JR.,	JONATHAN KNIGHT,
JOHN WORTHINGTON,	HENRY COMLY.

[1725.] From the above records we learn that
Friends were very willing to assist each other, and
we find that "superscriptions" were frequently
taken up in the Meeting for benevolent purposes.
In this year, one for "defraying ye expenses of a
family taken captive by ye Indians in New England;" also, one for "defraying ye charges to ye
healing of a young man that broke his leg at
Hasom." In 1736, there was another "to assist
Daniel Pennington to make up part of his loss—
he being burnt out."

[1727.] The crops of our forefathers appear to
have suffered from the ravages of destructive in-
sects; their corn was frequently injured by the
cut-worm, and their trees by the caterpillar. In

this year the latter became so numerous that they devoured nearly all the foliage of the trees, and wherever they passed left the woods as bare as in December. They did not confine themselves to the forest trees, but attacked and destroyed everything green that came in their path. It is probable that these caterpillars extended their depredations over a large extent of country, as we find an account of their having done much damage along the Schuylkill during the same season.

[1733.] In this year Byberry Meeting procured a "Book of Discipline" at the expense of fifteen shillings. About the same time a number of other works were added, and formed a kind of circulating library for the use of Friends. This appears to have been the first library ever established within the limits of either township, and was highly valued at that time.

Thomas Chalkley mentions an earthquake as having occurred in Byberry in 1737. It was not very severe, yet the shock was sensibly felt.

[1740.] This winter was remarkable for a great snow storm, which covered the fences. The crust on it was so hard that horses and sleds could travel over it in any direction, without following the course of the roads. Those who felled trees at that time were much surprised when the snow melted to find the stumps from six to eight feet high. A storm somewhat similar to this occurred in the winter of 1835–6. John Carver resigned his situation as clerk of the Meeting this year, and was succeeded by William Dunkin, who continued to act in that capacity until 1751, when William Walmsley was appointed in his place.

[1743.] A school-house is mentioned as having stood in Moreland at this time; but no account of teachers, or scholars, when it was built, or where located, has been found. About this time Samuel Jackson is mentioned as having sometimes preached in Byberry Meeting; and his name appears on the records for about two years, after which we hear no more of him. Thomas Walton, Jr., is said sometimes to have preached, but was never recommended. He was afterwards disowned, in 1764, for non-fulfilment of some contracts. One Will Knight, a half-brother to Giles, sometimes preached, but it was not well received. On one occasion some person pulled him down, when he remarked: "Thou needst not do so; for if it be of Christ thou canst not stop it, and if it be not of Christ it will die of itself." A more appropriate answer could scarcely have been found. Friends, however, showed their disunity with the matter, and he soon desisted.

[1746.] We find no account of any taverns in either township previous to this year. One is mentioned as having been then kept in the village of Smithfield, but no further account of it has been preserved. About this time an application for a tavern at Byberry Crossroads was made by Richard Carver, on which occasion several of the inhabitants signed a remonstrance against granting this application, in which it was stated that it would be an injury to the neighborhood; that there was no need of a tavern in the place, as three were already within three miles, and that it would only be a resort for idle persons, servants, and negroes. This was signed by John Jackson, Evan Thomas, Jonathan Knight, Crispin Collett, Daniel Knight, Benjamin Walton, Thomas Knight, Joseph Gilbert, Silas Titus, William Marshall, John Rush, and was probably effectual, as we find no account of the tavern afterwards until 1755.

[1748.] On the 25th of 6th mo., 1742, the Preparative Meeting "agreed to wall ye graveyard with stone, and Joseph Gilbert, Evan Thomas, Jonathan Knight, and Daniel Knight, were appointed to provide materials, employ workmen, and see ye work done." From some further accounts it would seem as if this wall was not built until 1748, and that the northwest end was left open so as to extend the yard in that direction. Friends at this time offered the privilege of burying to all who in any way assisted in the matter, and to their children; and several took advantage of this proposition.

[1749.] The first account of the appearance of the seventeen-year locusts, in Byberry, was in this year. They came in great numbers, and have appeared regularly every seventeen years since, generally first showing themselves about the 20th of June. From the accounts kept of them it would seem that they vary but little in the numbers which appear. They do much mischief by injuring the trees when about to deposit their eggs, and some instances of children having been poisoned by their sting have been met with.

[1753.] A collection was taken up to pay for covering the meeting-house, which was done the same year. Another collection was also taken up for making an addition to Byberry Meeting, by which we find that fifty-two persons contributed to that object. The addition made was thirty by thirty-five feet, and one story high. Two large fire-places were built in it; one in each corner of the east end. By means of these, the room was more comfortably warmed, and in winter was generally occupied for meeting purposes. Some time after this other improvements were made by introducing stoves, substituting wooden for the leaden sash, and putting shutters to the windows, so that the house was improved both in comfort and general appearance, and in this condition continued to be the place of worship for Friends until 1808, when the present building was erected.

Although the first settlers of Byberry were principally Friends, yet others of different persuasions came into the townships, so that by this time many of the inhabitants were of that class. Friends always made provision for their poor, but other societies were not so particular to do so; and as these increased with the increase of population, the township felt the necessity of providing for the maintenance of such as were unable to take care of themselves. From this time to 1800, about twenty persons were supported by the public, two of them being for the space of twenty-five years. The annual average amount of poor tax from this time to 1780, collected in Byberry, was

$99.67—all of which was spent in maintaining the poor.

[1755.] In this year a remonstrance was numerously signed against granting Jacob Buskirk the right to open a public house at the Byberry Cross-roads, which was probably without effect, as we find mention of a tavern called the "Three Tuns," kept at this place, in 1760. About this time there were two brickyards in successful operation in Byberry. One of them was on the farm now belonging to John Tomlinson, and the other on land belonging to George De Haven. These bricks were used instead of logs in erecting houses, and are said to have answered the purpose very well. For some years previous to this, a gun manufactory had been in successful operation on Byberry Creek, on lands now owned by Reuben Parry. The business was carried on by the Rushes, but seems to have gone down soon after this time.

During the French and Indian war, which lasted from 1755 to 1763, the people of Byberry and Moreland had a share of the troubles. As the government was in want of soldiers, several persons from Byberry entered the service, among which were some belonging to Friends. These latter were dealt with by the Society, and disowned for so doing. The people were kept in great apprehension for fear the Indians would come down from the mountains and destroy them, and some idle persons raised a report that they had come and destroyed the village of Smithfield. This news caused great consternation, and many of the inhabitants fled in haste to Dunks' Ferry, where they crossed into New Jersey. The report afterwards proving false, the fugitives returned not a little discomfited that they should have been so easily frightened.

[1758.] About this time Thomas Livezey made a survey and draft of Smithfield. He represented the town lot as containing about eighty acres, with the main street running diagonally across it. Among the owners of the lot at that time we find the names of Comly, Knight, and Walmsley.

As we have already observed, the great evil of human slavery was introduced into the townships in 1720; but it never became very popular. It probably was at its greatest height about this time, when the Yearly Meeting issued its testimony against keeping slaves. After this Friends were careful not to go deeper into the evil; but they did not manumit those already held until the Meeting became more positive in its directions, when most of those belonging to the Society set their slaves free; yet two or three who continued to hold their fellow-men in bondage were disowned therefor. When the slaves were liberated, care was taken by their late masters to provide for them, and to assist them in procuring a livelihood, also to encourage and aid them in educating their children. After Friends liberated their slaves, others became convinced of the evil, and many were induced to follow the glorious example of their neighbors, so that in a few years but few slaves were to be found in the townships.

[1759.] Benjamin Gilbert erected a grist mill on Byberry Creek near the centre of Byberry, which proved a great accommodation to the inhabitants. The old mill spoken of in Walter Forrest's Will had long ceased to exist; and for some years the only mills in Byberry were two bolting mills,—one near Reuben Parry's, owned by the Rush family, and that of Giles Knight. Some time after this Jonathan Knight, gentleman, built a grist mill on the Poquessing, several yards northeast of the one now in the possession of Jonathan Knight.

In this year we find that Friends concluded to hold afternoon meetings, with the hope of inducing the youth of the neighborhood to attend, instead of spending their time in a much less desirable way. They were held on the 2d and 4th First days of each month during the summer season, and were so well attended that they were continued nearly forty years.

[1760.] In this year we find a notice of a hotel, kept at Byberry Crossroads, with a sign of the "Three Tuns." It was kept at one time by Nancy Heaton, and at another by John Hilt. It had been customary to hold the township elections at the Byberry school-house; but some were desirous of having them held at the "Three Tuns," in hopes of continuing the hotel at that place. The officers of the election advertised it accordingly; but as none went except the officers, the plan entirely failed, and was not tried a second time.

This hotel was considered a nuisance by the neighbors, and but few of the respectable part of

the community had anything to do with it.   For
want of patronage, it was afterwards closed.

Nearly all the original surveys of land in Byberry and Moreland were made by Thomas Holmes,
surveyor-general.   He laid out the first farms in
regular parallelograms of fifty or one hundred
perches wide.   From the time of his death, with
the exception of Moses Moon and Nicholas Schull,
who did some surveying in the townships, we have
no account of any surveyors until Silas and John
Watts, of Lower Dublin, commenced the business,
in 1760.   They did nearly the whole business, until
1794, when Silas died, and John, finding himself
growing old, persuaded John Comly to take up the
matter, promising him assistance when needed.
He was successful; and continued to be the surveyor for over fifty years, until the infirmities of
old age prevented his continuance at the business.

[1763.] An earthquake was quite sensibly felt;
and on the 29th of November, 1783, another much
more severe occurred, and this one was again followed by another in about five hours.

[1767.] Milling seems to have been profitable
business; for most of the mill sites were soon after
this selected, and mills erected thereon.   In this
year a mill was built on the Poquessing by Thomas
and John Townsend, who commenced business
there, in partnership.   This continued for twelve
or fifteen years, when Thomas sold out his half to
John, in whose family it remained until within a
few years.   During that time it passed through

the hands of John, Ezra, and John P., successively, and is now owned by Levis Levis.

[1770.] The people of this section appear to have been very peaceable, as we find no account of any person's holding a commission as justice of peace until Alexander Edwards, in 1770. Previous to that time the little business in that line was done by Joshua Maddox or Isaac Ashton, in Lower Dublin. Difficulties and disputes among Friends were generally settled by the Meeting; and it was not until other denominations became more abundant that a justice of the peace was thought necessary.

[1772.] As has been already observed, but little opportunity was afforded to the children of the early settlers for obtaining an education, and many could neither read nor write; but it is believed that endeavors were used, as soon as circumstances permitted, to establish a place of instruction. At an early day, a log school-house was erected near the meeting-house, and in this a school was kept until 1772, when, being no longer fit for the purpose, it was pulled down. The school was then moved to the meeting-house, where it was continued until after the Revolution. Although the school appears to have been regularly kept since 1750, the affairs were very loosely conducted. During this year the subject of schools was particularly adverted to in the Preparative Meeting; and, after an interchange of views, James Thornton, Thomas Townsend, John Townsend, and Jonathan Knight, were appointed to have the school under their particular care. From this time for-

ward this important subject received its share of
attention ; and, owing to the judicious management of those who were appointed on such com-
mittees, an increased interest was soon manifest in
the neighborhood, and the facilities for obtaining
a good education were thereby much improved.
The meeting instructed its committee to employ
such teachers "as were not only in membership
with us, but who were well qualified for the business, and careful and attentive in the discharge of
their duties; and especially, that they be of sound
moral and religious principles, that by precept and
example they might inculcate useful sentiments in
the minds of those under their tuition." In the
year 1776 they employed Benjamin Kite to take
charge of the school at the meeting-house. He
was an excellent teacher, and is said to have
brought about a great change for the better, in
the manner of instructing the youth in Byberry.
He was a man of good judgment, with but moderate abilities; but had a peculiar faculty for im-
parting his knowledge, and kept the best school
that had then ever been in the township.

[1774.] This year was remarkable for the snow
storm which occurred on the 3d of May, and which
did much injury to the crops of the farmers in
Byberry and the adjoining districts. In the same
notes* we find that in February, 1779, the weather
was so warm that the bees swarmed and the peach
trees blossomed.

* Notes kept by Henry Tomlinson, of Bensalem.

[1776.] This year the "camp fever," as it was called, was very fatal in Byberry, and numbers of the people died of the disease. Among these were Richard Walton and Daniel Walton—the latter of whom owned a saw mill, situated in the meadow lately owned by Nancy Walton. When this mill was built is not known; but it was permitted to go into decay after Daniel's death. Some remains of the dam and race are still visible.

[1779.] According to the tax duplicate for this year, the number of taxables in Byberry was 82, and the value of property £179,690. Men were then required to swear or affirm that they had given in the right amount, and in case of refusal they were taxed double. Of the 61 property holders in 1779, 7 swore, 33 affirmed, and 21 were taxed double because they said nothing. Nine men were taxed $15 each because they had no wives.

[1780.] The census of the townships, taken this year, show only three persons held as slaves. They were rated from two hundred to three hundred dollars each; but it appears that their value soon afterward decreased, for, in 1784, only four years subsequent, they were worth but half that sum.

Previous to this time the colored people who died in the townships were generally buried in the orchards belonging to their masters or in the woods; but forty or fifty had been interred in a kind of a cemetery for them, on lands lately owned by Charles Walmsley. It was located in the field fronting the mansion house, not far from Watson Comly's line. All traces of it have long since been

destroyed, and hundreds have since passed over
the spot not knowing that they were treading upon
the graves of the long since dead. Another of
these graveyards was on the farm lately owned
by Mary Hillborn, where several slaves were
buried. The exact spot is not now known. Many
persons by this time had had their attention drawn
to the matter, and efforts were made to secure a
proper place for the burial of such people. Accordingly, in this year, we find that Byberry
Meeting purchased a lot of Thomas Townsend for
a burying place for the blacks, and the practice of
burying on private grounds was discontinued. The
record says the first person buried there was
"Jim," a negro belonging to Daniel Walton.

The land in Byberry and Moreland, as well as
all other land in Pennsylvania, was subject to a
quit-rent from its first settlement. This was not
very heavy, being only a penny to the acre, or a
shilling sterling to the one hundred acres. It continued until the Revolution, when the Assembly
of Pennsylvania passed an Act abolishing all quit-
rents; but as considerable opposition was made
by John Penn, then the principal proprietor, the
Assembly agreed to pay him £130,000 in lieu of
said quit-rent, and the landholders were thus released from further payment.

Having spoken of many circumstances that
transpired previous to 1780, it is now time to
glance at some of the events which occurred
within our limits during the time the Colonies
were struggling to throw off the galling yoke of

slavery to the Mother Country. We might speak
here of the noble cause in which they were engaged, and portray to our readers some of the exciting times connected with that period, but it
would be only repeating an oft-told tale, and we
must content ourselves with a mere glance at the
events as they were enacted in those days. There
is no account of our fair fields having been deluged
with blood, nor of any battle having occurred except the skirmish at Smithfield; and of that it is
said that about twenty-five Americans were, on a
certain occasion, in the vicinity of Bustleton, when
they were pursued by a company of seventy-five
British soldiers. As the pursuit did not continue
farther than Bustleton, the Americans thought the
danger had passed, and accordingly halted at Vanhorn's hotel, in Smithfield, to spend the night.
This company was under the command of Jacob
Humphreys, and on that very night allowed themselves to be surprised by one hundred British in-
fantry and twenty cavalry; and, in the engage-
ment which followed, one-half of them were either
slain or captured. The Americans scattered, and
were pursued by the enemy. One person, named
Glentworth, while trying to escape, fell over the
fence just as a soldier discharged his musket at
him, and, as he was supposed to be killed, the
enemy retired, and he escaped unharmed. On
that occasion several bullets were shot through
the front door of a house in the village, which belonged to a person named Vansant. He escaped
only by hiding himself under a hogshead. In the

morning several of the British went to Esquire
Comly's house, where they demanded breakfast,
which was at length furnished, much against his
will. They had with them a man named Krewson, whom they had taken prisoner the preceding
night. The same night the British visited the
house now belonging to Jacob Saurman, and a
person named Boucher, who had not time to escape from the house, crept into the chimney, and
his wife pushed the bed against it so as entirely to
conceal the fireplace. . They searched the house in
vain for their prisoner, but were finally compelled
to leave without him. They took the best of the
horses with them, but did not otherwise molest
the family. On one occasion, says a contemporary, a number of men, among whom was Peter
Yarnall, went to Byberry Meeting, while Friends
were assembling there, and took several horses
therefrom. They were afterwards returned to
their proper owners. During the whole of this
trying period, the inhabitants of both townships
were harassed by unprincipled collectors and law-
less bands of plunderers. Many of the people were
Friends, and were restrained by religious principles from joining in the contest. They suffered
the loss of much property, sometimes for the use of
the army, sometimes for military demands, and at
others without any pretext whatever. Horses,
sheep, hogs, wheat, corn, &c., were carried off.
Men were frequently seized and put in the army.
One Friend, who kept an account of the property
taken from him, stated that it amounted by fair

valuation to £150 sterling; another had his horses taken from the plow by the soldiers, and many of the household goods of a third were seized by the collector. On the 6th of March, 1778, a company of Lacy's men, numbering about six hundred, set fire to several barns and wheat-stacks near the Bristol turnpike, under pretence of fulfilling orders issued by General Washington, to prevent the grain from falling into the hands of the British, then in possession of Philadelphia. They burned some wheat-stacks belonging to James Thornton, near Byberry Meeting House, and some owned by his tenant, Robert Thomas, not far from Knight's mill, and supposed to contain three hundred bushels. A barn belonging to Andrew Singley, at White Sheet Bay, on the Delaware, and one owned by Thompson, at Prospect Hill, were also destroyed. One account says, that James Thornton met them near Joseph Knight's corner, and threatened to inform Washington of their proceedings if they did not desist; others say that a superior officer met them, and ordered them to destroy no more barns, after which they proceeded to the Billet. Shortly after this General Lacy caused many of the cattle and sheep to be driven into Bucks County under a similar plea. Some were taken as far as Doylestown, and others left near the Buck Hotel, in Southampton; but the owners going after them, nearly all were recovered. There was but little security for either persons or property, for wheat was taken from the granary, corn from the crib, fatted hogs from the pen, and even pork from the tub. One man left his corn in the shock until spring, thinking thus to save it; but it was taken as soon as husked. The same person, in order to save his wheat, had it ground, and the flour packed in barrels and hid under some buckwheat straw, where it remained all winter. In the spring he found a ready market among the poor people, who came up the river in boats, and walked across the country to his place. They first exhausted the supply at Howell's, now Comly's mill; and were then sent to this farmer, who always kept a barrel open ready to supply their wants. The flour was soon sold, and silver received in payment. The men, it is said, carried a half, and the women a quarter of a hundred, to the river, a distance of three miles. There was considerable difficulty in getting produce to market, as Washington had prohibited any intercourse with the British while they were in Philadelphia; yet, as provisions were high, and gold or silver paid for all that was purchased, many ran the risk of being captured, and when a successful trip was made, they seemed to be well repaid for the danger. They generally went along by-paths and across fields, and travelled only by night. A company of these men, when returning home, were bold enough to venture up the Bristol road, and when near Holmesburg were fired on by a body of soldiers, and one of their number, Tommy Price, was killed.

An old account says that Washington, while on the march to attack Cornwallis, at Yorktown, in 1781, encamped one night with the main part of his army on both sides of the Poquessing Creek, in the southern part of Byberry, and near the Red Lion Hotel.

Notwithstanding the great difficulty of getting their produce to market, and the losses sustained in various other ways, there were but few cases of failure among the inhabitants of either township. They made their expenses correspond with their income, and were generally prosperous; while some of the military collectors, who had taken undue advantages, afterward became very poor, and in one case reduced to actual want.

Many of the inhabitants were in favor of the old form of government, but they generally took no part in the contest, and but few were compelled to leave the townships on that account. It is said that William Walmsley harbored Joseph Galloway after he was compelled to leave his residence at Trevose, now Belmont, on account of his favoring the British, but Walmsley was not interfered with. Jonathan Walton, of Moreland, took an active part against the Americans, and was forced to go to Canada, but afterwards returned and was not molested. His property was not confiscated, and he sold it some years after peace was declared to Judge Sommers. Some of the tories in the adjoining townships were so active in their operations against the colonists, that they were forced to flee to Nova Scotia, England, and other places. After the war was closed, the new government passed an act requiring the oath of allegiance to it to be taken by all citizens, and denying to all who refused to do so the rights of citizenship. Some took the test without hesitation, but others felt some scruples about the matter. As the provisions of the new government became better known, the seeming objections were removed, and the inhabitants generally came into the measure, although some called it "swallowing the pill."

There was one act done by the people of Byberry which illustrates their true character, and deserves a place in this history. Benjamin Kite, who kept school at Byberry during the Revolution, gives the following account of this circumstance: "A singular civil arrangement took place in Byberry, with which no one who now lives is better acquainted than myself, which I think ought to be known. Soon after the Revolutionary War began, and with which the inhabitants being all Friends could take no part, some of the better class, convinced that the few poor of the township should be provided for, and the roads kept in order without applying to any of the constituted authorities, either of the old or new regime, for years held elections, chose overseers and supervisors, who regularly laid out and collected taxes, took care of the poor, and repaired the roads; and it is worthy of note that the taxes were never more regularly paid, though the collectors had no power to enforce their payment, nor were the poor ever more comfortably taken care of, nor the roads kept in better repair. The elections and the settlement of the officers' accounts took place in my school-room, and I, on those occasions, acted *ex-officio* as clerk."

During the war, as is well known, Congress issued "Bills of Credit" to a large amount. This was called Continental money, and soon began to depreciate, so that in a short time it was worth little or nothing. One man in Byberry, it is said, paid two hundred and fifty dollars of it for a tea-kettle, and another paid one hundred dollars for a mug of beer. Some, who were opposed to any change in the government, refused the Continental money, and hoarded up the old Province money, which they thought would be of full value after the war; but they were doomed to disappointment, it being entirely valueless.

Before closing this part of our history, we propose to notice some of the customs of the people at or about the commencement of the contest. The section of which we are writing the history had long since ceased to be a wilderness, and fine farms and fertile fields occupied the place of what was once lonely plains. The industrious white settlers had continued to increase, not only in numbers but in enterprise, until they had re-claimed the whole of the land; while the "red men of the forest," thus crowded out, had left the homes of their forefathers and moved onward toward the setting sun. These last had indeed sold out all their possessions to William Penn; but the lands thus given up had been the home of their childhood, and most of the important deeds of their youth had been enacted there. These lovely spots—their native grounds—around which so much that was pleasant clustered, were annually

visited by them; and when the storms and chill-
ing winds of winter had passed away, and the
spring, with her life-giving breath, had clothed the
earth with buds and blossoms, these rude sons of
the West were sure to come, bringing with them
the earthly wealth they possessed, to remain during the summer on the very spot where their early
days had been spent.   But as year succeeded year,
and these little bands continued to arrive, it was
plainly visible to all that the ruthless hand of time
was gradually removing them to another world,
and in a few years more none remained to keep up
this custom.   During such visits they occupied the
orchard belonging to Thomas Walmsley, and lately
owned by Charles Walmsley, subsisted upon what
game they could obtain from the woods and waters,
and the charities of their white friends around
them.

They roamed about the woods shooting small
game with their bows and arrows, or along the
streams in quest of the inhabitants of the waters.
Frogs, fish, and turtles were much sought after by
them, and even the land tortoises did not escape,
for they furnished many a feast to the Indian and
his family.   They looked upon the land as still belonging to them, and always felt a freedom to help
themselves to everything they met with in their
rambles.   We have no accounts of their having
disturbed any of the people, for they considered
the whites as their brothers, and ever held them
in the greatest respect.   It is said that the last
Indians who lived in the townships, were the two

squaws, who were buried in the old graveyard at Byberry Meeting, near the large cedar tree in the centre of the place.

With the disappearance of this race, and the conversion of their hunting-grounds into agricultural districts, the wild animals gradually disappeared. Wild turkeys, at first so numerous, were rarely seen after the Revolution. Bears, wolves, and wild-cats, also had sought safer places of retreat, or been destroyed by the inhabitants. Unceasing war had been waged against these animals, and particularly the wolves, as they had been so troublesome in destroying the sheep and hogs belonging to the inhabitants. Smaller game, however, seems to have been plenty; and we find accounts of myriads of pigeons frequenting this section. In 1764, they became so plenty that two young men, having no other employment, knit a net and commenced operations early in the autumn of that year. They were successful, and by the first of the following April had caught over twelve thousand, which were disposed of in Philadelphia at about eight cents per dozen.

If we were but to glance back at the condition of the country only a few years previous, great indeed would be the changes to be observed; and it is quite probable that in no one thing had those changes been greater than in the erection of buildings. The old mode of constructing houses by means of logs, and but one story high, continued in repute until about the year 1700, when some of the more enterprising commenced to erect houses of stone, and to make them two stories high. The last of the old log houses stood upon James Thornton's property, and was torn down only a few years since. Some of the first of the stone houses are still standing. Among these are the old Gilbert mansion in Byberry, now occupied by Thomas James, built in 1708, and the mansion, late the residence of Franklin Comly, Esq., in Moreland, built in 1702. The house on Thomas Townsend's farm was built previous to 1712, by James Carver. It was one and a half stories high, hip-roofed, and built of stone. It has since been materially altered. The houses of William Walmsley (now Edwin Tomlinson's), John Carver, Thomas Townsend, Jacob Eckfelt, and Reuben Parry, in Byberry, and those of Henry Brous, Charles Tillyer, and Jacob Saurman, in Moreland, are quite ancient, although some of them have been modernized in their appearance. Those belonging to Charles Tillyer and Jacob Saurman were built previous to 1720, and not having been materially altered since, furnish good specimens of the antique style of those days. The furniture in use was of the plainest kind, and the floors were without any carpets. The food of the inhabitants consisted principally of such articles as were produced on their farms, and but few luxuries, even such as are now to be met with in the most humble stations, were then to be had. The more common, yet indispensable articles, were cheaper than at present. Molasses sold for twenty cents per gallon, salt twenty to twenty-five cents per bushel; but sugar

was worth fifteen to twenty cents per pound. Beef
was 4 cents per pound, rum 14 cents a quart, and
sheepskins $1.75 a dozen. About the year 1750
the more wealthy began to adopt the fashions and
customs of Philadelphia. Silk and linen handker-
chiefs, silk for ladies' gowns, and fustian or cotton
velvet for coats, were introduced soon afterward,
but the general article of clothing for both men
and women was the "linsey-woolsey" made by the
frugal housewife. The men wore breeches only
coming to their knees: but these as well as their
shoes were often ornamented with silver buckles
of elaborate workmanship. As late as 1760, work-
ingmen wore pantaloons having no falling flaps,
but slits in front. They were so large that when
the seats were worn out the back part was taken
for the front, and by this means were made to last
much longer. Some of the gentlemen carried
muffs to keep their hands and wrists warm; and
the more elderly women wore bonnets made of
black silk, which, when on the head, is said to
have looked much like the top of a Jersey wagon,
and hence were denominated "wagon bonnets."

In 1744, breeches made of plush and lined with
sheepskin were in use, although many buckskin
breeches continued to be worn in Philadelphia
by men of rank, and sheepskin was worn by boys
as late as 1760, and in the country until after the
Revolution. These leather dresses were warm and
comfortable, and were very durable. One man
tried to wear a pair out, but after many years of
constant effort, he at last despaired of his pur-

pose and cut them into flail-strings. Breeches
went out of fashion in the early part of the present century. Before they disappeared the name
had become scarcely tolerable in refined society,
and those made of buckskin were contemptuously
called "leather organs." Tea and coffee were introduced about this time, but were at first used
only by the more wealthy, and then only on Sun-
days. Instead of these articles, people made tea
from garden herbs, and subsequently, during the
Revolution, when tea could not be obtained, they
used the Ceanothus Americana (New Jersey tea),
a plant growing abundantly in many localities,
from which a harmless beverage was made. In
the place of coffee, rye and wheat—but particularly the former—were used, and furnished a cheap
drink for all classes.

The children were not so carefully dressed as at
the present time; and the most of them, both male
and female, went barefoot about half the year.
Some of the more saving of the farmers usually
went without shoes, and when going to market
carried them in their hands until they reached the
city, when they put them on and wore them until
they got beyond the city's limits on their way
home; they were then taken off, and carried the
remaining distance. Many curious customs were
in vogue at this time. Umbrellas had not come
into use, and on rainy days it was the custom for
men to wear long oil-cloth cloaks; oil-cloth covers
for hats and bonnets were also common. Low-
crowned hats were at first in use, but when the

crowns were raised, the covers were carried in
them, ready in case of an emergency. In moderate weather men frequently wore overcoats to
meeting when there was any appearance of rain.
On one occasion a shower came up rather unex-
pectedly, and none were provided with a great-
coat except Edward Parry, who, on being asked
how it was that he had one, said, "Because I was
wise."

When umbrellas were first introduced it was
considered a disgrace to be seen carrying one, and
it was a long time before they came into general
use.

About this time (1770) it was customary to hold
fairs at different places in the fall and spring,
which were attended by a numerous concourse of
people, both male and female. These were sometimes held at Philadelphia, and at others at the
smaller towns, as Frankford, Bristol, &c. Many
went to make purchases, and others to see what
was going on, but by far the greater number for
fun and frolic. Horse racing, dancing, drinking,
stealing, and gambling, were carried on, and event-
ually were the cause of their discontinuance. At
a fair held at Bristol, a Frenchman was caught
while stealing a plug of tobacco, and was put in
the stocks and subjected to the scoffs and jeers of
the crowd. The young men, when the day was
propitious, went to the fair by hundreds, each
"with a bonnie lassie by his side." They were
generally in their shirt sleeves, with their coats
tied behind the saddle, and had on thin-soled shoes

in which to trip the "light fantastic toe." They
wore two pair of stockings, the inner one being
white and the outer one made of colored yarn,
with the top turned down so as to exhibit the inner
pair and guard it from the dirt. Boots were not
introduced until many years afterwards.

In those days the living was very different from
what it is now, and visitors were usually treated
with mush and milk, apple and peach pies, cheese
curds, home-made wine, and sugar, custards, &c.
This was good, wholesome fare, and some of it
would not be bad to take at the present time, particularly when one's appetite is sharpened by a
previous fast.

Many of the people at that time were unacquainted with the arts and sciences, and when anything occurred for which they could not offer a satisfactory explanation, it was attributed to the marvellous and the supernatural. Some firmly believed
in witchcraft, but we have no account of any one
having been punished on account of being a re-
puted witch. Many tales of witches have been
related and many a poor woman had the common
fame of being a witch, eighty or one hundred years
ago. What may now appear a strange fancy, the
spirits always selected the poor, thin, old, wrinkled
women as their subjects, while they carefully
avoided the young and handsome, the lady of
wealth and fashion, and the "sterner sex," whether
of high or low origin. One would suppose that it
was enough to bear the evils of time and the many
infirmities of age, without the ills following in the

train of witches, but as troubles are said never to
come alone, what else ought we to expect than
when the sunburnt faces became wrinkled with old
age, the temper soured by the cares and troubles
of time, when the teeth had fallen from their sock-
ets, the cheeks lost their youthful bloom, the head
whitened by the storms of many winters, and the
frail beings borne down to the very brink of the
grave, that they should be seized by the pestiferous
spirits who manifested their presence in trying
their charms upon the young people of the place,
exhibiting strange and unaccountable affection for
man or beast, haunting the abodes of the timid
and making unhappy the lives of the nervous. All
the evils that befell the people were charged to
their influence, and they were persecuted for crimes
that wrought no sympathy and of which they had
no knowledge. Ghosts, spirits, and apparitions
were objects of fear and apprehension. Many
would go a long distance around rather than pass
a burying ground at night, and places dark and
gloomy, said to be haunted, were carefully shunned.
A few persons more resolute than their neighbors
generally, sometimes caught the ghosts and horse-
whipped them so effectually as in the language of
the boys to make them *"hollar."* Sorceries and
incantations were in high repute; and "witch
doctors," both male and female, often enjoyed a
fair share of public patronage. Regular physicians
had not then settled in the neighborhood, and patent medicine venders were unknown, so that most
of the diseases were either treated by women doc-

tors—those good old souls who are still found in
every neighborhood and are always ready to wait
upon the sick or distressed—or the "charm doctors," as they were frequently called. The old
women generally resorted to teas, &c., made out of
garden vegetables; but when the patient got very
bad, some skilful son of Æsculapius from Frankford, Germantown, or Bristol, was called in and
paid a few visits, which often served to check the
disease. The influence of the moon was considered to be a settled thing; and all important acts,
such as planting seed, putting in the crops, cutting
timber, killing beef or pork, &c., were made to
correspond with the signs, phases, &c., of the moon.
We cannot, however, wonder at all this, for but
few had enjoyed the privilege of attending school,
or had had any opportunity afforded them for becoming better informed. Schools were very few
in number, and these few most miserably conducted, the teachers often being but poorly qualified
for the business. Another great want was books,
which were but indifferently suited to the purpose, and very expensive into the bargain. We
find it stated that a school had been established in
Moreland some time previous to this, but no account of it or its teachers has been met with. Byberry had but the one school, which was at the
Meeting House, and under the control of Friends.
This was kept up most of the time from 1711,*

---

* The following are the names of teachers engaged in Byberry
from 1711 to 1784: Richard Brockden, William Davis, John Wat-
more, Roger Bragg, Josiah Ellis, John Pear, Walter Moore, Tho-

but the number of scholars in attendance was usually small. Only the most common branches were taught, such as reading, writing and arithmetic, as far as "Practice;" and those who could write a legible hand and perform an example in "Double Rule of Three," were looked upon as having a good education. This school at that time was one of the best in the country, and its efficiency may be attributed to the fact of its having been under the care of Byberry Preparative Meeting, in which great interest for the welfare of the youth was always manifested.

Connected with this superstitious age were marvellous accounts of apparitions, ominous sights, and strange occurrences, and these were generally made the subjects of conversation during the long winter evenings when they were gathered around the fireside in social intercourse. The neighbors often met at these gatherings, when the mug of cider and plate of apples went freely round, and many a romantic adventure in pursuit of bears, wild-cats, raccoons, turkeys, &c., and many an interesting detail of the prodigious achievements of some Samson in felling the forests, husking the corn, or reaping the harvests, was related, to the infinite delight and satisfaction of the younger members present, who, with gaping countenances, eagerly drank them in as they fell from the lips of

mas Horner, Patrick Kelley, Joseph Walton, Isaac Carver, Benjamin Gilbert, Jr., Mahlon Carver, Thomas Marshall, and Benjamin Kite. Joseph Walton remained fifteen years and Benjamin Kite eight years.

the narrators. As but few books or papers were
then to be had, much more traditionary matter
was handed down than at present, and social feelings were more fostered as a matter of necessity.

It appears that, for some years previous to the
Revolution, the people of Byberry had become interested in the cause of civil liberty, and were
ready to resist what they considered any encroachments on their rights as citizens by all the means
consistent with their professed principles. The
inhabitants of both townships attended the elections in Philadelphia, and most of them belonged
to what was known as the "Assembly Party," in
opposition to that of the Proprietors, to which the
city people generally belonged. At these elections
disputes frequently arose, and in 1742 they came
to blows, when some of the Byberry and Moreland
people, along with others from the country, were
driven from the polls; but, arming themselves with
clubs, they returned and cudgeled the city party
without mercy. At these elections there was often
much difficulty about voting, owing to the great
numbers present; and, on one occasion, it is said
that an old man from Byberry, who could not get
near enough to vote, came home and went all the
way back again the next day for that purpose.

Prior to 1780 but few stores had been kept in
Byberry, and storekeeping was very profitable.
Giles Knight was the first who engaged in the
business; but, when James Thornton came over
from England, he brought some books for sale, and
soon after conceived the idea of starting a store in

Byberry. It proved to be very profitable, and he and his family continued in the business for the next forty years. It is said that he cleared £6000 in twelve years by the business.

We find that the people of these townships were not behind their neighbors in adopting improvements in agriculture. It had formerly been the custom to sow wheat among the corn, after which the latter was cleared off; but this practice was given up, and the ground where the corn had been the previous year was broken up and sown with wheat. After the custom of sowing oats was introduced, the corn ground was broken up in the spring, and a crop of oats gathered before sowing the wheat in the fall. This was a great improvement; but, as the crop of wheat sometimes failed, some one conceived the idea of sowing clover with the oats, and allowing it to remain over one season before putting it in with wheat. These two customs have remained in vogue ever since. The crops of wheat are said to have been very good, although but little manure was applied. Harvesting, for a long time, had been done with the sickle; but, about the year 1750, the scythe and cradle were introduced. Many objections were urged against this innovation on an old custom, and the older farmers determined not to use them; but, owing to their so greatly facilitating the labor of harvesting, they finally came into general use.

The first plows used were of the old English pattern; but an improved article, with Dutch shares and wooden mould-boards made of cherry, that naturally twisted in the right direction, afterwards came into use.* They worked very well, and would turn a smooth furrow; but the iron mould-boards soon came up, and the improvement, being so obvious, they were immediately adopted.

In early times people generally travelled on horseback; but about the year 1750 riding chairs were introduced, and, in 1764, Byberry and Moreland could boast of three vehicles of this kind only, kept for pleasure.

Formerly it was customary at Byberry Meeting for people to stand up when tired of sitting. When Samuel Sparold visited the meeting he observed in his sermon, "that if every one had to pay 2d. for each time of standing, he thought the practice would not be so common." This custom soon after went out of fashion.

During the Revolutionary War, there was a cave in the woods now belonging to Jacob Saurman. In this cave an old man lived alone for many years, and being very poor, depended upon the neighbors for food and clothing. Old Tommy Helveson's wife said she frequently carried victuals to the hermit, who is represented to have been very old, with long white hair and beard, but very harmless. Vestiges of the cave still remain.

Upon examining a list of the names of the inhabitants of these townships about the close of

---

* A person named Christian Zentman, of Moreland, Montgomery County, made most of the plows with wooden mould-boards used in the townships. After him Thomas Miles started the business at Fox Chase, and continued it about sixty years.

the war, one is much surprised to find so many unfamiliar names; but he is still more surprised at the absence of many of those so familiar as pioneers in the early history. Some families had been entirely removed by death, so that not a single representative remained; while others, delighting in change, and probably conceiving that other localities presented a better chance for them to become wealthy, had sold out their property, and moved to other places. We find, among those who thus emigrated, mention made of several of the Knights going to West Jersey, in 1717; the Comlys and Waltons to Horsham, from 1730 to 1740, and the Scotts and Comlys to Gunpowder, Maryland, in 1756. A few of these subsequently returned to their native place; but most of them remained, and their descendants may still be found peopling those places.

PART II.

FROM THE CLOSE OF THE REVOLUTION TO THE PRESENT TIME.

CHURCHES.

As we have already seen, Byberry, Horsham, and Abington Meetings were united to form "Abington Monthly Meeting;" but in the year 1782 Byberry and Horsham were detached from Abington, so as to form a separate Meeting, to be called "Horsham Monthly Meeting," which was to be held alternately at the two places. In 1786 the Monthly Meetings of Abington, Horsham, Gwynedd, and Richland, which had previously been attached to "Philadelphia Quarter," were united to constitute a new Quarterly Meeting, to be known as "Abington Quarter." The select members of Byberry at that time were James Thornton, a minister, Thomas Townsend, John Townsend, Susannah Walmsley, Grace Townsend, Agnes Walmsley, and Mary Knight.

In the same year the Preparative Meeting, having no Book of Discipline, paid £5 14s. for a manuscript copy of the same, and it was agreed to circulate it among Friends, "with caution and care to return it again in one month."

It is a matter of regret that so little is known of the religious labors of the ministers at Byberry, or of those who visited the place. Henry Tomlinson, who kept an account of many of the more important events in the neighborhood, in some of his notes on Byberry, makes mention of one Arthur Howell, preaching at Byberry Meeting, "and that he preached well, though a Whig." The same person states that in 1788, James Thornton, who was the most prominent minister at Byberry, obtained from the Meeting a certificate to go on a visit to his friends in England. On the occasion of his departure he preached a farewell sermon to a very large congregation of people, who had assembled in the meeting-house to hear him. He was absent about sixteen months; and on his return, the people again gathered in great numbers to show the respect they felt for him, as an honored neighbor and a worthy minister of the gospel.

In the year 1796, a census of the members of Byberry Meeting was directed to be taken for the use of the overseers; when it was found that there were three hundred and eighty-five members, including adults and children.

The old meeting-house, which was built in 1714, and reconstructed in 1753, began to have a very dilapidated appearance before the close of the eighteenth century, and by the year 1808 was in such a tottering condition that it was no longer tenable, and Friends in that year erected a new house near the locality of the old one, of the dimensions of 66 by 36 feet, and at a cost of about $2600. The whole of this sum was raised by subscription among the members, except about $60, which was given by Abington Meeting in consideration of a like sum formerly received from Byberry for a similar purpose.

About this time some Friends felt much concern in regard to the changeable modes of dress; and much was said to discourage Friends, and particularly the younger portion, from following the fashions of Philadelphia. High-crowned hats, narrow-waisted and sharp-tailed coats, lappel coats and sharp-toed shoes, were particularly animadverted upon. The girls were hardly allowed a cape to a black silk bonnet, a hood to a cloak, or any deviation from the old-fashioned shape and cut of a long gown; and Warner Mifflin was so much exercised in regard to ornamental show, that he carried a chisel and a saw with him when travelling about, so as to remove the superfluous carvings, &c., from furniture found in Friends' houses. At James Thornton's, he attempted to remove some ornaments from the clock; but the old lady interfered, and friend Thornton told Warner he had better give up the business.

About the time this matter claimed the attention of Friends, some discussion in regard to the use of spirituous liquors was introduced into the Meeting. Many Friends became very active in the cause; and through their influence the custom of handing around wine at social gatherings and furnishing distilled liquor to hands in harvest-time, was to a great extent abolished, and probably much good was done thereby.

The subjects of courtship and marriage also occupied the minds of many Friends, who urged the discontinuance of the custom of keeping company at unseasonable hours, after the rest of the family had retired, and some labored heartily to accomplish this end. Parents, who were very strict, enjoined the matter upon the young people; but others treated the subject rather indifferently, and kept to the good old-fashioned way in that very important and rather agreeable business.

The young people, contrary to their usual custom, were not in favor of the innovation, and expressed themselves as satisfied with sometimes waiting, when two only were in company, until the "wee sma' hours" when all but lovers are asleep. The old folks had served an apprenticeship to the delightful business, and why should not their children take pattern after them?

The number of members belonging to Horsham Monthly Meeting had increased so much, that, in 1810, it was thought desirable to separate the two Meetings, and since that time Byberry has had a Monthly Meeting consisting of its members only. From a census taken at this time, the members of the Meeting numbered four hundred and forty-six.

This year (1810) might be considered rather an important one in the history of the Meeting, as it was in the latter part of it that John Comly, afterward one of the most noted preachers of the So-

ciety, came forward in the public ministry. Some
others followed his example; and the Meeting
seems to have been more prosperous than at any
other period, and all things passed smoothly on
until the war of 1812, when a number of the members were drafted. Most of these refused to go,
and were accordingly court-martialed, and fined
from twenty to one hundred dollars each. They
could not conscientiously pay these fines, and therefore suffered distraints of their property, which, in
some cases, was taken and sold.

The prosperity of the Meeting at Byberry, and
indeed of the whole Society, continued for many
years; but there had been a difference of opinion
upon some important doctrinal points for some
time, and this spirit of discussion gradually increased until 1827, when it reached the crisis, and
a final separation was the result. Byberry Friends
seem not to have taken much part in the discussion until the time of the division. There was
then some difficulty in the Monthly Meeting, as
both parties desired to retain possession of the
Meeting's property, and to be considered the
Monthly Meeting; but it finally ended with the
Orthodox party withdrawing, and leaving the
Hicksite portion in peaceable possession. After
their withdrawal the Orthodox organized a Meeting for worship, which was held at David Comfort's house, in Byberry, until they had time to
erect a meeting-house, which they did in the latter
part of the next year, 1828, on a lot then belonging to Watson Atkinson, about a half a mile south

of the old meeting-house, for which they were to
pay a yearly rent of one ton of hay. In the year
1834, David Comfort, having purchased the property of Atkinson, deeded the lot to James C. Comfort and Thornton Comfort, in trust, for the use of
the Orthodox portion of Friends living in Byberry, both as a meeting-house lot and a burying
ground. It contained about one hundred square
perches, and was given with a proviso that if the
said meeting should be discontinued, and no meeting held there, the trustees were to sow it with
grass seed, and with the proceeds keep it in good
order. They continued to hold their meetings at
this place for several years, and until death had
removed most of those who took an active part in
the separation. The others then sold out, and left
the neighborhood; and, in the year 1859, meetings
ceased to be held at this place. The property is
now under the control of trustees appointed by
Frankford Monthly Meeting of Orthodox Friends.

This meeting-house is situated about fifty yards
from what is now the Byberry and Andalusia turnpike, and persons unacquainted with the circumstances would never think of its having been used
as a place of worship; but here, those who believed in the Orthodox creed, met together to worship the God of their fathers twice a week for
many a year. Their numbers were indeed few,
and their house small; but probably they felt as
if a small house with a few choice Friends was
preferable to a larger edifice, filled with strangers.
My recollections of this spot when a school-boy,

are, that seldom more than a dozen persons congregated there in the middle of the week, and
about twice that number on First-days.   Asa
Walmsley was their preacher, and often have we
seen him going to and from the Meeting.   He was
a portly old gentleman, his hair silvered o'er with
age, his dress neat but plain, and strictly corresponding with his profession, and his whole manners bespoke the kindness of a humane heart.   He
sometimes stopped to speak to us, when passing
through our play-grounds, and the impressions
made upon my mind on such occasions still remain.
There were two or three sheds connected with this
house, but they have been taken down, and the old
frame meeting-house now stands desolate and
alone, without a single tree or shrub around it;
and all those who met here in days gone by—the
Walmsleys, the Comforts and the Parrys—have
either removed to other localities, or are numbered
with the dead.

At the time of the separation the members of
Byberry Monthly Meeting numbered five hundred
and four, only thirty-nine of whom withdrew.   The
old Meeting still continues well attended; but to a
casual visitor it seems to be somewhat on the de-
cline.   It is a large stone edifice, two stories high,
and surrounded by a number of stately Lombardy
poplars, which are peculiarly interesting as relics
of former times, as most of this species so common
as shade trees around every farm-house twenty
years ago have since been cut down and the more
fashionable kinds planted in their place.   The ex-

terior of the house is neat but plain, and its appearance is sufficient to tell the stranger that it is a place of worship for Friends. In front of it, and only a few yards distant, is the " old graveyard " —the resting-place of many of the ancient inhabitants who now lie in undisturbed repose within its crumbling walls; to the south is the " new graveyard," which is fast filling up, and where every narrow cell will soon be tenanted ; and to the north is the " old school-house," where many of the present generation were educated, and in and around which many of the scenes of our early life are remembered with exquisite pleasure. The meeting-house yard contains about three acres of ground, all of which is nicely planted with shade trees, giving it a pleasant appearance and affording building-places for numerous birds, which, in return, make the spring and summer air vocal with their music. Long rows of sheds nearly surround the place, affording to the horses protection alike from the summer's sun and the winter's cold. The members being generally in good circumstances, go to meeting in their carriages; and on a fine summer's morning from eighty to one hundred neat vehicles, drawn by handsome and well-fed steeds, may be noticed occupying these sheds or fastened in the shade of the trees, while their owners and families are listening to the words of counsel and wisdom spoken within the sanctuary. Well do I recollect these scenes, and often does my spirit yearn to mingle with them once again.

Nearly all the more numerous families in and

around Byberry worship here, and the descendants of the Comlys, the Carvers, the Knights, the Gilberts, the Waltons, the Townsends, the Walmsleys, the Worthingtons, and the Tomlinsons—names found away back in the primitive settlement of the place—still compose the principal part of the congregation. Some of the names, familiar then, have not now a single representative left; and others, of whom we then had no account, now take an active part in the Meeting's affairs. The interior of this house is exceedingly plain, but there is withal a feeling of comfort that makes even a stranger feel that he is among *friends*. As I sat in the house a short time since, my thoughts wandered back to those who formerly occupied seats at the head of the Meeting, and it seemed to me that I could mentally see John and Isaac Comly, James Walton, and Joshua Gilbert, each with his own peculiar countenance, still sitting in the gallery, gazing at the back benches to keep some of us rollicking youngsters within the bounds of propriety and good order. I remember the solemn stillness that pervaded the whole assembly until John Comly arose to preach, when a slight bustle followed, but quickly died away, and the audience waited with suspense for the words of encouragement which all expected from his lips. All gave attention to the preaching; and as he proceeded in his discourse, one might see by their countenances that he was touching some of the many strings that are found in the human heart. The walls of the old meeting-house have at different times reverberated with the

voices of most of the great preachers belonging to
the Society, since 1808—such as Elias and Edward
Hicks, Priscilla Hunt, Mary Lippincott, Henry
Ridgeway, John Hunt, and a host of others—some
. of whom came long distances to fulfil their "mis-
sions of love." This spot is now, as it ever has
been, since the seventeenth century, the cynosure
of Byberry, and we hope that many ages will yet
pass away ere its walls shall crumble or its reminiscences be forgotten.

The great majority of the people of Byberry are
Friends, or friendly inclined, yet several of other
societies have of late settled there. In the village of Somerton and vicinity many of the Methodist persuasion have settled, and feeling the want
of a convenient place for religious worship they
started a meeting in that place at the old school-
house, several years since. As the society continued to increase in numbers and in wealth, they,
in the year 1848, erected a substantial stone church
in the east end of the village, and which ranks
among the improvements of the place. At first
this church was united with the one at Bustleton,
and a minister placed in charge of both of them,
who preached alternately at each place; but the
circuit was divided in 1858, and since that time
Somerton has supported a minister alone. This
meeting and the one at Byberry, are now the only
ones within the limits of the townships, yet many
of the inhabitants attend service at Pennypack
Baptist Church near Bustleton, or at All Saints'
Church on the Bristol turnpike, a short distance
from the southern extremity of Byberry.

PREACHERS OF BYBERRY MEETING.

While the Meeting was held near the Red Lion, in the southern part of Byberry, an old account says that a man preached there, and mentioned that, "as he was at the plow, the Lord came to him and told him to go to such a place;" that another man who was present immediately told the preacher "he lied; that the Lord did not come to him when at the plow, and tell him to go to such a place."

The first approved minister we hear of at Byberry was William Walton. In the minutes of Abington Monthly Meeting, mention is made of dealing with one William Hibbs, for not taking off his hat when William Walton was at prayer. William Walton was at the head of the Meeting for many years, and until his death, in 1736.

Thomas Walton, a nephew of the above-mentioned William, sometimes preached, especially when no other minister was present. He took a distinguished station in the meeting, but was never recommended. He was disowned about 1763, for not paying his debts.

Samuel Jackson preached about the year 1737, but probably was not recommended.

Ann Moore was an approved and celebrated minister. She resided in Byberry three or four years, but removed thence to Maryland, in 1753. She was one of the most popular and powerful preachers of her time, although she had but little education.

Walter Moore, husband of Ann Moore, sometimes attempted to speak in public meetings, but
his moral character was exceptionable. He received but little encouragement from the Society
to which he belonged, and was not held in much
esteem by them.

Jacob Scott appeared in the ministry about 1751.
He took some short religious journeys. He was
of the Scott family in Bensalem, and afterward
moved to Maryland.

Job Walton, son of William, made some attempts
at preaching in 1752. His conduct was irregular,
and he was disowned, probably for intemperance,
after which his life was unhappy.

Sarah, daughter of Isaac Bolton, of Southampton, was acknowledged as a minister of Byberry
in 1752. About 1757 she married and removed to
Maryland, where she died in 1783.

Abraham Griffith, an approved minister, became
a member of Byberry Meeting in 1752. He remained there about three years, and died near
Mount Holly in 1798.

James Thornton, an approved minister, settled
in Byberry in 1752, and became the most distinguished character of the place. He was much esteemed at home, and was very generally known
throughout the country.

Mary Comly, wife of James Comly, and sister to
old John Paul, was a frequent preacher, but her
sermons were generally short. She was not an
approved minister.

Margaret Porter, a native of Byberry, and an

approved minister, sometimes preached from 1762 to 1770. Afterward she removed to Frankford, where she died in 1815, aged 94 years.

John Gilbert, son of Benjamin Gilbert, the Indian captive, commenced to preach in 1769, but was never an acknowledged minister. He left Byberry in 1796, and died in Chester County in 1802.

John Davis, who had been a soldier in the Indian wars, was convinced of Friends' principles, and became a member about 1760, but was afterward disowned for getting intoxicated.

In 1804 he was reinstated as a member, and again became a preacher, but was never recommended. He resided in Jenkintown for many years, and was maintained by Abington Meeting. He died in 1819.

Mary Gilbert, wife of Joshua Gilbert, preached about 1780. Her communications were generally short. She is spoken of as being " a good kind of a woman, but often low-spirited." She died in 1813.

Ann Hampton, an approved minister from Wrightstown, became a member of Byberry in 1792. She had previously visited the meetings of Friends in New Jersey, Pennsylvania, and the States southward to Carolina. She was considered a pious woman, and her ministry gave much satisfaction to the Meeting. She died in 1796.

Hannah Yarnall appeared in the ministry in 1793, but was not recommended until 1798. She travelled considerably, and was much esteemed for sincerity and uprightness.

Ruth Walmsley, second wife of Thomas Walmsley (formerly Ruth Kirk), came to Byberry from Little York in 1794. She was an eminent minister, and died in 1798.

Peter Yarnall, an esteemed preacher, came to Byberry in 1797. He was considered one of the best preachers of his day, but lived only one year after his removal, having died in 1798.

John Simpson, a celebrated minister from Wrightstown, resided in Byberry from 1799 to 1803. He then removed to Ohio, where he died in 1811.

Ruth Cadwalader, who for many years resided in the Thornton family, commenced preaching in 1801. She was subsequently recommended, and was very lively in her discourses. In 1808 she married David Graves, and removed beyond Redstone.

David Comfort was born at Middletown in 1777, and moved to Byberry in the year 1800. He began to preach in 1810, and was recommended in 1817. He went with the Orthodox Friends after the separation, and subsequently removed to Philadelphia.

John Comly, probably the greatest preacher that ever lived in Byberry, commenced in 11 mo., 1810. In 1813 he was recommended, and continued preaching until his death.

Amos Hillborn, formerly a member of Wrightstown, came to Byberry in 1799. He began to preach in 1811, and was approved 1813. He frequently preached until his death, and was much respected.

James Walton, born in 1774, was for many years

9

an elder in Byberry Meeting, and commenced to
preach in 1812. He lived a consistent life, and was
much esteemed.

Michael Trump, from Horsham, resided in the
township for several years. He began to preach
in 1813, and was generally esteemed; but in 1814
he removed to Newport.

Mary Walton, daughter of William Walton, began to preach in 1816, and was recommended in
1818. She married Henry Pike, and removed to
Frankford in 1821, but is now living in Byberry.

Fanny Oram, a mulatto woman residing in the
family of James Walton, was religiously inclined,
and although not a member, spoke several times
in the Meeting in 1817.

· Sophronia Osborn, from the State of New York,
commenced to preach at Byberry in 1819. She was
considered a lively preacher.

Emmor, son of John Comly, was a preacher at
Byberry for several years previous to his removal
to Bristol. He now resides in Philadelphia.

Benjamin Tomlinson commenced preaching at
Byberry in 1854. He is now a recommended minister in the Society, and resides within the limits
of the Meeting.

Elizabeth, daughter of James Walton, commenced to preach in 1828. She has since removed to
Philadelphia.

James Brown, from Crosswicks, New Jersey,
came to Byberry in 1830. He frequently preached,
yet his sermons were usually short. He died at
Mechanicsville, 5th mo., 8th, 1858, aged 84 years.

Demas C. Worrell commenced to preach in 1832 at Byberry. He afterwards removed to Horsham, and was recommended.

Elizabeth, wife of Samuel Coleman, came from Trenton to Byberry in 1833. She was a frequent speaker. Her death occurred in 1836.

Elizabeth, wife of Samuel Newbold, came to Byberry in 1838. She was for many years one of the best preachers at Byberry.

Sarah, wife of Samuel Shotwell, a noted preacher from Middletown, came to Byberry in 1842. She continued to preach to the time of her death, which occurred 5th mo., 8th, 1862, in her 72d year.

Warder Cresson came from Philadelphia in 1819, and although but a youth, commenced to preach, and continued it for many years. He was never much esteemed; and some years afterwards he left his family and made a religious visit to Jerusalem, where he resided for several years, wandering about the country, and at times attempting to preach. By his strange conduct he lost the esteem of his former friends. He died at Jerusalem, in 1860, after having for a long time roved about the world.

Ann Knight, daughter of Thomas Knight, appeared in the ministry in 1819, but remained in Byberry only about one year afterward.

Benjamin Brown, a preacher from Philadelphia, settled in Byberry in 1820. He was not much of a speaker, although considered a very consistent man. He removed to Bristol in 1835, and has since joined the Methodists.

SCHOOLS.

As we have elsewhere observed, the principal school in the townships previous to the Revolution was at Byberry, under the control of the Preparative Meeting. Through the efforts made by Friends, this school was gradually improved in its character, and fully kept pace with those in the adjoining townships. In 1776, John Eastburn bequeathed to Byberry Preparative Meeting the residue of his estate, after certain legacies had been paid out, for the purpose of establishing a school fund which would make the school free. This amounted to £113 1s. 8d., or about $500. From the Meeting's record about this time, it would seem that the subject of free schools claimed more or less the attention of Friends, but nothing was done toward establishing such schools prior to 1800. Eastburn's donation appears, however, to have made the Meeting more alive to its duties, for in 1789 we find that Watson Atkinson, an able and efficient teacher, commenced teaching in a new school-house which was built on the Meeting's lot. It was only about twenty feet square, and was soon found to be entirely too small to accommodate the pupils, so that an addition was built to it in 1792. Atkinson was a man of considerable talent, far ahead of those previously engaged in teaching at this place, and did much toward improving the condition of the school by introducing the study of Mensuration, Algebra and Grammar. The principal school-books then in common use were Ben-

nett's Primer, Dilworth's Speller, Rose's Assistant, Fuller's Catechism, the New Testament, and
Æsop's Fables, all of which have since passed out
of use. In 1794, James Thornton died, and bequeathed £100 toward the fund to establish a
Friends' free school at Byberry; and John Townsend at his death, in 1800, left £50 to be applied to
the same purpose. These two legacies most probably induced Friends to take up the subject again,
when the plans were so far matured that a free
school, the first in the townships, was commenced
in the early part of 1802. It was placed under the
charge of John Comly, who was paid $15 for the
first month, but the salary was afterwards increased. The number of pupils immediately increased, and the usefulness of the school was thereby much extended. At the close of that year
Thomas Walton succeeded as teacher, and received
$253.33 for his year's work. In 1805, the salary
of the school was increased to $320 per annum, and
was continued at about that rate until 1812, when
the arrangements were altered, and the school
committee received the income from the fund and
disbursed the money instead of permitting it to be
paid to the teacher, as had formerly been the custom. John Comly taught the school previous to
its being a free school, and it is said while he was
teacher the school was much improved, and pupils
from a distance came to receive the benefits of his
instruction. He added Latin and Greek to the list
of studies, and several of the youth availed themselves of the opportunity to acquire a knowledge

9*

of these languages. Among others who studied
these branches, we may mention Alexander Knight
and Thomas Walmsley, two Byberry boys, who
afterwards studied medicine and became quite
noted in their profession. In 1795, after some consultation, it was concluded to start a girls' school,
and Hannah Thornton opened one at her house,
which continued for a few months only. Two
years subsequently it was revived, and Sarah
Samms was employed as teacher. It was opened
in the "Little Meeting-House," but was soon after
closed. It is stated that in 1797 a school-house was
built near the village of Somerton, and a school
has been regularly kept there since that time.
Among its teachers we find the names of Thomas
Knox, who taught the school for many years, and
was at the same time tax collector in Moreland;
Charles Dyer, William Cameron and James Bunting. This house was built of stone, and was torn
down only a few years since, although it had not
been used for school purposes since 1847. The idea
of a girls' school was not given up after the failure
at the "Meeting-House," and in 1804 John Comly
was induced to open a boarding school for girls at
his own house, and, for the accommodation of the
neighborhood, took in day scholars. At first it was
successful, but for some reason, in 1810, it was
changed to a boys' school. There were several attempts made at starting boarding schools in Byberry after this time, but they met with very little
success, and were all sooner or later discontinued.
Among the more prominent of these was one

opened by Thomas Samms, Jr., at his residence, in 1816, which was continued one year, and one kept by Eber Hoopes for six months, at Byberry Cross-roads, in 1813. This commenced with thirty-four pupils, but was discontinued for want of patronage.

Although the school at the Meeting-House was started as a free school in 1802, yet it was free only to those who contributed to the "fund," or to such as were in straitened circumstances. Others paid by the quarter, as they had previously done. Prior to 1813, the usual price was $2 per quarter, but in that year it was raised to $2.25.

In 1811, a few Friends associated for the purpose of establishing a school for girls. They provided a house, which was placed on a lot near the store, and the school went into operation under the supervision of the Association. This school was very successful, and was continued in the same building until 1827, when the house was sold and the school was afterwards kept in the second story of the school-house, on the Meeting's grounds, until 1838, at which time it was discontinued. The teachers of the school were Ann Barton, Rachel Parry, Hannah Barton, Elizabeth Walton, Lydia McCarty, Ann Webster, Martha Parry, Sarah Iden, Rachel Pasmore, Mary Edmundson, Ann Stevens, Elizabeth Knight, Mary Shourds, Ann Buckman, Ann Churchman, Deborah Shaw, and Mary Beans.

While Isaac Carver taught in the old school-house in Byberry, he was somewhat addicted to strong drink, and Benjamin Gilbert went around and persuaded nearly all his pupils from him, and

opened an opposition school in the "Little Meeting-House." Carver still continued to keep in the
old house, and the pupils attending the two schools
fixed upon a line to divide them. When either
party crossed this, the other one would attack
them and a fight would ensue. The school-house
stood on William Walmsley's ground, and it was
resolved, as Carver would not close the school, that
William Walmsley and Joseph Thornton should,
on the Seventh day following, when Carver had
no school, tear down the old building, and thus end
the trouble, which was accordingly done. On Second day, Carver, not knowing what had been done,
went as usual to his school, and to his surprise
found the house in ruins. He then went to Walmsley, and threatened to sue the perpetrator of the
outrage; but upon being told who did it, he was
satisfied to go no further than to scold very violently about the matter. After this Isaac kept a
school several years in his own house, where Richard Cripps now lives. This he continued until the
year of his decease, in 1786.

In the year 1826, Henry Pike opened a boarding school on Byberry and Bensalem turnpike, near
the village of Knightsville. It was at the house
lately owned by James Buckman, and was mainly
for small boys. It proved successful, and was continued until 1844, a period of eighteen years.

In 1832, Robert Pitman made proposals for opening a French school in the evenings at Byberry
school-house. His class was small, and consisted
principally of girls; but as the matter was dis-

couraged by many, it was soon discontinued. Several small schools, taught by females, were opened in different parts of the townships from time to time, but they were usually of short continuance; yet they had their use and their place in the great work of education. This subject was daily becoming more important in the minds of the people, and they felt a desire to give their children a better education than could be obtained at any of the common schools. Accordingly, several of the members of Byberry Meeting, after consultation, concluded to establish a school where the higher branches should be taught. It was established in 1836, and David Griscom engaged as its teacher. Through his wise administration, it rapidly rose in public estimation; pupils from other vicinities flocked to the school, and its success seemed settled beyond peradventure. Some, who were at the head of the matter, obtained the idea that it would pay to make a stock company of the whole concern, and to erect proper buildings for a first-class boarding school. These were built the next summer on a portion of James Thornton's land, at a cost of about $4000, and in the spring of 1838, the school was opened in the new buildings under very favorable auspices. But the change in the management of the affairs seems to have been unwise; and, before the project was fairly under way, David Griscom resigned on account of poor health, and John Lewis was selected as his successor. The school, however, was a failure; and in 1843 the company sold out the whole concern at public sale to James

Thornton for $1600. For several years after this a private boarding school was kept here, but was never very successful, and frequent changes were the result. Prominent among the proprietors were John Lewis and Samuel Smith, the latter of whom remained two or three years, and generally had a good school. It was for both boys and girls, but was discontinued after he left, and the school-house removed to the lot fronting Byberry store, and converted into a dwelling-house.

A school was started at Mechanicsville, several years since, and was for some years taught by Mary Gilbert, and afterwards by Abi Townsend. About the year 1849 a difficulty arose in regard to the black children attending the public schools, and Charles Knight, who was then one of the directors, had the school at Mechanicsville changed into a colored school, to be called the James Forten School. Abi Townsend was the first teacher of this school; after her were Susan McDowell and Hannah Clayton, the latter of whom is still the teacher. In 1855, this school was changed to one for white children, and the name is now Mechanicsville School. While it was a school for colored children but few of that class patronized it, but the most of them sent to the Friends' school at the meeting-house. For a number of years back no distinction has been made, and all, without regard to color, have been admitted into the public schools. For many years a school was kept at Pleasantville, and Charles Dyer was its last teacher. His salary, in 1846, was only two hundred dollars

per annum. It was discontinued in 1847, and the
pupils have since attended the school at Somerton.
The present school-house at the latter place was
built in 1847, on the lot within a few yards of the
old one. It is only one story high, is called the
Patrick Henry School, and will accommodate about
seventy pupils. James Bunting, its present teacher,
has been there for several years, and was the suc-
cessor of William Cameron, a Scotchman, who for
many years was considered the most learned
teacher anywhere in that vicinity. He was sometimes fond of indulging in "spirits," and on such
occasions would be very amusing to the pupils
under his charge. The only school now or for
many years kept in Moreland is on the road leading from the Lady Washington Hotel to the Red
Lion Hotel, on the Bristol turnpike, a short distance from where it crosses the Bustleton and
Somerton road. We have not met with any account of its early history, and, after considerable
inquiry, have been able to collect only the following
meagre sketch. There has been a school kept in
this place since 1790. It was for many years a pay
school, and was then taught by the following persons, probably in the order in which we give their
names: John Watts, Samuel Helverson, Alexander
Burke, John Bankson, Howard Trego, George C.
Bancroft, Jesse Wright, Charlotte Wright, Martha
Walton, J. E. Willis, and James Wheatland. In
1830, Howard Trego was the teacher of this school,
and is still spoken of as having been an excellent
one. The price of tuition then was two dollars

per quarter, and in 1835 three cents per day, the stationery and fuel being extra. This school was placed under the charge of the Controllers of the First School Section, about 1837. The old school-house was built of stone, and, by a system of packing, fifty or sixty pupils were frequently found within its walls. It was in a very dilapidated condition for many years previous to 1842, and a new building was badly needed; accordingly, soon after this date, the Controllers erected the present house on the site of the old one. At that time no deed for the property, and no record of any kind, could anywhere be found; the inhabitants of the township therefore met, and agreed to give up all right, title, &c., to the Controllers forever, on condition of their erecting a new building, which they did at an expense of eight hundred dollars. There were two old weeping willows that stood a few feet to the south of the old school-house, and these were the only shade trees on the ground. In the southern end of the lot was an open spring where the pump is now, and, as the lot was not fenced in from the public road, it afforded water to the road cattle as well as to the children, and was often in such a filthy condition as to be unfit to drink. The woodland back of the school-house then extended up to the lot, and was a favorite place of resort for the pupils, who usually spent most of their noons in rambling through it; but for many years back this has been inclosed, and the children not permitted within its limits. Since the new school-house was built, William A. Murray, John B.

Newell, George W. Fetter, John Murray, Lewis Felten, Joseph C. Martindale, William Cameron, William Burke, William H. Neville, and Joseph Morison, have been its teachers. The school is not so well attended as in former years, and the pupils not so far advanced.

A school was kept for several years at Knightsville, on the Byberry and Bensalem turnpike. It was always small, and was at first in a part of the house since owned by Judge Knight. Afterwards it was kept in a small tenement nearly opposite to where John Bevan now resides. After the new school-houses were erected in Byberry, in 1847, it was discontinued, and the old house was moved back into John Tomlinson's orchard, where it is now used as a sort of store-house in general. The principal teachers of this school were Susan Albertson, Mary L. Packer, Charles Sayre, and Jane Hillborn.

A school was kept for a short time on what is now the Byberry and Andalusia turnpike, in a small house on Emmor Comly's farm. The house is now used as a dwelling. It was called Byberry Primary School, but continued only a few months. Jane Hillborn, I think, was the only teacher. About the year 1842 a boarding-school for girls was commenced by Sarah Comly at her residence, in Byberry. It continued about three years, and was pretty well attended, numbering as its pupils nearly all the larger girls in the neighborhood. In the year 1800 a school-house was built at Powelton, on the Byberry and Moreland line, on a lot given by Silas Walton and Edward Duffield, for school purposes; and during the same year, a log house was erected thereon. It was called the Byberry and Moreland School, and has been kept up regularly since that time. In 1854 the Controllers had the lot conveyed to them, and a new stone building was erected near the site of the old one. The lot is beautifully situated, having a gentle slope to the road, and an abundance of shade trees. Many of these are maples; hence, when the new building was erected, it was designated as the "Maple Grove School." Soon after this the old log house was sold at public sale to Isaac White and taken down, and nothing now remains to tell where it stood. Pupils from both of the townships attend this school, yet it has always been rather small. We have met with no account of its teachers, and can now recollect only the following: Joseph Naylor, Richard Burke, Samuel Jones, Jacob Sides, Monroe L. Vansant, Francis Tomlinson, James Houseman, Elwood P. Dudley, John W. Saurman, and William Wheatland, the latter of whom still imparts wisdom to the rising generation under his care.

About the year 1847, Naylor's System of Geography was introduced into the townships, and a class was started at Byberry Hall by Henry Laffert. By this system the geography of the whole world was taught in three weeks, the class chanting the names of the towns, rivers, islands, &c., from large outline maps. Soon after this, James Thornton, Jr., started a class at the "College," and afterwards had another at the Byberry school-house, both of which were well attended. A school of the same kind was afterwards started by Abigail Roberts, and the system was finally introduced into the public schools, but it did not answer well there, and was long since discontinued. In the year 1816, some of the people in the northern part of Byberry became dissatisfied with the school at the meeting-house, and desired to have a school-house built in a place more convenient to them. After considerable noise respecting the establishment of this school, it was finally agreed that one should be erected on land which James Walton and Mardon Wilson were willing to sell for that purpose. This lot was situated on what is now Byberry and Bensalem turnpike, opposite to the woods lately owned by Charles Walmsley. It contained about half an acre of land, for which was paid sixty dollars, and it was always left open to the public road, so that it was a rendezvous for sheep, cows, &c. The house erected thereon during the same year was a small one-story stone building twenty by twenty-five feet. It would seat about forty pupils uncomfortably, and cost only one hundred and fifteen dollars. Joseph Comly, John Roberts, James Bonner, Israel Walton, James Walton, Mardon Wilson, and Josiah Walton, were among the prime movers in this matter. The school was placed under the care of Byberry Preparative Meeting, and trustees were annually appointed by that body to have charge of it.

The yard was a few feet higher than the road, and was filled with trees, several of which were

walnuts, hence the beautiful and appropriate name
of "Walnut Hill," by which the school has ever
been known. This spot has been the scene of
many joys in times gone by, and many now living
can revert with pleasure to their school days at
Walnut Hill. In front of the lot was a piece of
woodland containing several acres, belonging to
Charles Walmsley, through which the school children rambled at pleasure to pluck the earliest
spring flowers that shoot forth almost from beneath the snow, or gather a bouquet of asters and
golden rods even after the chill November winds
had caused all others to wither and die. To the
east, and only a few yards away, a little brook
flowed merrily along, affording to the boys a fine
opportunity for constructing mills, milldams, water-
falls, &c., and it was seldom in the summer-time
that some of these could not be seen along its
course. A few fish also sported beneath its clear
surface, and the little boys who were fond of
angling often, with a thread and crooked pin,
spent an entire noon in the vain attempt to draw
a minnow or a redfin from beneath the roots that
overhung the stream. Some fine old chestnut trees
stood along the meeting-house road by the woods,
and these, as well as the orchard belonging to
Watson Comly, were frequently visited by those
who were fond of chestnuts and apples—and what
boys are not?—much to the detriment of the
owner. But the palmy days of Walnut Hill are
gone, for not a walnut tree now remains on the lot,
and the old school-house stands desolate and alone,

—a wreck of its former usefulness. The cheerful voices of merry children no more are heard within its walls, for it is now only a receptacle for posts and cordwood; and the greensward on which hundreds of rollicking youths have whiled away many a happy hour, has been turned down by the plow, and all traces of their childlike games, like many of themselves, are gone forever. When last we passed that way the door stood open; one shutter was gone and another much broken; the fence had been removed from the lot; and there was but little left to remind the traveller that it had ever been a school. There have doubtlessly been several teachers at this place, but we have met with the names of but few of them. These few are Mary Walton, Ethan Wilson, Joseph Wilson, Aaron Ivins, Dubre Knight, Charles Dyer, Catharine Dermot, Howard Trego, Randall Myers, Mary Beans, George W. Huntsman, Maria Houseman, John Lewis, Albanus Groom, John Reese, and Benjamin Walton. Ethan Wilson was among the first teachers at this school, and did not give entire satisfaction, so the trustees told him "to quit" at the end of the quarter. Ethan, however, thought differently, and refused to go. The trustees reasoned with him, but as he would not do their way they thought it best to do his, and he went when he got ready. Ethan was very fond of arguing, and attended all the debating schools in the vicinity, where many a Demosthenes was forced to

"Own his skill,
For even though vanquished he could argue still."

10*

Charles Dyer taught the school for many years, and was much esteemed as a good teacher; but like most others who follow that profession for a long series of years, he became very cross in his old days, and the mischievous boys often rued their conduct when the flexible hickory fell unsparingly upon their backs.

On one occasion the stovepipe fell down, and the old man, while putting it up, unfortunately burned his fingers, when, in order to alleviate the pain, he flogged all the boys who were in the school-room at the time. But with all his harshness he was a kind old soul, and his many good deeds will continue to live after his few errors are forgotten. This school was discontinued in 1847, when the new school-houses were finished, and most of the pupils were transferred to the Godfrey School, at Lazy Lane. Some few attempted a private school there under the charge of Benjamin Walton as teacher, but a few months sufficed to close the school, to be opened no more. Some years after that an Act of the Legislature was obtained by Israel Walton, John P. Townsend, and others, to sell the property; accordingly it was sold, and now belongs to David Dyer. The money arising from this sale, amounting to $200, has been put at interest so as to create a fund for procuring better accommodations for Byberry Library.

In 1847, the Controllers of Public Schools concluded, for the better accommodation of the children in Byberry, to build three new school-houses, —one at Somerton, one at Lazy Lane, and one at

Cresson's Corner. The one at Somerton we have already spoken of in a previous paragraph. The other two were opened, in 1848, by the directors, Charles Knight, John Tomlinson, and Lewis Rumford. The erection of these school-houses was violently opposed by many of the inhabitants, who refused to avail themselves of the opportunity to school their children at the public's expense. The schools, and all connected with them, were denounced in the most bitter terms, and the children who attended were styled pauper children. One man went so far as to declare that he would never permit his children to attend the public schools while he had "an under garment" for his back, yet in a few months his children were sent to the identical school, and the gentleman, it is presumed, wears a shirt to this day. So odious were those institutions to some, that they forbade their children even to walk across the school-house grounds; but *time*, the great assuager of all evils, real and imaginary, and *self-interest*, the producer of the "second and more sober thought," soon induced them to patronize the new schools, which have since become their pride rather than their disgrace.

The school at Lazy Lane was built upon a lot purchased of Watson Comly, by the city, and was named the Godfrey School, after the inventor of the quadrant, Thomas Godfrey. It is beautifully located; and as the yard was planted with shade trees soon after the erection of the building, there is now plenty of shade to shield the pupils from the burning heat of the summer's sun. The teachers at this school have been James Ivins, Robert Ivins, Edward Ivins, Robert Eastburn, Francis Tomlinson, Henry Tschudi, J. C. Martindale, Charles A. Singer, E. A. Singer, Robert Barnwell, John B. Iredell, James W. Lear, and Charles Roberts, the latter gentleman still occupying the situation.

The school at Cresson's Corner was built on a lot purchased from Lewis Rumford, by the Controllers, and was named the Benjamin Rush School, after Dr. Benjamin Rush, one of the most noted of Byberry's citizens. The school was first taught by Jacob Sides, who remained there for several years, and was accounted a good teacher. He is now Principal of the Newton Boys' Grammar School, in West Philadelphia. The next teacher was J. M. Van Arsdalen, who has since studied law, and now is a member of the bar in Bucks County. Since his time the teachers have been Wallace Dudley, George M. Sayre, John W. Saurman, George Gilbert, Charles G. Freed, and Jacob H. Lukens. This school is not so well located as that at Lazy Lane, and the attendance is not so large.

We have now given a short account of all the schools within the townships except the one at the meeting-house, which is known as Byberry School, and which is the most ancient as well as interesting institution of learning in either place. We have already spoken of some of the early teachers of this school, and of some of the difficulties which

impeded it in its career of usefulness; but owing
to the liberal opinions of the Society of Friends,
who have always fostered institutions of learning,
its progress has been onward, and generally in advance of all its contemporaries. The old house
built in 1792, and which is still remembered by
some of the older inhabitants as the one in which
they obtained the major part of their early education, remained standing until 1823, when the present building was erected in its place. This house
is about twenty feet wide by thirty feet long, two
stories high, and is built of stone. The lower floor
is now occupied for school purposes, and will seat
about fifty pupils, but on the second floor a small
room has been partitioned off for the Byberry Library. The remaining part still has the school
furniture in it, although no school has been kept
here since the year 1847. In the lower room a
single row of desks were formerly placed around
next to the walls, so that all the pupils sat facing
the stones and mortar, and mostly had their backs
to the teacher. The benches consisted of a number of stools, without backs, fastened to a plank
ten or twelve feet long, and so arranged as to suit
the desks. On these the pupils sat from morning
till night, leaning over their desks in front, but
without any support whatever for their backs.
The desks had lids, which could be lifted up when
it was desired to examine the contents within;
and the boys and girls might often be seen with
the lids resting on their heads, much to their detriment in the way of study. In the centre of the

room, previous to 1840, stood the old wood stove, in which many a cord of oak and hickory had been consumed. It was then the duty of the larger boys to split up enough wood to keep the room warm; and when an arm-load was wanted, one of them was detached for that duty, and soon returned with the required amount. At noon-time the boys and girls took turns in sweeping out the school-room; but neither this nor the splitting of wood was then considered a hardship, although they might occasion a little "grumbling" if enforced at the present day.

Then, too, we had the good old quill pens, which were regularly mended by the teacher after each lesson in writing, which was generally given morning and afternoon. The copies, too, had to be ruled by him—a task never imposed upon the teacher now. Soon after this the steel pen was introduced, and at first the price was as high as ten cents for a single pen. The school-room then had but little furniture, and for many years after I commenced going, we had not an outline map, a chart, or a blackboard in the school. The first blackboard I ever saw was one made of poplar boards, planed smooth and painted black, and brought to the school in 1845 by John Williard. It answered the purpose as long as I attended the school. On it the teacher, at long intervals, performed an example in arithmetic; but the principal use made of it was to teach the smaller children their tables.

The books then in use were Pike's and Rose's

Arithmetics, the New Testament, the Introduction, English Reader, Sequel, Cowper's Task, the Expositor, Comly's Speller, and Olney's Geography. All of these have long since been discarded for the much better ones now published. Very little explanation of any kind was then given by the teacher, and the only wonder now is that the pupils learned anything at all. This school, as well as all others in the townships, remained under the control of Byberry Preparative Meeting until about the year 1837, when the Court of Quarter Sessions appointed Charles Knight and John P. Townsend directors for Byberry; and Jacob Shearer, Jr., and Thomas Reading, for Moreland. In 1840, John P. Townsend, Charles Walmsley, and Yarnall Walton were directors for Byberry, and Jacob Shearer, Thomas Reading, and Jacob Saurman for Moreland.

Soon after this they ceased to be appointed by the Court, and have ever since been elected by the people. The following are the names of the teachers since 1784, as far as we have been able to obtain them : Christopher Smith, Watson Atkinson, John Comly, Thomas Walton, Ethan Comly, Benjamin Moore, Joshua Gilbert, Isaac Moore, Robert Parry, Charles Hampton, Eber Hoopes, Job Lippincott, Nathaniel Pettit, Mardon Wilson, John Maule, John Dickenson, Charles Atherton, Joshua V. Buckman, Joshua Gilbert, Howard L. Trego, Seth Trego, William Wood, Ruth Banes, Joshua Fell, Hannah Fell, Sarah Fell, James Ivins, George A. Newbold, Elliot Smith, Watson C. Martindale,

Jane Hillborn, Rebecca Buckman, Elizabeth Comly, Hughes Gourley, and Achsah Blakey.

John Comly was probably the most prominent among this list of teachers, and is said to have improved the school more than any of his predecessors. Joshua V. Buckman is spoken of as having been an excellent teacher. After he left Byberry he was for some years principal of the grammar school at Bristol, and is now a resident of that place. Howard L. Trego, who commenced there in 1834, was a teacher much beloved by his pupils, and was held in high esteem by his employers. He was very much interested in the study of natural science, and was one of the founders and most active members of the Byberry Philosophical Society. He was probably one of the best botanists that have ever resided in the townships, and is spoken of by those who frequently enjoyed his company while rambling through the woods and meadows, as having a very familiar acquaintance with the flora of that vicinity. He was fitted as a close observer of Nature's laws, and could detect differences in the forms of plants, and arrange them under their proper orders, with more facility than most persons. This love of flowers he carried with him to the school-house, and on each side of the door might be seen a flower-bed containing many beautiful floral specimens, which he tended with his own hand. He was kind to his pupils, and in return they loved and respected him. After leaving the Byberry school he started a boarding-school on the Bristol turnpike, near Andalusia, and after residing there a few years he went out West, where he was killed by the fall of his house, during one of the terrible hurricanes that sometimes sweep over those western plains. He was succeeded by Seth Trego, a man of violent temper, and one totally unfit to be an instructor of youth. The large pupils were permitted to do as they pleased, while the smaller ones were abused without mercy. He remained but a few months; yet his conduct toward us was so unkind that I never think of him but with feelings of regret that he ever was my teacher. While here, he, along with some others, sent up a balloon from the lot in front of the store. It went about a mile, then lodged in some tall trees, from which it was soon after obtained by those who sent it up. It created considerable excitement in the neighborhood at the time. The next teacher was William Wood, who lacked the necessary nerve to preserve good order. At that time many large boys attended the school; and it was no uncommon thing, in the winter season, to have upwards of seventy pupils in attendance, and twenty of these over sixteen years of age. On one occasion, one of the large boys got into trouble with the teacher, when a scuffle ensued, and the teacher, aided by one of the other pupils, gave the offender a "sound drubbing." Joshua Fell came about 1840, and continued to be our teacher for upwards of six years. He was a successful teacher, and advanced the pupils more rapidly than any of his predecessors. He kept excellent order, and was generally beloved by his pupils.   But few pranks were played while he was there, for

> "Full well the boding trembler learned to trace
> The day's disasters in his morning's face ;"

and full well did we all know that his word was law, and that his dignity was not to be trifled with.   After leaving the school, he commenced the mercantile business in Bucks County, where he still resides.

In 1848, this school was given up by the Controllers of Philadelphia, and it has since been under the charge of the meeting, and been supported by the school fund.

Connected with my school-boy days, at this place, are some reminiscences which I cannot neglect to chronicle here, for

> "In my poor mind it is most sweet to muse
> Upon the days gone by—to act in thought
> Past seasons o'er, and be again a child."

As this school-house is on the meeting's property, the pupils have always been allowed the entire range of the grounds during their hours of recreation, and well have they used it for their enjoyment.   In the winter-time and in rainy weather the long rows of sheds offered a most glorious place for playing ball: and during the summer the large yard, so well filled with shade trees, furnished to all an opportunity for recreation and amusement such as the pupils of other schools have seldom known.   Fronting the house, and only a few yards from the door, stands a large white oak, which has endured the storms of many a winter; and at each end may still be seen a large willow tree, whose leaves have kept off the rays of the morning and evening sun for upwards of half a century. A little to the south is the pump, shaded by a smaller willow, which has grown from a small limb stuck there while I was a schoolboy. In the northwestern part of the yard stands a noble old oak, under whose wide-spreading arms we have spent many an hour, sometimes listening to the sweet songs of the birds in its branches, and at others stretched out upon the greensward, and with half-closed eyes listlessly musing upon the events of our boyhood life. At the south end of the lot are two large buttonwoods, near which the old schoolhouse formerly stood, and under which is the well, though now covered up, at which our fathers and grandfathers often slaked their thirst. Some of the small trees, up which we often climbed and bent over till their tops touched the earth, are now of such dimensions as would require an hour's hard labor to fell them to the ground. The whole of this yard is covered with grass, and has been the playground for thousands of happy children who knew no sorrow. Well do I recollect those joyous hours, when in company with my playmates we leaped the cat-gallows, hid the handkerchief, played blind man's buff, chased the flitting butterfly, or whipped the humble-bee's nest—hours fraught with pleasures, unmarred by their usually accompanying pains; but those joyful moments, almost the only real happy ones of life, are past

and gone, and many who were then participators,
now sleep beneath the little mounds of the silent
graveyard, while others are still roaming o'er the
wide world to seek a fortune or a name. Yet,
amid the turmoils and cares of this life, we often
revert to the past, for

> "How sweet to every feeling heart
>   Is the mem'ry of the past;
> To think of days when love and joy
>   Around our hearts were cast;
> To let our thoughts swift take their flight
>   O'er days when life was new,
> To roam through haunts of pleasant youth,
>   And all those scenes again renew."

ASSESSMENTS, &c.

The names of nearly all the early settlers of the
townships have been lost, for want of some chroni-
cler to hand them down to future generations; but
a man's necessities will sometimes compel him to
do what he would otherwise have but little taste
for, and such seems to have been the case with
Thomas Knight, who kept a store in Byberry, in
1775. It was customary then as now for men to
buy on credit, and Thomas was forced to enter
their names on his books, together with the articles which each one purchased. These books contain over one hundred names, which is the earliest
list that we have found. Among these we find the
Waltons, Townsends, Parrys, Willards, Greens,
Vankirks, Edwardses, Fosters, Rodmans, Free-
mans, Woodingtons, Streets, Enochses, Stateses,

Grooms, Walmsleys, Hibbses, Dungans, Vande-
grifts, Gilberts, Tomlinsons, Randalls, Comlys, Hal-
lowells, and Wilsons.

Prior to the Revolution, the population of Byberry was rather sparse, as there were but ninety
persons registered as taxable in 1779. At the same
time the real estate was assessed at £180,850, and
the rate of taxation fixed at fifty shillings per
£100. Money at interest was taxed at three pence
per pound. In 1783, the assessment gave 5618
acres, which was divided into fifty-three farms and
lots. There were 122 horses taxed at $37.33 per
head, 114 cows at $10 per head, and 230 sheep at
ten shillings each. Two tan yards were assessed
—one to Giles Knight, at $140, and the other to
Abel Kelley, at $160. John Jackson and John
Britton had each one slave, and Dr. Edwards two,
which were taxed at $133.33 per head. The num-
ber of slaves appears to have increased subsequently, for, in 1786, eleven were assessed, seven of them
to Dr. Edwards, at $200 each.

The people of Byberry, in common with their
neighbors, felt the good effects of a peaceful
country, and basked in the sunshine of prosperity.
Business of all kinds was much improved, and the
population increased so rapidly, that in 1814 the
number of taxables was 183; in 1830 it was 225;
and in 1863 it was 264. The enumeration of the
inhabitants of Byberry, made under the direction
of Congress, resulted as follows: in 1800, 579 persons; in 1810, 767 persons; in 1820, 876 persons;

11*

in 1830, 1018 persons; in 1840, 1055 persons; in 1850, 1130 persons; and in 1860, 1168 persons.

In 1840, there were three white persons over twenty-one years of age who could neither read nor write, and two in the township who were deaf and dumb. In 1860, out of the 1168 inhabitants, 1101 were white and 67 colored; 114 were of foreign birth, one was blind, three idiotic, and six were paupers. There were but 214 houses, five of which were unoccupied. The live stock consisted of 321 horses, 8 mules, 2 oxen, 395 cows, 173 sheep, and 359 swine. Of the crops raised, there were 16,063 bushels of wheat, 707 of rye, 28,417 of Indian corn, 27,089 of oats, 15,883 of potatoes, 34 of barley, 446 of buckwheat, 82 of clover seed, and 53 of timothy seed. Of the other products, there were 37,885 pounds of butter, 31 pounds of cheese, 30 gallons of molasses from sorghum, 105 pounds of honey, 5 pounds of bees-wax, and 550 pounds of wool.

EVENTS RELATING TO THE WAR OF 1812.

In the midst of the peace and prosperity which had smiled on the land since the dark days of the Revolution, the whole country was plunged into a war with Great Britain. Although armies were necessary then as now, yet few people in either township enlisted in their country's cause, preferring to remain at their more agreeable vocations at home. People in other sections were equally

unpatriotic; and the Government found it necessary to make a requisition upon the States for
troops. Several in this section were drafted, and
ordered to report at head-quarters, below Philadelphia. Most of these declined going, and were
afterward court-martialed, and fined sums varying
from twenty to one hundred dollars each. Friends'
discipline not only disapproved of wars, but of all
connection with them; and members who had been
drafted could neither go nor pay fines imposed
upon them in lieu of service. Many, therefore,
suffered distraints of their property, which was
taken off and sold to meet the demand; the friends
of others interfered, paid the demands, and had
the property returned to the owners.

As nearly all intercourse with other parts of the
world was interrupted, many articles in daily use
became scarce, and the prices high. Sugar was
sold at thirty-three cents per pound, coffee at forty
cents, and cotton and woollen goods at almost fab-
ulous prices. In this state of affairs many ex-
pedients were suggested, either through motives
of economy, necessity, or patriotism. Rye coffee
came into general use, and sugar was almost entirely dispensed with. A short time after the
commencement of the war the banks stopped
specie payment , and soon all kinds of specie, from
a cent upwards, passed out of circulation. In
order to supply the want of small change, the
banks issued notes of less denomination than one
dollar; and private individuals, in many cases,
issued small notes, payable in goods or in bank

notes. In one instance some schoolboys set a number of these bills afloat, and they circulated as well as any until their character was discovered. The Legislature, at its next session, passed an act against issuing this kind of money, and most of the notes were called in; but considerable loss was sustained by the holders of them. As the whole country was flooded with paper money, things seemed to work well, and prices of real estate as well as all other things were very high This continued for some years after the war ended; so that, in 1816, we learn that wheat sold at $3 per bushel, corn $1. 25, and oats 75 cents. But a reaction soon ensued, when depression followed depression, and every article of produce was so reduced in value that embarrassment and ruin to hundreds was the result. The price of land fell nearly one-half, and wheat sold for seventy-five cents, corn for thirty, and oats for twenty cents per bushel. During the prosperous times, many persons who had saved a little money invested it in property, paying often less than one-half of the purchase price, and giving a mortgage for the re-mainder; and others had in various ways con-tracted debts, with a fair prospect of being able to meet their engagements. But the reaction was too great for them, and they were forced to see the savings of many years of anxiety and toil swept away to satisfy the demands of urgent cred-itors, and now, having passed the meridian of life, to commence the world anew, without a single cent to call their own. But few persons in the townships became so reduced as this, yet all felt the effect of the change of times, and were to a greater or less extent sufferers. In order to obviate these difficulties, more attention was paid to the cultivation and improvement of their farms, unnecessary expenses were curtailed, and habits of economy became the order of the day, so that, in a few years, they were once more in the old channels, moving along smoothly and prosperously.

AGRICULTURE.

We have already spoken of some of the more important improvements in agriculture, previous to the close of the Revolution, and now we desire briefly to sketch its history since that period. Byberry and Moreland are agricultural districts, the whole surface being divided into farms of from thirty to one hundred acres each, and the population composed almost exclusively of farmers, or such mechanics as are necessary in a farming community. Such being the case, a short account of the agricultural changes is deserving of a place in these sketches.

In 1780 the Hessian fly—that scourge of the wheat crop—first made its appearance in the vicinity. Previous to that time the crop had been good, and a failure of it was seldom if ever known; but now the ravages of this destructive insect were very great, whole fields were so injured as not to be worth harvesting, and many persons entertained apprehensions that the wheat crop was not to be depended upon again, and they accordingly stored up the crop on hand for future use. The rye crop entirely escaped from injury, and it was at once substituted for the wheat. It answered a very good purpose for bread, but the pies and cakes were not so palatable, and the people began to look anxiously for a remedy for the evil which had befallen them. One was soon found in the application of manure, for when that was judiciously applied an average crop seldom failed, and farmers began to gather all the weeds, straw and rubbish that could be procured, in order to increase the amount of that necessary article. Previous to that time, large quantities of buckwheat were raised, but the straw was thought to be useless, and was, therefore, generally burned in the field. In 1786 one farmer had thirty-five acres of it, and in the spring following sold the whole lot to Dr. Edwards for two dollars, and it was thought to be well sold. Several experiments, in the way of farming, were tried about this time, and for the purpose of comparing notes, an agricultural society was started in 1789, and several of the Byberry farmers became members. It is said to have done considerable good, and many of the most valuable changes which took place at this time were owing to experiments made by the members of this society. It is still in existence as the Philadelphia Agricultural Society.

Before the application of manure became common, the main dependence for hay was upon meadow bottoms, or low grounds, along streams.

Water was frequently carried in ditches along the sides of the hills, and at proper intervals let out to irrigate the soil, so that these spots always produced heavy crops of hay. No grass-seed was sown, as is now done; but the white clover, which is native to the soil, and which will always grow when not choked out by other plants, sprung up in the wheat fields, and furnished pasture for the next season. Meadows were then considered very valuable, and were the only parts of the farm which produced hay for winter use. In 1791, plaster of Paris (sulphate of lime) was first introduced here as a fertilizer. It was tried on Indian corn, and proved advantageous, but on the meadows it was of little use. A little red clover had previously been cultivated, and upon this it acted almost like a charm, so that the next step was to procure clover-seed, and the upland fields were soon luxuriant with its growth. Seed was at first very scarce, and was bought and sold by the pound, rating at about fifty cents. Plaster was sold at $1.10 per bushel; but dear as were these articles the application was made, and the harvest exceeded all expectations. The custom of mowing the upland fields soon after this became general, and furnished much better hay than had been obtained from the meadows. Timothy was soon introduced, and, in time, it and clover were mixed together. By this course of farming the amount of produce was greatly increased, and farmers were necessitated to erect hay-houses, or enlarge their barns so as to hold all their crops. The meadows and low bottoms soon

ceased to be considered the most valuable portion
of the farm, and were either turned into pasture-
grounds or permitted to grow up with rushes and
other worthless plants. About the same time lime
began to be used, and this, together with the plaster, the timothy and the clover, and the increase
in the price of all agricultural products, brought
wealth into the community, and made them more
prosperous than at any former period. As a result
of this increase of wealth, there was an improvement in the farm buildings, and new houses and
barns of an approved style soon began to occupy
the places of the old ones. Shortly after this, the
cultivation of potatoes, as an article of profit, was
commenced. Previously, they had been cultivated
only for home consumption. The first varieties
raised were the cut-throats, Spanish potatoes and
lady-fingers; these were followed by the Thompson
potatoes, brought from England by Joseph Thompson, in 1793; Scotch grays, blue-skins, fox-eyes and
mercers—each succeeding one being an improvement upon its predecessor. This last variety was
introduced about 1820, and has been very generally
cultivated ever since—a period of more than forty
years—and they still retain many of their original
good qualities. It is said that two hundred bushels per acre was considered an average crop fifty or
sixty years ago; and that, when properly attended, they oftener raised more than less than that
amount, and as they were never diseased, the crop
was a profitable one. About the same time broom
corn began to be raised, and brooms to be manu-

factured for market. Benjamin Atkinson was the first who made it a regular business, and he was induced to do so about 1790, through the influence of James Simpson, a Quaker preacher, then residing in the neighborhood. He found it a profitable business, and, about 1805, he admitted Bezaleel Croasdale as a partner, and they jointly monopolized the trade until 1816. The brooms were sold in Philadelphia, New York, Baltimore, Lancaster, and Trenton. The brooms were made round, and with a horn on the neck, confined to its place by a wooden peg, instead of twine as now; the handle was of oak, roughly shaved with a drawing-knife. During the war of 1812, the brooms brought $4.20 per dozen, wholesale. From 1830 to 1840 an average of sixty thousand brooms were annually manufactured in Byberry alone, for the Philadelphia market. In 1819, Bezaleel Croasdale made some improvements in the manner of manufacture, for which he obtained a patent, and carried on the business successfully for several years. Charles B. Comly was the first person in Byberry who made broom handles for sale. For many years the annual sales amounted to about 175,000 handles. Of later years, broom corn has not been grown so extensively, and the sales now do not amount to over 75,000 per annum. Oats were raised to a very limited extent, and several years elapsed before they were considered a profitable crop. Buckwheat was a staple production, and large quantities were raised by every farmer; but as the opinion of its impoverishing the soil gained ground, its culture decreased, and comparatively little has been raised during the last twenty years. There was also much attention paid to the improvement of the breed of horses, and the subject was a favorite topic of conversation among farmers and the young men generally. The old-fashioned breed was too small—scarcely any being more than fourteen hands high—and in many other respects was defective; so that a change was deemed needful. Horses with more bottom, bone and sinew, were wanted; and in order to secure animals of this kind, men studied all the important marks of a good horse as well as those of a poor one, and a full knowledge of the diseases, &c., to which the animal was subject, was considered necessary. Thomas Simmons, taking advantage of this change in opinion, spent a short time in study, and set himself up as a horse farrier—the first in the townships—and soon obtained a good practice. The result of all this was a larger and better breed of horses, and an improvement in the quality of the stock generally.

While the great changes which we have just narrated were going on, farmers had become more deeply interested in their business; and in order to have as much land under cultivation as possible, swamps and low grounds were reclaimed, and timber cleared off. So much of the latter was sold that many men were much concerned for fear the next generation would not have sufficient wood for fencing and for domestic purposes. To economize, it was proposed to plant the Virginia thorn (Cratœgus cordata) for hedges; and Joseph Comly, in particular, took much pains to obtain a supply of seed and raise the young plants for that purpose. Through his efforts many were induced to plant hedges, and for several years they answered an excellent purpose; but like every other living thing, their period of life drew to a close; and while they were in the last stages—which often lasted several years—they were worse than useless, and farmers have generally grubbed them up and set post-and-rail fences in their places. In the year 1816, the Long Island hay-rake was introduced, and found to be a labor-saving implement. Some years afterward the re-volving rake was brought into notice as a great im-provement, and has been in general use since. In 1817, the crop of Indian corn was much injured by the *grub;* and as this was believed to be the natu-ral consequence of killing off so many of the in-sectivorous birds, several persons here entered into an agreement to prohibit gunning on their farms, which arrangement was enforced for many years, although much opposition was manifested on the part of some of the gunners. About the year 1820, a mowing machine was introduced into Byberry by Samuel Newbold; and soon after this James Thornton purchased a similar machine. They were drawn by four horses, but did not work well, and were soon thrown aside. James Thornton cut ten acres of grass in one day with his machine. In 1840, another pattern was introduced much bet-ter than the first, but it did not answer, and, like its predecessor, was soon laid aside. After this we

hear no more of mowing machines until the introduction of Ketchum's patent, in 1850, by James
Thornton, Jr., since which time they have come
into general use, and almost every farm is now
supplied with one of them.   In the year 1840 was
the first appearance of the potato disease here,
and many farmers that season lost nearly their
whole crop.   Since that time they have been more
or less affected with the rot; but as many have of
late years been planting them much earlier than
formerly was the custom, they have not suffered
so much from the disease as they did at first.
Threshing machines were introduced in 1830, by
Edward Duffield.   Previous to that time all the
threshing had been done by the flail, and the sound
of the threshers might be heard in the winter re-
sounding from almost every barn.   At first the
four and five-horse powers were used, but these
have generally been laid aside, and their places
supplied by the railroad powers, which combine
many advantages the others do not possess.   The
farmers of this section generally have kept pace
with their neighbors in introducing all the modern
improvements in their vocation; and their farms
at the present time are as well stocked with all
that is necessary to their business, as are those in
any other section of our country; and as a class
they probably enjoy as much prosperity and happiness as usually fall to the lot of mortals.

ROADS.

We have but little account of the roads, bridges, &c., in Byberry and Moreland, hence our remarks must be limited. It is quite probable that the Bristol turnpike, as it is now called; the road leading from Byberry Cross-roads to the Red Lion; what is now the Byberry and Bensalem turnpike, and the Bustleton and Somerton turnpike, are the oldest, and were laid out prior to the Revolution. Mention is made of the Bristol turnpike road as early as 1700. The Byberry and Bensalem turnpike road was formerly known as the King's highway, and was the main road leading from Philadelphia to Growden's mansion, now C. W. Taylor's, in Bensalem. The owner of the mansion placed mile-stones along this road, three of which are still standing in Byberry. Jacob Myers said that when he came to Byberry sixty years ago, the road leading from Byberry Meeting-House to Townsend's Mill passed through the woods near Carver's house. The present road was laid out soon afterwards.

Many years since a turnpike was made from the Rocks, near Frankford, to Somerton, a distance of eight miles; but owing to imperfect construction it became very rough, and was shunned by travellers; hence the company was soon dissolved, and the road left in charge of the Supervisors of the townships. This continued until 1842, when the present company was incorporated. They took possession of the road and put it in good condi-

12*

tion, at a cost of $8000 per mile, since which time it has been much travelled.

The Byberry and Bensalem turnpike was chartered in March, 1848, and was open for travel in 1852. It is 5¼ miles long, and cost $11,442.

In 1790, the inhabitants of Byberry and Southampton met to decide which part of the county line should be mended by each township, when it was agreed that Byberry should take the upper and Southampton the lower part.

In 1793, John Swift, Edward Duffield, William Walton, and Isaac Comly, met in regard to mending the road between Byberry and Moreland, when it was agreed that Byberry should mend the lower and Moreland the upper part.

In 1798, supervisors were, for the first time, allowed a compensation for collecting the road-tax.

The Byberry and Andalusia turnpike was chartered in 1857. It was covered with gravel to the depth of eight inches. It is about two miles long, and cost $5000.

In 1816, a road was laid out between John and Evan Townsend's land, extending from a road leading to Minktown to the road from Townsend's Mill to Mechanicsville.

POST-OFFICES.

For a long time after the first settlement of the townships, the nearest post-office was at Philadelphia; but as the villages of Frankford, Bustleton, and Holmesburg grew up into importance, post-offices were established there for their convenience, and the people of Byberry and Moreland resorted to them for the little business they had through that channel. As Byberry became more densely populated and the circulation of newspapers began to increase, the people felt the want of a more convenient post-office, and, in 1826, one was established at Byberry Cross-roads, with a weekly mail. This answered for a short time; but, in 1832, the office was removed to the store near the meeting-house, and a daily mail arrived from Andalusia. In 1834, this was changed to a tri-weekly mail, and so continued until within a few years, since which they have had a daily communication by mail with Philadelphia. In the year 1858 the post-office was removed to Mechanics-ville; but as this was very inconvenient to the citizens, it was soon removed to the tailor shop near the meeting-house, and Jackson Brown appointed postmaster. Here it gave general satisfaction, and was continued until 1862, when it was again taken to the store near by, where it still remains. The office has at different times been under the care of Oliver Parry, Cyrus Pierce, Jackson Brown, William Penrose, and Ross M. Knight. It is now under the charge of the latter gentleman. The mail route was formerly by way of Bustle-ton and Somerton, and was for many years carried by Silas Vanarsdalen. Since that time the mail-carriers for Byberry have been Joseph Fell, Nathan Webster, Jackson Brown, Charles B.

Comly, Peter States, Isaac Knight, and Theodore Hawk. It is now brought up by the Philadelphia and Trenton Railroad Company to Andalusia, and carried to Byberry by the last-named person. The amount of mail matter to this office has been gradually increasing since its first establishment, and for the quarter ending June 30th, 1863, was as follows: Letters received, 1496; sent, 1095; newspapers received, 4019; sent, 40. A daily mail to Somerton was established many years since, and has proved a great blessing to the people in that vicinity. It reaches the city by way of Bustleton, and is carried by George Birkman. For many years the postmaster was Benjamin Comly; but it is now under the charge of William Hoot. The village was formerly called Smithfield; but when the post-office was established it was named Somerton, in honor of Judge Sommers, who resided near by.

OVERSEERS OF THE POOR.

Byberry and Moreland have always maintained their own poor. Previous to 1752 this was done entirely by the members of Byberry Monthly Meeting, but since that time each township has taken care of all except the poor belonging to the Society of Friends. At no time since the above date have the people been entirely free from persons depending upon them for support; some for a short time only, while others were for a long term of years. Among the latter were a husband

and wife, both of whom were maintained fifteen years; Timothy Hibbs, an idiot, twenty-six years; one aged widow, thirteen, and another twenty-five years; one spinster, Hannah Howard, thirty-three years; Rebecca Adams, who died in 1818, at the advanced age of ninety years, for several years; and Mary, familiarly known as "Old Molly Jerden," nearly sixty years. These were all in Byberry. In Moreland, there was Susan Quee,* for about fifty years; "Black Hannah," for several years, who died about 1857, aged nearly one hundred. The first Overseer of the Poor in Byberry was John Worthington, elected in 1752, to serve one year. In 1753, Job Walton and Richard Walton were chosen to perform the duties of that thankless but necessary office. Since that time two persons have annually been elected in each township, and a regular account of their expenditures, &c., in Byberry, has been preserved in the township book. The accounts in Moreland we have not been able to obtain. From these books we find that from 1761 to 1809 the average annual amount of poor-tax was $143—the least being in 1776, when it was only $10. Since 1809 the largest amount spent in any one year was in 1851, when $998.50 were required. In 1860, six persons only were supported by the townships. This account does not include the poor belonging to the Society of Friends; for we find the Meeting has paid $100 per annum, on an average, for the support of its

* I believe still living.

poor since 1761. When Lower Dublin created their poor-house many persons wanted Byberry and Moreland to join with them; but the latter townships preferred to maintain their own poor by boarding them in the neighborhood. It is the duty of the Overseers to provide the necessaries of life to all who are unable to procure them, and not let any suffer; and to lay and collect an annual tax to pay all debts thus contracted. It is probable the poor are better and more comfortably provided for than where poor-houses have been erected in which to give them quarters.

BYBERRY LIBRARY.

After peace was declared between Great Britain and the American Colonies, and wars and rumors of wars had died away, the people in the vicinity of Byberry began to turn their minds more and more to educational matters. The schools were much improved, and a taste for general reading created in the community. Books of all kinds were expensive, and few persons at that time possessed much of a library. In order to make up this deficiency, and to furnish each other with reading matter, it was proposed by John Comly, Ezra Townsend, Thomas Townsend, Benjamin Walmsley, Asa Walmsley, and James Walton, to establish a circulating library. After considerable discussion, and not a little opposition on the part of some of the women Friends, the constitution of the Byberry Library Company was adopted, 12th mo. 29, 1794. A clause in the constitution "prohibited the introduction of all atheistical or deistical works, all novels, plays or romances, and every other book that has an immoral tendency, or that is prejudicial to the Christian religion." For this reason the Library now contains a better selection of useful volumes than is usually found in such places. The constitution was signed by twenty-three persons, some of whom resided in Moreland and Bensalem, and each paid in the sum of $4, the most of which was used in purchasing books; so that when the Library was opened it contained about seventy volumes, exclusive of several loaned by the members. It was first placed at the house of Ezra Townsend; but in 1798 was removed to Byberry School-house, where it remained until 1816. It was then taken to Gilbert's store, while the Library Company were fitting up a suitable room for it in the school-house, whither it was removed in 1818. When the new school-house was built, in 1823, a room was finished expressly for the Library, and it has remained there ever since.

The books are arranged according to their size, whether quarto, octavo, or duodecimo, and members are permitted to keep them out from one to eight weeks, varying with the size and contents of the volume. Members have access to the Library at all times; but they can take out only two volumes at a time, and these must be returned before others can be had. The members pay an annual tax, usually about $1 each, to defray the expenses of the Company and procure new books. Those owning shares in the Library now number about forty; and the annual tax, together with the fines received for keeping books out beyond their time, amounts to over $50, so that probably about thirty volumes are annually added to the collection. This library is one of the best to be found outside of the city, and now contains over two thousand volumes, which treat principally of religious, historical, or scientific subjects, and affords an excellent opportunity for all to acquire much valuable and useful information. The price of the stock has been raised to $6 per share, and new shares are from time to time created, to meet the wants of the people.

This library has been of great value to the neighborhood, and much of the information diffused among the citizens of the place is attributable to this source. Many of the young people avail themselves of this opportunity for reading; and many of them, along with the writer of this, have had occasion to feel thankful to those liberal-minded persons who originated and bequeathed to us this invaluable legacy.

BURIAL-PLACES.

The proper interment of the dead has always been felt to be a solemn duty devolving upon every Christian, and places suitable for the deposit of the bodies of those who had served out their earthly pilgrimage early claimed the attention of the people, and lots were set apart by our forefathers for this purpose. Among the first of these was a lot of one acre, which was bequeathed, May 30th, 1786, to Byberry township, by John Hart, grandson of the ancient John Hart, as a burial-place for the poor of the vicinity forever. This is still the township burial-ground, in which, at long intervals, some unfortunate mortal whose life had probably been imbittered by the strange vicissitudes of fortune is laid in the narrow grave, without so much as a friend to shed a sympathizing tear. It is located in the lower end of the township, near the Red Lion Hotel, and from the number of persons annually placed therein, will serve the township as a burial-place for at least another century.

This might indeed be made a beautiful resting-place for the dead, but for many years there has been little care taken of it, and brambles, weeds, and small cedars cover the ground, giving it a forlorn and repulsive appearance, strangely contrasting with the far more attractive spots of the kind around Philadelphia. The last burial I recollect at this yard was that of a friendless old man who was taken sick near Knightsville, in Moreland, and found his way to a neighboring barn, where he soon afterwards died. No one knew him; and his name, as well as his history, has remained unknown to us to the present time. A single one-horse market wagon composed the procession, and two men beside the driver, were all that followed

13

the mortal remains of the deceased stranger to this "Potter's Field," where it has since reposed undisturbed by the bickering world around it. As I surveyed this procession I thought how sad is the life of the pauper, for he is grudgingly cared for while living, and when about to be buried,

> "They rattle his bones over the stones,
> Because he's a pauper whom nobody owns."

The graveyard for colored persons, previously mentioned as being situated in the eastern part of Byberry, is still kept for that purpose. Some years since a portion of this yard was plowed up, and most of the "little mounds" were levelled with the earth around, so that the exact spot where many of this race were buried can no longer be seen. What a pity that man should ever be willing to disturb the resting-places of the dead in order to add to his coffers! Of late years more care has been taken of this place, and it is now kept in good order by Byberry Meeting.

There was, also, a burying-place for slaves on William Tillyer's farm, in Moreland, which was continued until within the last twenty years. The lane leading to the dwelling-house then went in opposite to the school-house, and made a sharp turn about two hundred yards from the road to get to the house. At this bend the graveyard was located. It was a small triangular lot, and had been used as a burial-place for many years. Jacob Saurman informs me that it had a Swede fence around it when first recollected by him, but that in later times it was left open, and as it was overgrown with grass, weeds, and briers, the cattle of the farm were permitted to roam over it at pleasure. He remembers that two colored persons were buried there, one of them while he was Overseer of the Poor in Moreland. About a dozen graves were then visible, and the place remained in this condition until the death of William Tillyer, when the route of the old lane was changed, and the "old graveyard" was destroyed, so that not a vestige of it now remains to mark the last resting-place of the ancient dead. Connected with its history is the following: On one occasion a black dog in the neighborhood died, and the children attending Tillyer's school, on account of the color of the animal, obtained the body and made preparation for its burial in that yard. Twelve o'clock (noon) was the appointed hour; and punctually at that time the pupils, young and old met, and, forming themselves into a procession, solemnly followed the remains, borne by two pall-bearers and accompanied by a chaplain, to their "final resting-place," where they were decently interred and a eulogy pronounced on the good qualities of faithful old Tray, after which they returned to their usual pastimes at the school.

The "old graveyard" belonging to Byberry Meeting, and of which we have frequently made mention in this history, contains one acre of ground, and is situated in front of the meeting-house, about fifty yards distant. It is surrounded by a stone wall about four feet high, and has two entrances on the eastern side. It has been full for many years, and the last of those buried there were Margery Knight, 1st mo. 27, 1841, aged eighty-three years, and Elizabeth Townsend, 7th mo. 7, 1841, aged seventy-five years. Among those first interred were two Indian squaws, in 1692, and whose graves are under the large cedar tree* near the centre of the yard, where they have slept for nearly two centuries.

A graveyard should always be the most inviting and lovely spot on earth, for as we all love the beautiful while living, it is a pleasing thought that when our journey through life is over, we shall be laid amid the pleasant scenes we love so well. It is said of Alexander Wilson, that his last wish was to be " laid beneath a shady tree where the song-sters that charmed him while living might come and sing around his tomb !" And poor John Fitch, the great American mechanic and inventor of the steamboat, prayed that he might be buried on the banks of the Ohio River, so that he would be near the many steamboats which his hopeful spirit led him to believe would one day glide up and down that stream ! A cemetery should, therefore, be the type of our thoughts and our religion, and in this respect the old graveyard, with its quiet air and its absence of gorgeous tombs and other memorials of the dead, is highly characteristic of the people

---

* This tree was planted by Joseph Gilbert at the head of his wife's grave, about 1750. Isaac Comly, who died in 1823, aged fourscore years, recollected seeing him come there to water it. Isaac at that time was a small boy going to school.

who now slumber within its walls. In ancient
times they rarely marked the spots where their
families were buried, but within a few years many
have been careful to have headstones placed at the
graves of their families and friends, and in this respect the new graveyard differs from the old one.
The absence of these little memorials in the latter
makes it far less interesting to the present generation who may wish to spend an hour

"Where the rude forefathers of our township sleep."

Very few stones, indeed, are found in the yard,
and only about fifteen of them have dates to tell
us when those who lie beneath paid the debt of nature. Two of these have the names in full, while
all the rest have the initials only. But one marble
stone is in the yard, and that is less than one foot
high. After some difficulty in deciphering the initials and figures on the stones—for they were covered with moss and lichens—and in making reference to some notes, we learned that the following
persons had been interred there previous to the beginning of the present century: Jonathan Knight,
son of the first Giles and his wife Jane, in 1745;
Thomas Knight, brother to Jonathan, 1774; Joseph
Knight, another brother, 1762, aged eighty-two
years, and his wife Abigail, 1764, at same age;
Giles Knight, son of Joseph, 1799, and his wife
Elizabeth, 1766; and Samuel Scott, 1761.

But little care is taken of this yard, and tall
briers and rank grass are permitted to grow and
cover the whole surface so as nearly to obliterate

13*

the little mounds and hollows beneath. Most of the graves have sunk so that it is difficult to tell where they are, and the wild Indian or wood-grass has become so firmly rooted that not a single wild flower can unfold its beautiful petals there. In one corner of the yard a family of elders have taken quiet possession, to the exclusion of everything else. Scattered here and there over the whole surface are a few small cedars, and in the centre stands a large tree of the same species, whose trunk has been scarred by the thunderbolts of heaven, and through whose top the wintry winds moan sadly:

"For it is ever sad when others' grief is fled,
And still remains the constant mourner of the dead."

No walks have ever been laid out in this yard, and the visitor to this full-tenanted resting-place of the long-since dead must make his way as best he can among the little mounds. This yard contains nearly all of our early ancestors, and it has been estimated that not less than four thousand sleep beneath its sod. When it was nearly filled, another lot of about one acre, a little to the south of the meeting-house, was purchased from the property now owned by Robert Purvis. The first persons buried there were in February, 1832, scarcely one-third of a century ago, yet it is now more than half filled, and contains not less than two thousand graves. Margery Walmsley was the first one buried there, and she was followed in a few days by Joseph Carver. It was for several years the only

burial-place in either township, and was used by
nearly the whole neighborhood, whether Friends
or not. It is beautifully situated, and forms an
appropriate resting-place for departed friends; and
around it are a number of trees,

> " Which make a lone and silent shade,
> Where none but reverent footsteps tread;
> Where many friends are calmly laid
> To sleep the slumbers of the dead.

> "Oh ! sadly sighs the evening breeze,
> As it sweeps o'er the lonely place,
> And sadly droop the murm'ring trees
> As tho' they mourned the slumb'ring race."

The sextons at Byberry graveyard have been
Benjamin Atkinson, 1793 to 1796 ; T. Simmons,
1796 to 1797 ; Griffith Street, 1797 to 1819, then removed to Ohio ; Watson Atkinson, for about one
year ; James Jenks, from 1820 to 1850; and William
Forrest since that time.

After the Methodists became more numerous
and built their church in Somerton, the question
of having a churchyard attached occupied the attention of the people; but after some years spent
in considering the matter, it was finally agreed to
form an association, and to purchase ten acres of
land near the village for a cemetery. A very appropriate spot was selected to the east of the village, and the grounds were neatly graded, the walks
laid out, and it fitted up for the purpose. Many of
those in the vicinity have purchased lots there, and
a large number have already been buried in the
place. The ground is called the William Penn

Cemetery, and was opened in 1855. The first interment there was Thomas Dyer's child, 11 mo., 7, of that year, since which time it has been growing more and more in favor with the people. It is situated just out of the village, and the serenity and quiet beauty of the spot

> " Affords a calm for those who weep,
>   A rest to weary pilgrims given,
> Where they may softly lie and sweetly sleep
>   Beneath the vault of Heaven."

PHILOSOPHICAL SOCIETY.

The minds of many of the Byberry people seem to have taken quite a literary and scientific turn in the early part of the nineteenth century. They had been educated by such men as Watson Atkinson and John Comly, who had taken great pains to impress their minds with a proper estimate of the value of scientific and literary knowledge to all persons, whatever their walk in life might be. They comprehended the broad bearing of the sciences upon their social callings, and had made good use of the valuable but small library just started in their midst, during the long winter evenings, when, released from their daily toils, they gathered round the social board; but this did not satisfy them, and some of the more enthusiastic conceived the idea of forming a society having for its object the diffusion of scientific knowledge. While this matter was being discussed, Joshua Hoopes, of West Chester, through the invitation of some per-

sons in the neighborhood, proposed giving a course
of twelve lectures on Astronomy. A class of thirty
members were soon obtained at two dollars each,
and the lectures were delivered in Byberry School-
house. At the close of these lectures Dr. Isaac
Comly proposed "that an association be formed
for the purpose of delivering lectures on scientific
subjects." After some further conference on the
matter, a constitution was adopted Tenth month
26, 1829, the preamble of which states that the
"Society is for the acquisition and promotion of
scientific knowledge," and is to be designated "The
Byberry Philosophical Society." The meetings
were held weekly during the winter season, when
some one of the members usually delivered a lecture to the Society. The first course was upon
Natural Philosophy, and it appears to have been
very popular, for the meetings were regularly attended by many who were not members. These
proceedings continued until Twelfth month, 1832,
when the constitution was so altered that the Society could form a cabinet of natural curiosities,
and the work of collection commenced at once.
The cabinet was at first placed in a room belonging to Isaac Comly, where it remained until 1834.
It was then removed to James Thornton's house,
and afterwards to a school-house in the neighborhood, where it remained until 1840, when the Society erected a convenient building for it near the
Meeting-house, and removed it thereto. Lectures
have at different times been delivered in the Society's room, and when these were not going on,

conversational meetings were frequently held by the members. From 1854 to 1860, popular lectures were delivered at "Byberry Hall," under the auspices of the Society, and were well attended by members and others. Considerable interest was manifested when the cabinet was first started, and everything of interest that could be found was collected and neatly labelled, then placed in the collection. Great pains were taken to procure and stuff all the birds found in the vicinity; many curiosities were also obtained from various sources; and the science of mineralogy, in particular, received the close attention of many of the members, so that in a short time the collection became quite valuable, and annual contributions were rendering it still more so. But as the originators of it either left the neighborhood or were removed by death, a lukewarmness sprung up, and as the younger members care but little about the matter, nothing has been added to the museum for several years. The specimens have been left uncared for until many of them are entirely spoiled; and unless some of the young members give it a little attention, the whole collection will soon be worthless. The specimens number about two thousand, and they should be the pride of every one who is in the least interested in the works of nature.

ADELPHIAN SOCIETY.

In the latter part of 1799, a number of the younger portion of the community met and formed a literary society, to be called "The Adelphian Society," the object of which was the "promotion of useful knowledge among the members." Orations were frequently delivered by the members, and discussions upon various subjects often engaged the attention of the association. Much interest was manifested in it, particularly by the young, and many of the written essays read at these meetings have since been published, and reflect no discredit on their authors. After a time the interest at first manifested began to wane, and at the end of two years it was discontinued, yet it was undoubtedly productive of much good to those who took a part in its proceedings.

DISTINGUISHED CITIZENS.

Although Byberry and Moreland have but a limited territorial area, yet they have become somewhat renowned in history for having been the birth-place and residence of some of our most distinguished men. In early times, Benjamin Gilbert, a polemic writer of considerable note resided here. Since then William Cooper, afterwards a member of Congress, and father of the distinguished novelist, J. Fennimore Cooper; Dr. Enoch Edwards, an officer in the army of the Revolution, and subsequently a Judge in the Court of Common Pleas for the City and County of Philadelphia; and Dr. Walmsley, a prominent medical and scientific man—have all dwelt within the limits of the township. The gallant Decatur, and his father, Captain

Decatur, with his family, were residents for several
years previous to 1798, when President Adams
called them into the service of our country. Byberry can also boast of having given birth to Dr.
Benjamin Rush and his brother, the Hon. Judge
Rush, both of whom are too well known to need
any encomium here. The house in which they
were born is still standing on the farm now owned
by Reuben Parry. They were both much attached
to their place of nativity, and frequently visited
it during the latter part of their lives. Besides
these was Edward Duffield, of Moreland, who was
noted for the high position he held among scientific
men.

AUTHORS.

Several of the people of this district have at different times given their thoughts to the world in
the form of lectures, essays, addresses, poetical effusions, and elaborate works upon various subjects.
It is not our intention to narrate all these; but we
shall mention only a few of the most prominent
ones. Some of these works still survive their
authors, while others have passed into oblivion,
along with the ephemeral literature of their day.
Of the merits of these productions we are unable
to speak, having met with but few of them; but
many are highly spoken of by contemporary writers, and others have stood the test of time, and
are still acknowledged as among the best works on
the subjects of which they treat.

The first of these, of which we have any account, was John Hart, who, in conjunction with Thomas Budd, published an "Essay on the Subject of Oaths," in 1692.

Benjamin Gilbert published "Truth Defended," 1748; "Discourses on Perfection," 1769; and "Further Discourses on Sin, Election, Reprobation and Baptism," 1770.

Dr. Edwards published "A Charge to the Grand Jury," and "An Essay on Agriculture," in the "American Museum," 1788.

Edward Duffield, "Some Observations on the Application of Plaster of Paris," 1797.

James Thornton, preacher, left a memorandum of his Life and Travels, which was published in "Friends' Miscellany."

Peter Yarnall, M.D., left a "Journal of his Life and Ministry," portions of which have been published in "Friends' Miscellany."

John Townsend published an "Essay on Education," and "Some Observations on the Ministry," in the same work.

Grace Townsend wrote several poetical essays which evinced considerable talent, but were not published.

Dr. Walmsley published "An Essay on the Absorption of Medicine," 1803, and, subsequently, several other medical papers in "Barton's Journal."

William M. Walmsley, "An Account of the Wheat Moth," in "Barton's Journal," 1804.

William Walton, the original narrative of "The Captivity and Sufferings of the Gilbert Family."

Joshua Gilbert, several excellent essays, signed a "County Friend," in the "Advocate of Truth," about 1827.

Warder Cresson, "An Address to the Select Members of Abington Quarterly Meeting," 1827; "Babylon the Great is Falling," 1830; "Jerusalem, the Centre and Joy of the Whole Earth," 1844.

John Comly, one of the most gifted of Byberry authors, published, among other things, English Grammar, 1803; Spelling Book, 1806; Primer, 1807; Sermons, 1827; Epistle to Friends, 1832; Spelling and Reading Book, 1842; Book of Useful Knowledge, 1844; and, with his brother Isaac, edited and published "Friends' Miscellany," in monthly numbers, twelve volumes, from 1831 to 1839.

Isaac Comly published several "Sketches of Byberry;" also, "Easy Lessons for Juvenile Readers," 1807; "Philadelphia Primer," 1808; and "A New Assistant," 1809.

DISEASES.

The early part of the year 1793 was somewhat remarkable on account of the prevalence of typhus fever in both townships. It was a dangerous form of the disease, and many who were attacked died. In the latter part of the same summer the yellow fever prevailed in Philadelphia, and many persons removed to the country to remain until the danger had passed. There was scarcely a house in either township which had not some boarders from the city. One of these died of the fever at John Gilbert's, and was buried on his farm without even so much as a coffin. The neighborhood was a second time visited by the typhus fever, in the summer of 1813, and many persons were afflicted with the disease; but from the skilful treatment pursued by Dr. Worthington, of Moreland, then the principal physician, very few died. A dangerous form of dysentery prevailed here in 1819 and 1820, and several persons died, one of whom, Ezra Townsend, was a valuable citizen, and his loss was much felt in the community. In 1849, the cholera broke out and caused great consternation among the people. Many were attacked by it, and a few died. Rachel, daughter of James Knight, was attacked while in Byberry Meeting, July 15th, and could not be removed to her home. She died there, July 20th, and was interred in the new graveyard. During that summer nine cases of cholera occurred in Somerton, four of which proved fatal.

Intermittent and bilious fevers were common many years ago, but since the forests have been cleared off, the lowlands drained, and the soil generally cultivated, these diseases have nearly disappeared. The townships, however, have always been remarkably healthy, and the inhabitants have enjoyed as long and as happy lives as the people in any other section of the country.

MILLS.

At the present time there are six mills within the limits of Byberry township, two of which have saw-mills attached. Five of these mills are located on the Poquessing Creek, and one near the centre of the township, on the Byberry Creek. This latter mill is now known as Comly's Mill, and is owned by Charles B. Comly, one of the most enterprising citizens of Byberry. The first mill at this place was built by Benjamin Gilbert, in 1759. It was a small structure, and probably remained standing until it was purchased by Robert Phillips, in 1837. Previous to this time it had been in the possession of Ephraim Howell and Amos Hillborn. In 1838, Robert Phillips erected the present building. It is a convenient mill, and has an eighteen-foot over-shot wheel, with four run of stones. In the year 1846 this property was again sold, and John Comly, Sr., became its owner. In 1850, at his death, it passed into the hands of his son, Charles B. Comly. The stream upon which it is located is rather small, and during the dry weather of summer does not furnish sufficient power to run the mill. In order to obviate this difficulty, in the summer of 1855 an addition was built to the mill, and a steam engine of twenty horse-power placed therein, and so arranged as to be used when there was a scarcity of water. Since that time the business at this mill has been much increased, and now does more work than any other mill in the township. In 1857 many of the farmers had begun to raise sugar-cane

(sorghum saccharatum), and in order to accommodate them wooden rollers for crushing the cane
were attached to this mill. After the cane was
crushed the owners took the juice home, and boiled
it down in their kitchens; but the result was so
unfavorable that they became discouraged, and no
more was raised for several years. In the spring
of 1863, John Comly, who now has charge of the
mill, became interested in this matter, and distributed sugar-cane seed to the farmers in the vicinity,
at the same time offering to put up suitable machinery for manufacturing the syrup, &c. This
machinery consisted of a heavy iron crusher, with
three rollers, and a furnace over which is a copper
evaporator twelve feet long and four feet wide. In
the autumn of that year these works were put in
operation, and eight hundred gallons of syrup and
fifty pounds of crystallized sugar were made that
season. This was the first sugar made from sugar-
cane in either township. In 1864 the amount of
syrup made at this place was 5500 gallons. The
steam engine at this place is the only one in use in
the townships, and judging from appearances it
has been a profitable investment.

The mill in the northern part of Byberry, on the
Poquessing Creek, known as Carter's Mill, was
built by James Carter, Esq., in 1838. It is run entirely by the stream on which it is located, and is
now occupied by Elmer Carter. A saw-mill is attached to it; and at both it and the flour-mill considerable business is done. In 1864, machinery for

14*

crushing sugar-cane and making syrup was obtained, and is now in successful operation.

The next mill below this, on the same stream, is known as Townsend's Mill. From information obtained through Mahlon Carver, a descendant of the first John Carver, and much interested in the ancient affairs of the township, the first mill at this place was built by Lawrence Growden. It was on the Bensalem side of the Poquessing, about three hundred yards above the site of the present one. In order to obtain water-power for this mill, a small dam was constructed on the Poquessing, opposite to the farm now occupied by Edwin Tomlinson. From this dam the water passed through a race over a mile in length before it reached the mill. No traces of either the dam or the old race now remain. The present mill on the Byberry side is fed from a dam about two hundred and fifty yards up the stream. This was for many years in the possession of the Townsend family, and was sold about 1845. It has since been owned by Edwin Knight, Jesse James and Levis Levis. About one mile below this mill, at Mechanicsville, a saw-mill was built by Evan Townsend in 1794. For many years it was used as a saw-mill only, and part of the time owned by William Bennett, who carried on an extensive business there. After Noah Shull purchased it, a hominy mill was attached, and some of the farmers raised white corn, expressly for making hominy. The present owner, Charles Buckman, has attached a mill for grinding feed. Farther down the stream, about one and a half miles, is Gordon's Mill, built by John Hill-born, in 1825. For several years this was owned by John Gordon, but since his death has passed into other hands. Ephraim Howell said that the first season he lived at what is now called Gordon's Mill, the dam broke. It had no waste-place originally, except at the east corner. He erected a framework there, but in the morning after its completion he was surprised to find that the water had forced a passage through it, and the dam was nearly empty. Plenty of fish were caught in what was left, and he found the track of an animal in the mud supposed to be that of an otter. He then dug stone and got Jesse James to build the present stone-work of the breast of the dam, about 1776. The only mill not yet mentioned is on the same creek, in the southern end of the township. It was long owned by Samuel Smedley, and often goes by the name of Smedley's Mill. It is now owned by Jonathan Knight, and is conveniently located for doing business. Being located on the Poquessing, within two miles of its mouth, its wheels are seldom still from want of water. It is probably the oldest mill site in the townships, but we have been unable to find any account either of the time when a mill was first erected there, or of its subsequent history.

NEW COUNTY.

The people in the rural parts of the city have, for many years, desired to be separated from the

built-up portions, and various attempts have been
made to accomplish that end. In 1812 it was proposed to make a new county from portions of Philadelphia, Montgomery and Bucks counties, and the
Legislature petitioned to that effect; but it was a
failure. In 1841 the project was revived with some
hope of success; but the Legislature thought proper not to grant their request. In 1856, soon after
the Consolidation Act went into operation, a third
attempt at separation was made, and nearly every
person exerted himself to obtain what all so much
wished. Many meetings were held, and delega-
tions sent to Harrisburg; but all without avail.
The people of the townships are too valuable not
to be citizens of a great city like Philadelphia, and
therefore the representatives of the people concluded that it would, for the interest and welfare
of said inhabitants, be best for them to remain
connected with the "largest city in the world;"
and "Penn County," with all its advantages, lives
only in the wishes of the people.

REMARKABLE OCCURRENCES, ETC.

In the autumn of 1812, a violent hurricane passed
across the townships, and did much damage. The
roof of the academy at Bustleton was blown off;
Jacob Wilson's barn, in Byberry, was blown to
pieces; Joseph Knight's wagon-house was over-
turned, and a part of Thomas Gilbert's house unroofed; fences were blown down, trees uprooted or

snapped off a few feet from the ground, and orchards nearly destroyed. In 1820 and '21 similar storms visited the townships, and did equally as much damage. On the 2d of April, 1841, a very violent storm occurred about sunset. It unroofed Asa Walmsley's barn, destroyed a threshing-machine house for Charles Martindale, moved two long rows of sheds at the meeting-house, and blew over several trees in different parts of the townships. On the 12th of the same month snow fell all day and part of the night, and was on an average about twelve inches deep.

Since 1841 the townships have been visited by several hurricanes, which have done much damage by uprooting trees, &c.

A remarkable instance of the sagacity of a dog is mentioned as occurring in 1820. Jesse Knight removed with his family from Byberry to Zanesville, Ohio, and took his dog with him. After arriving at his destination, the dog was very uneasy, and appeared dissatisfied with his new home. Accordingly, he took " French leave," and started for his old friends and comrades in Byberry, where he arrived in due time, having travelled more than four hundred miles, and crossed several large streams of water in his journey. He was very tired and quite thin when he reached his old quarters, but in other respects he was none the worse for his long journey.

LARGE TREES.

Among the large trees in Byberry and Moreland we find mention of a large chestnut tree on the farm of the late Franklin Comly, Esq. It was twenty-seven feet in circumference. It was struck by lightning and killed, after which it was cut down by Isaac Krewson.

A very large willow tree was blown over on Jabez Wilson's house, April 2, 1841; and during the same year a large white oak, about eleven feet in diameter, was cut down. It stood between the house and the creek, and made over seventeen cords of wood.

A very old pear tree on Watson Comly's farm was cut down in the year 1854. It was nine feet nine inches in circumference, fifty feet in height, and made over three cords of wood. It was over one hundred years of age, and produced fruit until it was cut down.

A large chestnut tree, six feet in diameter, on John Carver's farm, was cut down by Watson Comly in 1855. It made ten cords of wood and one hundred and eighty posts.

The largest tree of any kind in the townships was, without doubt, the "old elm" which stood in front of John Carver's house, and about one hundred yards distant. It was, on account of its great size, a curiosity, and sojourning strangers often went to view its gigantic form. It stood alone in all its majesty away from surrounding trees, and

was a noble specimen of that noble species now so
seldom seen around our dwellings. It measured
twenty-five feet in circumference, was forty feet
up to its branches, and its topmost limbs were one
hundred and ten feet high. How long it had stood
none could tell ; but for several years previous to
its destruction it had been gradually decaying. In
the autumn of 1856, the "old elm" took fire from
some burning brush, and, being dry, it burned so
rapidly that it fell the next day. The limbs burned
for three days, and were finally extinguished by a
shower of rain ; but the roots burned for over one
week. Mahlon Carver states that the tree made
twenty-five cords of wood. For many a long year
the branches of this venerable old elm were waved
by the passing breeze, and beneath its shade thousands of human beings stood to view its gigantic
form ; but the old tree—a connecting link between
the present and the long-since past—has, like a
mighty monarch, fallen.

> " Then hail to that elm ! that brave old elm !
>   Our last lone forest tree,
> Whose limbs outstood the lightning's brand,
>   For a brave old elm was he !
>
> "For seven score of full-told years
>   He bore his leafy prime,
> And like a relic of the past
>   He told of the olden time.
>
> "But the raging fire felled his giant form,
>   And we ne'er shall see him more ;
> So here is a tear to the memory
>   Of the elm before the door."

A large poplar tree formerly stood on Nicholas Helverson's, now James Tomlinson's farm. It was 130 feet high, 50 feet up to the lowest limb, and 16 feet in circumference near the ground. It was cut down by Silas Roads, and sawed up for bedsteads. It stood near Jacob Saurman's line some distance back from the turnpike.

A very tall hickory tree grew in Jacob Saurman's woods. It was 120 feet high, and when cut down made over four cords of wood.

On John Carver's, now Colonel Burling's farm are two pear trees, still standing, which were brought over from England by the first John Carver in 1682, and are consequently over 174 years old. One of them is still alive and bears fruit.

On the late Alfred Worthington's farm stands a chestnut tree that measures 28 feet in circumference. It is still in full vigor, and probably the largest tree now standing in either township.

BIG WOMAN.

Although the people of Byberry are generally shrewd, and by no means can be called " green," yet some of ye ancient ones were led into snares, and listened to the " lo here's " and " lo there's." Several ludicrous accounts of their gullibility have been preserved, one of which, we think, deserves a passing notice in this history. Some fifty years ago one or two wags in Byberry, for want of better employment, raised a report that some hunters in the Far West had discovered a family of giants,

consisting of a man, his wife and child. The man
was unwilling to be captured, and resisted them so
fiercely that they were forced, partly in self-de-
fence, to shoot him. After his death the wife and
child, considering resistance useless, submitted to
their captors, and were brought eastward to be
exhibited to the wondering people inhabiting the
towns and villages in Pennsylvania. The man
was covered with hair, like the wild animals of his
native forests; but, unfortunately, his precious
body lay buried near the spot where he so gal-
lantly fought for his dear wife and child. The
latter were brought on in excellent health, and
were said to be on exhibition at Flourtown, a small
village in Montgomery County, about ten miles
distant. The mother was sixteen feet high, and
the "little one," though only six months old, was
six feet high. It required one barrel of flour per
week to keep the woman in bread, and the child
drained the udders of three cows, besides the nour-
ishment obtained from the mother. Wonderful
and improbable as were these stories, they were
credited by many people, and several of the more
curious procured the necessary conveyances, and
started for Flourtown to see the "show." It is
said they felt much inward satisfaction while on
the journey there, and speculated much upon the
appearance, &c., of the lady; and one or two, who
were basking in the sunshine of "single blessedness," expressed themselves as satisfied that the
husband had been slaughtered. As they neared
the village their excitement increased, and, whip-

15

ping up their "nags" into a John Gilpin pace, they entered the town and drew up at the principal hotel. Not finding a very large crowd in attendance, and but little excitement, they, after refreshing, cautiously asked "if there had not been a show there?" but their amazement was indeed great when the landlord stated "he had not heard of any except one of a *learned goat*." Their spirits becoming more and more depressed, they refreshed once and again, and, with fallen countenances, started home. After this party had fairly started, the wags raised a second report that the "show" had been removed to Jenkintown, several miles nearer. As soon as this was heard, several others, mostly on foot, started for that place, determined not to let such a favorable opportunity pass to see so great a *natural curiosity*. They trudged on, with high hopes and great anticipations, and in due time arrived at Jenkintown, where they saw their fellow-dupes and the *learned goat*, but nothing of the "Big Woman." After much "smiling" to keep up their depressed spirits, they turned toward home wiser, if not better men. The hoax was too good to be kept, and soon was in everybody's mouth; but it grated harshly upon the ears of those whose credulity had been practised upon, and for many years afterward it was much safer, before mentioning the "Big Woman" in the presence of any of the victims, to be certain that there was room for a retreat in the rear, for it seldom failed to create a pugnacious spirit in the humbugged person.

ACCOUNT OF A FEW BIRTHS AND DEATHS IN BYBERRY AND VICINITY.

	Born.	Died.	Age.
Joseph Knight, . . .	1680	1762	82
Abigail, his wife, . . .	1682	1764	82
Mary Thornton, their daughter,	1723	1793	70
Giles Knight, their son, . .	1719	1799	80
Elizabeth, his wife, . . .	1717	1766	49
Henry Tomlinson, . . .	1721	1800	79
Sarah Titus, ...	1713	1792	79
Thomas Townsend, . . .	1720	1794	74
John Townsend, . . .	1723	1800	77
Catharine Singley, . . .	1702	1802	100
Sarah Bolton, ...	1698	1784	86
John Paul, ...	1715	1786	71
Edward Parry, . . .	1725	1792	67
Susanna Walmsley, . . .	1715	1795	80
Nathaniel Samms, . . .	1718	1796	78
Grace Townsend, . . .	1721	1803	82
Jonathan Parry, . . .	1743	1809	66
Rachel Bolton, . . .	1728	1810	82
Thomas Ridge, ...	1728	1810	82
William Walton (Jersey Billy),	1725	1807	82
Daniel Brittin (Smithfield), .	1690	1760	70
Elizabeth Brittin, . . .	1687	1766	79
John Brittin, son of Daniel, .	1715	1795	80
Thomas Walmsley, Sr., . .	1674	1754	80
Mary, his wife, . . .	1676	1755	79
David Jones, an ancient man, .	——	1756	—
Thomas Walton, . . .	1658	1758	100
Henry Walmsley, . . .	1671	1759	88
Thomas Tomlinson (Bensalem),	1688	1764	76
Joanna, his wife, . . .	1702	1772	70
Joseph Gilbert, . . .	1675	1765	90
Thomas Rush, ...	1685	1771	86
William Ridge, . . .	1696	1776	80

	Born.	Died.	Age.
Thomas Walton, . . .	1693	1777	84
William Croasdale, . . .	1689	1777	88
Samuel Allen, ...	1701	1785	84
✓William Homer, . . .	1707	1786	79 ✓
Isaac Carver, ...	1721	1786	65
Phebe, his wife, . . .	1718	1793	75
William Hibbs, . . .	1700	1789	89
John Carver, ...	1717	1791	74
Ann Davis, ...	1715	1798	83
Giles Knight, ...	1720	1799	79

We find, upon looking over the list of subscribers to defray the expenses of Byberry Meeting,
that of the seventy-four persons mentioned in
1806, not one is now living; of the seventy persons mentioned in 1807, James Paul only is living;
of the seventy-four persons mentioned in 1809,
Jeremiah Comfort, James Paul, and Robert Parry
only are living; and, of the eighty-five subscribers for building Byberry Meeting-House, in 1810,
John P. Townsend, Jeremiah Comfort, Mary Pike,
and Robert Parry only are living. Thus in a few
short years the present generation will have passed
away, and the places which know us now will then
know us no more forever.

NOTES OF EVENTS EXTRACTED FROM OLD
MANUSCRIPTS.

[1753.] John Holgate on the township.
A legacy of £17 3s. 8d. left to Byberry by Philip
Honey.

[1754.] The township Dr. to 100 hobnails bought of Thomas Maul for Holgate's shoes, 4d.

Making two shirts for Holgate with thread, 3s. 4d.

Making breeches for Holgate with thread, 3s. 6d.

Making shoes for Holgate, 7s. 6d.

Drawing a tooth for Holgate by Thomas Townsend, 9d.

The township Dr. to Thomas Mardon for keeping with victuals, drink, washing, lodging, and mending, the said Holgate from May the 4th, 1754, till March the 25th, 1755, £5.

Thomas Mardon and William Homer were Overseers of the Poor for the year 1754. The following letter to them will show one of the customs of that early day :

"April the First, 1754.

"Friend Thomas Mardon and William Homer, you are hereby desired, according to your lawful commissions, to consider, grant, and warn or forewarn, one Jonathan Wright and his family either to inhabit quietness, or else forbid them from having my plantation for this year, according to our lease.

"From WILLIAM HOMER."

"He was accordingly forbidden by the aforesaid Overseers."

[1759.] Paid lawyer Moreland £1 17s. 6d. for advice and assistance on account of ye poor.

[1760.] John Keen killed by a fall from a horse.

15*

Justice Austin paid for swearing Jane Cox.

Sarah Dykes, Jane Cox and child, and Joan Smith on poor list.

Paid 9s. 4d. for 1½ yards of bearskin for Holgate's jacket.

Paid 8s. for Holgate's shoes.

Paid lawyer Galloway for advice, £1 2s. 6d.

Paid lawyer John Ross, £3 2s. 6d.

Paid lawyer Moreland, £3 10s.

Third mo. 16, a very great snow fell.

[1761.] Paid Joseph Galloway for advice, £2.

Bought linsey woolsey at 3s. per yard.

Paid £1 to William Folwell for tending Court at Newtown ten days, to prove Jane Cox's husband served four years, by indenture, with him in Jersey.

[1762.] Samuel Swift noted as a doctor.

Joseph Galloway paid 17s. 6d. for removing a trial from the Quarter Sessions to the Supreme Court.

[1764.] Josiah Foster killed by a wagon.

Joan Smith removed to Abington.

Daniel Boileau's wife killed by thunder.

[1765.] March 22, a very great snow began to fall, which lasted till the 29th, at night.

[1767.] Mary Grimes killed by a riding chair.

Thomas Homer killed by a cart.

[1768.] John Holgate died.

[1769.] April 20th, a very smart shower of snow.

[1770.] 10s. received of Alexander Edwards for profane swearing.

7s. 6d. paid to Mary States for extending kindness to Catharine Hickey in time of labor.

[1771.] John Johnson fined 5s. by Alex. Edwards for profane swearing.

[1772.] John Humphreys fined 5s. by Alex. Edwards for profane swearing.

[1775.] 8 mo. 5, Peter States killed by the fall of Gill's house when it was raining.

[1776.] 1 mo. 9, Mary Tanner departed this life about 4 o'clock in the morning, being about 89 years of age.

[1777.] 2 mo. 4, Priscilla Walton buried; died with the small-pox.

5 mo. The First of this month Howe's army is to come—Robert Croasdale told Jonathan Wilson.

5 mo. 1, Abel Knight died from a hurt received from a cart.

6 mo. 9, Benjamin Walton, Jacob Roads, and William Peart stole a blanket from me, —— Carver.

[1779.] 2 mo. 16, Rachel Carver heard the shadfrogs.

3 mo. 24, a deep snow, and a very snowy day.

6 mo. 28, began wheat harvest, and finished 7 mo. 8.

[1780.] 2 mo. 6, a tea-pot cost £31 17s. 6d. Continental money.

3 mo. 30, snow all day long—the snow eleven inches deep in common.

4 mo. 2, went to meeting in the sleigh; it was tolerably good going; some came four miles.

5 mo. 19, a remarkably dark day, with smoke.

7 mo. 13, began to cut wheat.

8 mo. 15, eat common red cherries.

10 mo. 7, a new tea-kettle bought for £112 10s.

12 mo. 4, ground covered with snow.

12 mo. 19, green flies plenty.

[1781.] 2 mo. 3 and 4, trees covered with ice to admiration.

7 mo. 20, finished hauling wheat—lateness occasioned by wet weather and heavy wheat.

9 mo. 15, finished sowing wheat.

[1782.] 9 mo. 7, John Carver finished sowing forty-five acres of wheat.

12 mo. 9, in the morning it began to snow, and continued until midnight, snowing very fast most of the time. It was near fourteen inches deep.

[1783.] 1 mo. 9 and 10, a very great snow storm, about twelve or fourteen inches deep.

5 mo. 21, the locusts began to come out of the ground in great numbers.

8 mo. 29, began sowing wheat.

[1784.] 4 mo. 9, the cistern froze.

[1785.] Frogs heard for first time, 3 mo. 1st.

4 mo. 16, there was a hard, black frost, and the little, still ponds were frozen over.

4 mo. 19, a great hail storm.

12 mo. 18, the weather very warm.

12 mo. 19, heard the bluebirds.

[1786.] 4 mo. 4, hail and snow fell to the depth of 5 inches.

5 mo. 18, a white frost.

12 mo. 4, about ten inches of snow fell upon an average, if it had not drifted.

12 mo. 8, it snowed and hailed, with a very high wind. Snow drifted to a great height.

12 mo. 25, Isaac Carver departed this life with the small-pox.

[1787.] 4 mo. 21, a very smart snow; the ground in the evening covered white with snow; the trees in full bloom; and it froze near an inch thick, and looked awful.

6 mo. 23, Mary Carver taken ill with the small-pox.

12 mo. 22, the roads dry and dusty.

[1788.] Second Month, eighteenth day,
   Our boy, James Anderson, ran away.

7 mo. 16, began harvesting; the first of the fly to our knowledge.—John Carver.

9 mo. 1, Thomas Roberts killed by falling out of a tree.

[1789.] 2 mo. 19, a very deep snow, near fourteen inches, if it had not drifted.

7 mo. 30, a great flood.

8 mo. 2, 3, and 4, there were four stout freshes in Poquessing Creek.

[1790.] 4 mo. 28—this morning the ground was covered with snow, and some of it lasted till night.

[1791.] 10 mo. 18, the trees were covered with sleet. It snowed and hailed and rained. The sleet lasted all the day long.

[1792.] 5 mo. 19, a large frost.

[1793.] 12 mo. 3 and 4, it snowed and blowed very hard. The snow was thought by some to be fourteen inches deep.

[1795.] 6 mo. 2, a hail storm.

[1804.] 3 mo. 29, thunder and great rain.

[1806.] First snow 12 mo. 3 ; moon twenty-three days old when the snow fell.

8 mo. 23, a great rain.

11 mo. 1, nothing in garden yet killed by frost.

[1807.] 4 mo. 25, the first thunder of the season.

[1829.] 9 mo. 17, Isaac Comly saw a land turtle on his farm which was marked I. C. (Isaac Comly), 1790 ; E. C. (Ezra Comly), 1795 ; J. C. (Joseph Comly), 1799. This turtle had been seen in 1811, 1812, 1815, and 1819. On the same day he found another turtle, which he had marked I. C. in 1789, forty years previous.

MISCELLANEOUS.

The good people of these townships were probably without a Justice of the Peace prior to 1770, when Alexander Edwards took out a commission. Previous to that time, those in need of such services resorted to Bustleton or Holmesburg. Edwards died in 1777, and his son, Dr. Edwards, succeeded him in the commission ; but in 1792 he removed to Frankford, where he died in 1802. Dr. Edwards was very useful in the neighborhood in keeping order among those needing restraint, and especially among the large boys, who congregated on the Sabbath for unnecessary and often pernicious practices. Prior to the Revolution no physician had thought proper to locate in either of the townships ; but about that time we find Dr. Swift settled in Moreland and engaged in an extensive practice. Soon afterward Dr. Edwards located in Byberry, and although considered a skilful physician, he gave up the practice after the Revolution, and turned his attention to politics and farming. The next one of note was Dr. Samuel Knight, in the lower end of the township. He was much beloved, and had the confidence of all classes until his death, in 1796. After this physicians became more plenty, and the townships have since always been well supplied with members of that useful profession. In 1784 a stone barn, the first in this vicinity, was built by Isaac Comly, on a place known as "Old Sod," and since then the property of his son Isaac, and now owned by Dr. Comly. A part of this is still standing, the walls being good, but the woodwork is nearly gone. In 1796, the barn now belonging to John P. Townsend, in Mechanicsville, was built. About the same time Edward Duffield built a barn in Moreland, near the village of Somerton. These were the first barns with stabling underneath and a bridge to get to the floor and mows. They are generally known as "cellar barns," and have been the fashion ever since.

In former times tailors and shoemakers did not work in shops as they do now, but they went from house to house to accommodate their employers; this was called "whipping the cat." The farmers would buy a sufficient quantity of leather, and the shoemaker was engaged to come once a year, when each member of the family was supplied with a pair of new shoes. As he boarded with the family his charges were moderate; although it was often very inconvenient for both parties. The tailor, also, was sent for as soon as the cloth came from the weaver's, and while there usually made up a suit of sheepskin breeches for lads and buckskin for men. About one hundred years ago square-toed shoes and boots were the tip of the fashion in this section. The same fashion has prevailed three times in the last fifty years, and is now "all the go." Almost every farmer thought it neces-sary to raise a portion of flax, from which were manufactured sheets, shirting, and all other neces-sary articles of clothing. One acre of good flax would produce enough to clothe ten or twelve per-sons, and could be raised at a trifling cost. When the tow was spun it was dyed different colors, and then sent to the weaver's, who wove it into cloth. This furnished material for nearly all the common clothing; but the "Sunday" clothes were made of finer materials, such as velvet, corduroy, &c. The apparel of the female portion of the family was generally made of wool, and some itinerant wool-comber and spinner was engaged every autumn to prepare the wool for weaving. From the first introduction of sheep in the township there was more or less loss sustained from having them killed by the dogs. Almost every man kept one, and some as many as half a dozen worthless curs, which were of no use to anybody, but always doing some mischief in the neighborhood. In or-der to recompense the owners of the sheep for their loss, some persons, in 1826, petitioned the Legislature and obtained from it an Act for taxing all the dogs in the township. The tax was to be collected by the Overseers of the Poor, and the money to be applied to paying for all sheep killed or injured by the dogs. From the passage of the Act, in 1826, until 1858, a period of thirty-two years, the sum paid for sheep thus killed amounted to one thousand and fifty-six dollars, being an average of thirty-three dollars per year, a sum greater than the real value of all the dogs in the township. On the night of the 19th of September, 1848, a dog killed twenty sheep for Watson Comly, and the next night the same dog killed twenty more for Morton Walmsley. The latter sheep were in a pen having a high fence around it. Into this the dog got by jumping off the barn bridge near by; but after doing the mischief he was unable to escape from the pen, and in the morning was dispatched by the owner of the sheep. Several others suffered in the same way, and fewer sheep have been kept since that time, partly on account of the danger of having them killed by the dogs.

Various schemes for getting rich in a shorter time than is possible in the ordinary way, have from time to time been tried; but all of them have uniformly proved failures, and left the experimenters in a worse, instead of a better, condition. Among these we hear of John Hopkins' scheme for getting rich by raising mustard, John Hancock's plan of cultivating castor beans to make " cold expressed castor oil ;" and John Livezey's culture of the Cayenne pepper-plant to supply the

16

people with that article. In 1838, the famous morus multicaulis was introduced, and extensive plans for raising silk were entered into. David Comfort erected a large frame building, thirty by fifty feet, for a cocoonery; but the bubble burst; so that in the latter part of the same year the trees were worthless, and could not be sold at any price, the cocoons could not be given away, and all the glorious expectations vanished like snow beneath the summer's sun. Several were plunged into irretrievable ruin, and their properties soon advertised by the sheriff. Comfort's cocoonery was sold in 1843 at less than one-fourth of its original cost, and was purchased by Charles Martindale, who employed Joseph Comly to move it to his farm, a distance of half a mile. This required four days; but was finally accomplished without any injury to the building.

About the year 1836, an anti-slavery society was established, and persons employed to lecture on the "Abolishment of African Slavery." These lectures were kept up for several years, and during that time some attempts were made to improve the condition of the blacks in the vicinity. Under the auspices of this society a Sabbath school for their instruction was established at the school-house in the meeting-house yard, and continued for several months, but it gradually declined. The members also lost their interest in the society, and it survived the school but a short time. It was the intention of this society to establish an anti-slavery library, and several volumes were purchased for that purpose. These were kept at the house of Samuel Kirk, in Mechanicsville, where most of them still remain, although no new ones have been added for many years, and but little interest is now manifested in regard to it.

In 1792, a society for debate was started by the young men of Byberry. At first they met at Thomas Walmsley's house, and afterward at the school-house. It was generally called "The Congress," and lasted only one winter. In 1796, another was started under the name of "The Fraternal Society," with Asa Walmsley as president, and John Comly secretary. It lasted one year. From this time till 1820 a debating school was in operation nearly every winter. One of these, in 1807, met at Byberry Cross-roads, and was composed of nearly all the inhabitants in the vicinity, whether good, bad, or indifferent. Many ludicrous anecdotes of their meetings are still in existence. William Plumley was the president; and on one occasion, when one of the members accidentally got intoxicated, he was fined one dollar, which sum was immediately paid. In 1858, the Byberry Literary Society was established, with eighty-four members. The proceedings were of an interesting character, and attracted much attention, so that the meetings were well attended. A paper known as the *Literary Record* was connected with the society, the articles to which were contributed by the members. Some of these compositions were very creditable, and evinced considerable talent on the part of the writers. After the commencement of the late rebellion several members left the neighborhood, and most of those remaining lost all interest in it, so that it was closed in 1862.

In 1864, this was again revived under the title of " Byberry Institute;" and through judicious management on the part of the members has become more popular than any such institution previously established in the township. The sessions are held weekly in the Byberry Hall, and generally attract full houses. This society held its first annual reunion in a romantic spot along the banks of the beautiful Neshaminy, in August, 1865. On that occasion several hundred invited guests assembled to listen to the dialogues, essays, and orations which were delivered by the members. The day was favorable, the exercises were good, and the whole affair passed off with so much satisfaction, that the first annual reunion of the Byberry Institute will long be remembered with pleasure by all who participated in its enjoyments. The second annual reunion of this society was held in August, 1866, and was still better than the first. These societies are to be commended as being the means of diffusing useful knowledge in the neighborhood, and we hope that this one may be long continued.

About thirty years ago a "debating school" was started in Moreland, and the meetings were held in Tillyer's school-house. It continued for several years, and was attended by most of the people in the vicinity, some of whom learned right well how " to spout." In later times a society for debating was started in Somerton, and became so popular as to attract speakers who lived six or eight miles away. It was closed in 1863, and has not since been revived.

When we look back, even for a few years, we find that great changes have taken place in almost every locality, particularly in the buildings and the general appearance of the country. Three houses formerly stood along the Bustleton and Somerton turnpike, near where the creek crosses above Byberry Point. The one on the west side was built of stones and logs, and but one story high, and was for many years occupied by Conrad Lingerman. The other two were on the east side, about fifty yards apart, both being on the farm of Thomas Chappell. One of these was a frame house two stories high, with but one room down stairs, and was occupied by Thomas Clark, in 1820. The other was stone and log, and occupied, in 1822, by Joseph Force; soon after this the house was torn down. At Byberry Point a very old frame and log house stood for many years, and was at one time occupied by George Duffield. It was taken down eight or nine years since by Jesse Clewell, its present owner, and a more commodious one erected in its place. A blacksmith shop formerly stood at this place, but has been gone over twenty-five years. Between this and the creek, on the west side of the road, was a woods, which I remember as a dark, gloomy place. Just above the point on the Byberry turnpike was a woods on the west side, and near by an old frame dwelling owned

and occupied for many years by "Bulger" Worthington. After it came into the possession of George
W. Saurman, most of the timber was sold off, and
a new house built in the woods, in 1855. The old
house has since been removed, and the place much
improved. At Knightsville, the old house occupied
by Leonard Knight, Esq., was torn down in 1856,
a short time after the Squire's death. The old
school-house which stood nearly opposite to John
Roberts's tenant-house has been moved back into
John Tomlinson's orchard, and is now used as a
wagon and store house. Opposite Tillyer's school
a very old log house stood where Mrs. Thomas
now lives, and was owned and occupied for many
years by Thomas Helverson. The present dwelling was built by his son Sammy, who for many
years taught the school opposite. An old house
stood on the farm now owned by Andrew Erwin,
not far from the present farm-house, but nearer the
creek. This was the residence of Susan Albertson
for several years, and until her death at a very
advanced age. The present house was built by
Squire Dawes.

The house on the farm now owned by William
Potts is very old, and was at one time occupied by
William Wainwright, and afterward by Dr. Worthington, who removed thence to Somerton, about
1823. The farm-house on the property owned by
the late Thomas Worthington was built by Thomas
Banes, grandfather of Joseph Banes, of Bustleton, in
place of a very old log house formerly there. Nearly
all the ancient houses in Somerton have been torn

down and new ones erected in their places, so that
the village presents rather a neat appearance. Four
old huts in this village were torn down several
years since by the neighbors, in order to get rid of
the occupants, who occasionally visited the " hen-
roosts " and " wood-piles " in the vicinity. At
Byberry Cross-roads there has been great change.
There was a large tract of woodland where Silas
Tomlinson's house now stands, and which extended
along the turnpike nearly to the little stream
crossing some distance below. In the west corner
was a store, kept previous to 1817 by the Carvers,
but during that year they sold out to Isaac Bolton.
It was afterwards kept by Josiah Walton, Thomas
R. Martindale, Charles E. Clayton, and others. A
blacksmith shop stood in the north, and a small
tenement in the south corner. All of these have
been removed, and a new set of buildings erected
in the west corner by Silas Tomlinson, the present
owner. This spot formerly had the euphonious
name of " Plumbsock," but is now called " Byberry Cross-roads." An old house formerly stood
under the walnut tree opposite to Charles Martindale's orchard, and a blacksmith shop stood in the
orchard, near the road. The well near the dwelling-house remained open until about twenty years
ago. It had been filled with stones to within six
or eight feet of the top, and was thus left, until
one day when they were plowing in the field, one
of the horses backed into it. After considerable
trouble he was taken out with a few bruises, and
the old well was filled up on the same day. An

old log house formerly stood near George Dehaven's line, on land belonging to Mr. Wilmer. It
was built by one of the Waltons. Another log
house stood where H. Humphrey's house now
stands, and was torn down only a few years ago.
On John Roberts's farm stood an old house for
many years occupied by Benny Peart. The buildings on the farm belonging to Charles Martindale
formerly consisted of an old stone house and a log
barn. The barn fell down near thirty years ago,
and the house was demolished by the present owner
about 1848. A blacksmith shop formerly stood at
the corner of Comly's road and Bustleton turnpike, near James Tomlinson's house. It was removed many years ago. A blacksmith shop stood
at Byberry Point, and for many years belonged to
George Duffield, but it was removed thirty odd
years ago. An old still-house, in which many a
gallon of whiskey was distilled, formerly stood on
the late Judge Sommers's farm. The whiskey business became so unprofitable that it was given up
about forty years ago, and the still-house converted into a wagon-house. A still-house also
stood on John Lingerman's farm, then belonging
to John Dyer, but this, too, has long since passed
away.

The road leading from Byberry Store to Townsend's Mill had a woods on both sides of it for a
considerable part of the distance. That on James
Thornton's place, now owned by Richard Cripps,
was for many years left open as commons, and
was a place of resort for the older part of the pres-

ent generation when they went to school. It was
filled with cow-paths; and one of those who then
frequented that spot has remarked "that the tink-
ling of the cow-bell, mingled with the shouts of
happy school-children, when he was a boy, still
come fresh to his memory, although like the old
woods they have long since departed forever." The
woods on Charles Martindale's place, between his
orchard and John Barney's, has been cut down
since my memory, although as far back as 1837.
Further on were extensive tracts of woodland on
the farms of John Carver and Evan Townsend,
which abounded with rabbits, squirrels and partridges. As gunners were not permitted there,
game was plenty, and the boys in the vicinity had
much pleasure as well as profit in trapping and
snaring it in the fall and winter; but the old oaks,
chestnuts and hickories, which thickly covered the
ground, are all gone, and only here and there a
stump remains to tell the tale to passing travellers. The east side of the road from Byberry Hall
to Vanarsdalen's Corner was cleared off only a few
years since; and a large tract of timber on the
road from the Benjamin Rush School-house to Gordon's dam has been removed within the last twenty
years, and several houses built where it stood.

In the latter part of 1816, a society of young
women was formed in Byberry, the object of which
was to afford relief to the poor. They held meetings in order to increase their funds, and not only
made contributions themselves, but solicited them
from others. Various articles of clothing were

made up and distributed among the needy, and did much toward alleviating the sufferings of the poor.

In 1817 the corn was much injured by the grub-worm, so that it did not yield more than half a crop. Prices that year ranged as follows: wheat, per bushel, $1.87; rye, 80 cents; buckwheat, 55 cents; corn, 75 cents; oats, 35 cents; flaxseed, $1.90; cloverseed, $12; potatoes, 50 cents; butter, 31 cents; apples, 60 cents; and eggs, 20 cents.

July 21, 1817, was remarkable for the violent storm of wind and rain which occurred, when a large number of trees were uprooted or twisted off, fences were blown down, the corn much injured, and the fruit blown off the trees. Several days in the beginning of May, this year, were observed to be very smoky, but the cause was not known. Previous to 1840, militia trainings were very common in the townships, on which occasions many of the inhabitants "turned out and drilled," to obviate the necessity of paying militia fines. On the 13th of May, 1816, about fifty persons assembled for this purpose, and elected Seneca Hibbs as their captain. At such times considerable liquor was drunk, and, when under its influence, quarrels were of frequent occurrence.

The majority of the people were never much in favor of "training days," and toward the last of them the greatest "ignoramuses" in the neighborhood were usually elected captains, brigade inspectors, &c.; and their actions while in office caused no little merriment to the lovers of fun. Isaac Comly remarks that "many of the old resi-

dents recollect the achievements of Colonel Galla-
gher. On one occasion at Milford, Bucks County,
the Colonel was rigged out in a cocked hat, military coat, and a sword four feet long, made of an
old scythe. He rode Giles Knight's jackass, and
the sword dragged on the ground. The jackass
would not go across the bridge over the Neshaminy, so the fellows carried the Colonel, jackass and
all over, much to the merriment of those present.
Some objections were made to the Colonel's eating
dinner with the other officers, but his company
pushed him on and he went through. This was
the last training in this section."

• The summer of 1816 was remarkably cool, and,
from some notes made at the time, we find a frost
occurred May 16, so as to kill the garden vegetables,
corn, &c.; and, on June 11th, frost was noticed in the
low places generally. During the same year the
crops were below the average yield, and one of
the poets of the day noted the fact in the following lines:

> " The grass tho' short the laborer's mowing ;
> The corn is small, but fast is growing ;
> The winter was hard upon our rye ;
> The wheat's much injured by the fly ;
> Now and then we have a storm,
> A few days cold, and then it's warm."

In 1819 land sold at least $30 per acre lower than
it had done in 1814, and many who were forced to
sell were entirely ruined. During the winter which
followed, the laboring men found but little to do,
and several were hard beset to get along. The as-

sociation of ladies was very active, and the sufferings much mitigated. The poor in other places were much pinched, and we find many went round with briefs to collect money. One of these was to enable John Brooks to build a house; another to enable Thomas Ridge to go to Ohio. A Dutch woman from Frankford went around to collect money for the same purpose, and when questioned as to why she came to Byberry, she said she was advised to "because it was considered a good place." Emigrating to Ohio became very fashionable, and several families left their native place; among these were Isaac Tomlinson, William Plumley, Griffith Street, John Adams, and Joseph Croasdale, Jr.

Some time during the latter part of this summer a balloon passed over a portion of Moreland; and as things of this kind were rather uncommon, people speculated upon the cause. Some were at a loss to conceive what it could be; but others saw in it the resemblance of a cow, which had in some supernatural manner been provided with wings, and was then journeying over the country in order to see the fine farms and happy people around Philadelphia.

The collection of the tax assessed upon the people for military purposes has always been a matter attended with serious trouble in the townships. Most of the inhabitants are Friends, and their principles would not permit them to pay money for such purposes. In many places the collectors did nothing more than ask for the tax; while in others they

adopted every means in their power for obtaining
it. Sometimes they seized upon such property as
they could find, such as carriages, harness, grind-
stones, horses, cows, hogs, &c.; all of which were
sold at public sale, after which the overplus was
returned to the several owners. Those who refused to pay were often taken to jail, where they
were sometimes kept for several days, and until
they or their friends paid the amounts assessed to
them.

The summer of 1818 was very sickly, and many
persons died. Help was very scarce, so that the
neighbors had to assist each other. Joseph Comly
was sick nearly all summer, and as he was unable
to attend to his farm, the neighbors assisted him.
On one occasion they assembled to the number of
thirty-five, and cut down thirty acres of grass and
grain for him in one day. During this year John
Black kept a hotel at Smithfield; and we find that
he brought a suit against several individuals, to
recover twelve and a half cents for liquor furnished
them by way of treat at the militia muster. He
obtained judgment in his favor, and they had the
debt to pay as well as the costs. This year Conrad
Snyder, from Bensalem, was through Byberry
collecting money to pay a doctor's bill! Lucky
doctor!

August 29, 1818, we find it stated that Elizabeth
Barton was at Byberry Meeting, and preached on
the subject of "The sun's softening wax and hard-
ening clay."

Some of the geniuses of the townships are spoken

of as trying their skill at invention during this year. Their thoughts were influenced by the ambitious desires of Fulton and others; and Benjamin Willard, of Mechanicsville, spent some time in making a wagon to go by steam; but, unfortunately for the reputation of the village and the purse of Willard, the wagon did not go.

There is still in use in Byberry a pair of cart wheels, the hubs of which were part of a wagon belonging to William Walmsley, great grandfather to Silas Walmsley. The wagon was taken to carry stores to the English army engaged in the French and Indian War in 1759. The following occurs in William Walmsley's account book: "Ye 30th day of ye 6th month, June, 1759, John Vanhorn and Thomas Webb pressed my wagon, and took it away to carry military stores to Ohio, and brought the wagon back ye 29th of ye 9th month, 1759." These hubs "are made of quartered white oak, and are the last of the military matters of those days. Could these hubs speak to their *felloes*, what feats of arms and deeds of valor done in olden time would they portray!"

After the Revolutionary War wild animals became very scarce, and panthers, wolves, or wildcats were seldom seen. A panther was shot in Moreland about the year 1790. Some wild turkeys were seen there in 1792, and in 1835 William Webster shot a wild-cat near the Bristol turnpike. Game, such as partridges, pheasants, rabbits, squirrels, &c., were plenty until within a few years; but as their haunts have been destroyed, they have gradually decreased in number until but few are now found.

Exciting accounts of some wild animals have from time to time been circulated, and a few of the timid ones have been so frightened that they could not be induced to expose themselves to the danger after nightfall. Although the tracks of bears, panthers, otters, beavers, &c., are said to have been seen, yet none of these animals have been captured.

In the year 1853, a company of Chippewa Indians, consisting of a chief, his squaw, and two sons, visited Byberry, and encamped in Morton Walmsley's woods, where they remained nearly the whole summer. In order to raise money they gave several entertainments in Byberry Hall, which were well attended, and furnished them with as much as sufficed for their wants. They roamed through the fields and woods, but were very civil, not molesting anybody.

The Independent Mutual Fire Insurance Company was chartered in 1843. This is not confined to the townships alone, but extends over a portion of Bucks, Montgomery, and Philadelphia Counties. The first meeting respecting this company was held at Somerton in 1842; and at the next session of the Legislature a charter was obtained. Franklin Comly, Esq., was the President of the Company until his death in 1860; since that time John Smith, Esq., of Huntington Valley, has been its presiding officer. Watson Comly, Esq., has always been its secretary. It commenced with an insurance of

$200,000, but the amount now insured is over
$2,800,000, and is steadily increasing. Nearly all
the property in both townships is insured in this
Company. The losses by fire are paid by assess-
ments upon the property insured.

We have now traced all the more important
events of the townships from their earliest settlement down to the present time. In the first part
of the history we have probably collected nearly
all events of interest that have escaped the ravages
of time; but during the last few years various
things have transpired which we have not noticed,
although they would be interesting to many persons. It is, however, probable that few, if any, in
the townships, have preserved an account of the
events of the last twenty years—a matter particularly to be regretted, as Isaac Comly faithfully
chronicled all events of interest from about the
the year 1790, until his death, in 1847, and a portion of this history has been obtained from such
accounts as he from time to time published.

TOPOGRAPHY, GEOLOGY, ETC.

The surface of Byberry has a general slope to
the south, the most northern part being sufficiently elevated to afford a good view of the
greater part of the township and of the country
lying on both sides of the Delaware River. All
the larger streams take their rise in this locality,
and flow in a general southerly direction. Just

above the northern boundary of the township the
Poquessing, one of the most beautiful and interesting streams in the vicinity, takes its rise; and, as it
flows onward through a rolling country, forms the
entire eastern boundary. It has several small tributaries from Byberry, the most important of which
is Bloody Run, which empties into it above Carter's
Mill, Black Lake Creek at Mechanicsville, and Gilbert's Run, about a mile below. It passes through
a beautiful district, well suited to agricultural purposes, the country being moderately rolling, and
the soil fertile. Its banks, for the most part, are
skirted with timber, and but few dwellings of any
description are near it. Much of the scenery along
its course is picturesque, and it affords considerable matter of interest to the traveller. From its
source to its mouth, a distance of about twelve
miles, there are no fewer than eight mill-dams,
which furnish water-power to as many mills. This
can be said of but few streams in this vicinity. Of
these mills five (one saw-mill and four grist-mills)
are in Byberry, and are all on the western bank of
the creek.

The Byberry Creek, the next stream of importance, rises in the "timber swamp," in the northern part of the township, a little to the southwest
of Somerton, and flows through the middle of the
township, receiving several small tributaries in its
course. One of these—Ellwood's Run—comes from
Silas Tomlinson's land, and unites with the main
stream, or Wilson's Run, on Horace Smith's farm;
while the only other one of moment rises in More-

17*

land, flows a southeasterly course, and empties into •
the main stream on Nathaniel Richardson's farm.
Soon after receiving this stream the main creek is
turned to the southwest, around the base of a
range of hills, forming part of the western boundary, and finally comes back on the south side of
the same range, meeting with the Poquessing at
the extreme southern end of the township, about
one mile from where it empties into the Delaware.
This stream has but one mill on it—Charles Comly's—near the centre of Byberry. By these streams
and their tributaries the whole of Byberry is
drained.

The surface of the country is generally level, except along the eastern boundary and in the southern part, where a few moderate elevations are
found ; yet these are so limited that no part of the
surface can be said to be hilly or rough. The geo-
logical features, therefore, present nothing striking ;
and, so far as I have examined them, but little
worth inserting in sketches like these. In the
northern part the soil is a little sandy and mixed
with mica, and contains some of the common gar-
net, though the specimens are usually small. This
is underlaid with rocks of mica slate, which seems
to be the most common formation in the northern
part of the township, and from the amount of gar-
net found in it might be denominated garnetifer-
ous mica slate. This is well shown along the
course of the Poquessing. Nearer the middle of
the township the gneiss formation is generally
found, composed of quartz, feldspar and mica, and

underlying the whole surface. These ingredients
are blended in different proportions, and along
with them hornblende and talc occasionally occur.
Along Black Lake Run hornblende is found mixed
with the gneiss; and in the same vicinity I found
some specimens of that mineral, where *talc* had
taken the place of the mica, forming a rock called
protogine. Soapstone, or talc, is also found on
farms belonging to Jonathan Leedom and William
Carter, near Somerton. On the farm belonging to
Silas Vanarsdalen, two or three rocks, weighing
several tons each, have been found, presenting
very much the appearance of Edge Hill stone.
These are gneiss, containing more than the usual
quantity of feldspar, blended with the quartz and
mica; the latter in very small quantities, giving to
it the appearance of Edge Hill stone, which is a
mixture of feldspar and quartz intimately inter-
fused. From its spotted appearance it has been
denominated porphyritic gneiss. It also contains
a little tourmaline or schorl. Professor Rogers, in
his report on the geology of Pennsylvania, remarks
" that where the feldspar is the predominating mineral, it exhibits a remarkable tendency to pass to
the condition of kaolin by decomposition." Specimens of this last-mentioned mineral occur on the
road leading from Mechanicsville to Gordon's Mill,
just below Thomas James's house, only a few hundred yards from the rocks on Vanarsdalen's farm,
and probably have been formed by such decomposition. The kaolin is in small quantities, and too
impure to be of any value for manufacturing pur-

poses. In some localities, particularly along the Poquessing, where this formation is exposed, the laminated structure is somewhat remarkable for its tortuosities and irregularities; but in others it is very regular in its arrangement, and affords excellent material for building and other purposes. On Silas Tomlinson's farm there is a quarry of hornblende, which furnishes excellent stone for turnpikes. This mineral has also been found in several other places in the townships.

Along the Poquessing, about half a mile below Mechanicsville, on the Bensalem side of the stream, there is a projection or mound about twenty-five feet high, and covering near a half acre of surface. It is composed of gneiss, the feldspar of which has mostly changed into kaolin, and contains here and there a few crystals of schorl. This mass has the appearance of having at some former time been united with the rocks on the Byberry side, its composition and general appearance being similar to them. It is, therefore, not improbable, but that the Poquessing may once have passed around to the east of it, and that the projection was undermined by the action of the water, and fell into the valley where it now lies, and that the stream has formed a passage between it and the rocks to which it was attached. This change probably occurred many years since, as the mound is now covered with earth, in many places four feet deep, in which the remains of large trees may still be seen.

In the meadow lately owned by George Weiss, there are two large masses of rocks, composed of

asbestiform actinolite, in which impressions similar to those made by a man's foot appear. A similar print has been observed in a rock near the
mouth of the Poquessing, which has given rise to
the belief by the superstitious "that they were
made by the Devil when he leaped over the Delaware into the Jerseys."

Bog iron ore occurs in several places in the
northern end of the township; sulphuret of iron in
small crystals also is found, intermingled with
other minerals. Some very pure specimens of
black mica occur along the Poquessing in several
localities, but they are usually small. A few specimens of green quartz, or *prase*, probably colored
by actinolite, have been found in the vicinity. On
Nathaniel Richardson's farm some specimens containing sulphate of copper have also been found.

A peculiarity in the water-courses exists which
deserves to be mentioned. They are all found to
the western side of the valleys through which they
flow, and, consequently, that bank is generally
skirted with hills made up of the gneiss or mica
slate. From this circumstance it is rare to find a
good quarry on the eastern banks of any of the
streams.

The lower end of Moreland generally slopes to
the south, being drained by the tributaries of Byberry Creek. The soil in that section is generally
argillaceous, and only moderately fertile. The
prevailing formation there is micaceous, yet few
quarries are found. In the northern part the land
slopes to the west, the surface being sufficiently

rolling to carry off the waste water. The soil here
is either a sandy or gravelly loam, except that
part in the vicinity of the "timber swamp," which
is argillaceous. A small stream rises in this swamp,
and drains the clay bottom in the vicinity; while
to the north another stream rises in the rolling
ground. After flowing about a mile across the
township in a westerly direction, they unite and
form a pleasant little stream which finds its way
to the Pennypack, near Verreeville. Some quarries have been opened along this stream, from
which excellent building-stone is obtained. The
geology, &c., of Moreland, is similar to that of Byberry, and affords but little of interest to the general reader.

VILLAGES, ETC.

Babylon, about half a mile southeast of the Byberry Meeting-house, is a scattered village lying
on both sides of the road, and containing eight
dwelling-houses, besides a few other buildings.
The late Thomas Gilbert was the first settler in
the place.

Black Lake is a small stream, one branch of
which rises on John Carver's place and the other
on James Thornton's, and, after flowing nearly a
mile, unite on land belonging to Charles Martindale. It then flows a winding southeasterly course
for another mile, and empties into the Poquessing
at Mechanicsville. The water in this stream has
a very dark appearance, and is probably colored

by vegetable matter along its course. This will account for the name of "Black," but why called "Lake" is not known. The name, however, has been used from time immemorial, and we are not disposed to change it. There is a tradition that stonecoal was found along this stream on the farm now owned by Charles Martindale, before the Revolutionary War, but no evidence of it has since occurred.

Byberry Point, in the western part of Moreland, is at the junction of the Bustleton and Byberry turnpike roads, about three-fourths of a mile from the former place. There is but one house here.

Byberry Cross-roads is where the Southampton road crosses the Byberry and Bensalem turnpike, about one mile north of Byberry Meeting-house. A tavern was formerly kept here with the sign of the "Three Tuns," but was afterwards converted into a store, which was kept by different persons until within a few years. At one time several mechanics were located here, and the place was called "Plumbsock;" but these have all disappeared, and the place is now known as Byberry Cross-roads.

Carter's Mill is on the Poquessing, in the northern part of the township. It was built by the late James Carter. Several houses are in the vicinity. A saw and a grist-mill are in operation here, both doing a good business.

Amos Knight's Corner is on the Byberry and Holmesburg road, one mile southwest of the Meeting-house. It was named after its late proprietor,

Amos Knight, who lived here many years, and was noted for his eccentricities.

Ellwood's Run is a small stream emptying into Byberry Creek on Morris Penrose's place. Its source is on land owned by Silas Tomlinson, about one mile from its mouth. It was named after Thomas Ellwood, who for many years lived in a small tenement near it.

Gingerbread Field is west of Knight's Mill, near the Poquessing, on a part of the original Ellis's tract of five hundred acres. On this Ellis had his habitation; and in the garden attached both he and his wife were buried. The graves were for a long time inclosed by a fence, but now no vestige of them remains.

Kaintuck, composed chiefly of meadow-land, is situated in the northern part of Byberry, near the foot of Edge Hill, and extends along the west branch of the Poquessing Creek for half a mile.

Knight's Mill is on the Byberry and Andalusia turnpike, in the southern part of Byberry. It is on the Poquessing, and was erected about 1770, by Jonathan Knight, gentleman; it was rebuilt in 1815. There are five or six dwelling-houses near by, also a county bridge over the Poquessing.

Knightsville is situate on the Byberry and Bensalem turnpike road, where the Moreland road crosses it, near the thirteenth mile-stone. It is a village containing six dwelling-houses and some other buildings. It was named in honor of Leonard Knight, Esq., and Jonathan Knight, Judge, who for many years resided here. A school was formerly kept at this place.

Minktown, a village of two houses, is situate on the Poquessing, near Townsend's mill-dam. The house was built here over seventy years ago, by Benjamin Adams, weaver, and contained but two rooms, in which was brought up a large family of children. It derived its name from the number of minks found here a few years since. Opposite to this place is the burying-ground for colored people.

Pleasantville, on the county line, about one mile east of Somerton, is a village of ten or twelve houses. It was formerly noted for the store kept there by Edward Worthington, and was then called Tortleburg, or, more politely, Terrapin-town. These names have of late been discarded, and from its being a pleasant place is now called Pleasantville.

Perth is a small village near Bloody Run, on the road leading from Somerton to the county line. It has become noted for being the place where Hart was attacked and seriously injured, for which the Mansons were tried and acquitted.

Ridge's Mill is on the Poquessing, near the north corner of Byberry. It has a long mill-race, but no dam, yet considerable business is done here.

Townsend's Mill, on the Poquessing, one mile northeast of Byberry Meeting-house, was built in 1767, and remained in the Townsend family from its erection until within ten or twelve years. It is a valuable property, and capable of grinding 15,000 bushels per year. There are several dwellings and a smith and wheelwright shop near it. During the exciting presidential canvass of 1844 it was called " Coonville," on account of the emblematic raccoons kept there in connection with the cause of Henry Clay, and has since frequently gone by that name.

Timber Swamp. This is a large tract of woodland reaching from the west corner of Byberry near Andrew Ervein's, northeast along the Moreland line almost to the Somerton road. This was formerly one vast tract of woodland, the largest in the vicinity, and was a noted hunting ground. Raccoons, opossums, squirrels, and birds were found there in abundance, and even bears were sometimes seen. The last Bruin found there was in 1780, and was shot by Jersey Billy Walton. It was formerly a great place for ghosts, &c., and many marvellous tales have been narrated as occurring in the " timber swamp." Much of the timber has been cleared off within a few years, and its limits thereby greatly contracted.

Powelltown, at the junction of the Moreland and the Holmesburg roads, is a village of five or six dwelling-houses, a school-house, and some other buildings. The school-house is a new building, and an ornament to the place. This village is named after a family of Powells, who resided there for many years.

Comly's Mill is the only one on the Byberry Creek, and is near the centre of Byberry, about one mile south of the Meeting-house. This stream not furnishing sufficient water-power, the enterprising proprietor, Charles B. Comly, introduced steam, and the mill is now run by it instead of water, and does an extensive business. A few houses have been built near by, mostly by Robert Phillips, the former owner, giving the place the appearance of a village.

Somerton, the largest village in the township, is situate on the Bustleton and Somerton turnpike road, about three miles from the former place, and thirteen from Philadelphia. It is partly in Moreland and partly in Byberry, and extends a quarter of a mile along the turnpike. A public school-house and a Methodist church have, within a few years, been erected here. Besides these, the place contains three hotels, two shoemakers, one saddle and harnessmaker, two stores, one wheelwright, one blacksmith, one undertaker, two carpenters, one tailor, and one doctor. It contains about thirty-five dwelling-houses, and a population numbering about one hundred and eighty persons. A post-office has been established here, and is connected with Philadelphia by a daily mail. A little to the east of the village is the William Penn Cemetery.

Byberry Store, now owned by Ross M. Knight, is the chief emporium of Byberry, and is near the centre of the township. A post-office was established here in 1832, and it is now in daily communication, by mail, with Philadelphia. Near by is Friends' Meeting-house, in which many important events of bygone times have transpired, and around

which much that is dear to every native of Byberry still lingers. Byberry Hall and the Cabinet
of Natural Curiosities belonging to the Byberry
Philosophical Society are here; and the old school,
established more than a century ago, and which
for a long time was the only one in the township,
is still kept open for the education of the youth.
A tailor and a shoemaker shop are near at hand;
and two or three dwelling-houses also help to give
importance to the place. It is now as it has been
ever since the first settlement, the centre of at-
traction in Byberry.

Mechanicsville, next to Somerton in point of size,
is situate on the Poquessing, where Black Lake
Creek empties into it. It was named from the
number of mechanics settled there, and is a place
of considerable importance. It contains about
twenty dwelling-houses and several other buildings, which are scattered on both sides of the
valley through which Black Lake flows; and it
numbers about one hundred and fifty persons in
population. In it the trades are well represented,
as carpenters, masons, storekeepers, machinists,
butchers, wheelwrights, saddlers and harnessma-
kers, scriveners, and farmers are found within
its limits. A mill for sawing lumber and grinding
feed, and a public school, are in successful operation here. Opposite to this place, on the Bensalem side of the Poquessing, is Elizabethtown, a
small village containing several dwellings, all of
which have been erected within twelve or fifteen
years. A substantial county bridge connects these
two places.

BIOGRAPHICAL SKETCHES.

JOHN HART.

JOHN HART, born at Whitney, in Oxfordshire, England, November 16, 1651 (O. S.), was among the earliest settlers, having come over with Penn, in 1682. He purchased four hundred and eighty-four acres of land, bordering on the Poquessing Creek, in the southern part of Byberry, on which he settled and spent several years of his life. He was a man of rank, character, and reputation, had considerable influence, and was several times elected a member of the Assembly. He was a leading member of Byberry Meeting, and at one time considered a good preacher. He manifested great interest in promoting the views and doctrines of George Keith, his name being attached to many of the papers published by that party against Friends; and at the separation, all his nearest neighbors, and some of those more distant, joined him in opposing the principles maintained by Friends. After the separation, in 1691, he preached to a society of Keithians that met at the house of John Swift, in Southampton; but, in

1697, this meeting was broken up, and he, along with many others, embraced the principles of the Baptists, and was baptized by Thomas Rutter. In 1702, they joined the meeting at Pennypack, where Hart became assistant minister, but was never ordained. He was, however, considered a pious Christian and a good preacher, and continued to officiate at that meeting, and at a Baptist Church in Philadelphia, from 1707 to 1720. He sold all his possessions in Byberry in 1705, and removed to Southampton. His wife was Susannah Rush, by whom he had five children : John, Joseph, Thomas, Josiah, and Mary, who married into the Crispin, Miles, Paulin, and Dungan families, and mostly settled in Lower Dublin.

JOHN RUSH.

JOHN RUSH, the patriarch of the Rush family in Byberry, was the commander of a troop of horse in Cromwell's army. After the war was over, he married Susannah Lucas, of Harteen, in Oxfordshire, in 1648. In 1660, he embraced the principles of the Quakers, and along with his whole family, consisting of seven children and several grandchildren, came to Pennsylvania in 1683, and settled on Byberry Creek, near where Reuben Parry now lives. In 1691, he and his family became Keithians, and, in 1697, most of them joined the Baptists. He died in 1699, leaving ten children, seven sons and three daughters. His sword and watch have been preserved by his descendants; also, his family Bible, containing the names of his children, in his own handwriting.

JAMES RUSH.

JAMES RUSH, son of John and Susannah Rush, was born in Oxfordshire, England, in 1678, and was brought over with the family to Pennsylvania, in 1683. He never married, but remained at the family mansion, where he died in 1727, aged forty-nine years, and was buried in the ancient graveyard in the southern part of Byberry.

WILLIAM RUSH.

WILLIAM Rush, son of John and Susannah Rush, came over with the family in 1683. He was married while in England; but his wife, Amelia, died in the latter part of the same year of their arrival, and was buried at John Hart's burying-ground on the Poquessing. William died in 1688.

HENRY ENGLISH.

HENRY ENGLISH, brother-in-law to Giles Knight, came over to Byberry some time previous to 1690. While in England he married Hannah West, in 1685, and with her came to America, and settled on his half of his father's purchase in Byberry. He was a member with Friends, and gave one acre of ground for the use of the meeting. But little is known of him except that he lost his first wife, and that he married Hannah, widow of William Hibbs, in 1712. In March, 1711, a year previous to this marriage, he made a deed of his property

to his intended spouse, which expressly stated
"that it was in consideration of the love, good-will
and affection which he had and did bear toward
his loving friend, Hannah Hibbs." He died about
1724, but probably left no children.

JOSEPH ENGLISH.

JOSEPH ENGLISH, one of the original settlers,
came over with Penn, in 1682, and settled in Byberry. He married Joan, widow of Henry Comly,
of Bucks County, in 1684. He died 8th mo. 10th,
1686, and his wife, 10th mo. 20th, 1689.

WALTER FORREST.

WALTER FORREST came over with Penn, in 1682.
He took up a large tract of land in New Jersey;
also, some land in the southern part of Byberry,
bordering on the Poquessing. On this little tract
he settled, and built a mill near where Thomas's
Mill now stands. He was a member with Friends,
and his name frequently appears in the early records of the Society. He held considerable property at the time of his death, but it is probable
that he left no heirs, as none are mentioned in his
last Will.

ABEL KINGSTONE.

ABEL KINGSTONE, one of the earliest settlers in
Bensalem, lived near the present residence of Joseph Knight. The earliest account of him extant
is, that in 1706 he was appointed one of the Overseers of Byberry Preparative Meeting. He was

continued in this service for several years; and, between 1717 and 1735, was repeatedly chosen to visit Friends' families, in which service he gave great satisfaction. He was appointed an Elder by Abington Monthly Meeting, in which capacity he continued twenty-eight years, and was the first person chosen to this station under the discipline. He is uniformly spoken of by his neighbors and contemporaries with much respect, and was considered a valuable and worthy Friend. He was an approved minister in the Society for many years previous to his death, which occurred 11th mo., 1747. He left several daughters, one of whom married John Cadwallader, of Horsham; and another (Susannah) married George James, of Philadelphia, in 1717, and had two children, Abel and Elizabeth. Abel was afterward a noted merchant in Philadelphia, and Elizabeth married Giles Knight the second, in 1738, and became owners of the Kingstone estate in Bensalem.

GEORGE JAMES.

GEORGE JAMES was a tailor, and followed that business at the old Kingstone homestead in Bensalem. He buried his first wife, and, in 1738, married Sarah Townsend, of Long Island. She was a widow, and the mother of Thomas and John Townsend, who were afterwards noted members of Byberry Meeting. George James was a member of the Society of Friends, and by them was much respected. His wife Sarah died about 1773, aged about 83 years. The date of his death is not known.

WILLIAM HIBBS.

WILLIAM HIBBS was among the early settlers from England, and his land laid northwest of the tract belonging to Henry English. He remained with Friends after the Keithian controversy, but seems to have had some difficulty with his neighbors. He died previous to 1711.

DUNCAN FAMILY.

The DUNCANS settled north of Byberry, in Bensalem. They were noted in their day as solid and exemplary Friends. Among these were John Duncan, Edmond Duncan, and William Duncan, for many years Clerk of Byberry Meeting. The last of the family was a "learned old bachelor," who died at an advanced age, in 1808.

JOSEPH FOSTER.

JOSEPH FOSTER was among the early inhabitants, and we find it stated that in 1731 he purchased of Josiah Ellis a part of his tract in Byberry, and erected a log house thereon, near the residence of the late Isaac Comly, where he lived several years. He left eight sons, from whom most of that name have descended.

WILLIAM HOMER.

WILLIAM HOMER settled in Byberry in 1713. He was a member with Friends. He married Mary Walton in 1729, but left no children.

WILLIAM BILES.

WILLIAM BILES came from England in 1678, and took up his residence in Bucks County. He had considerable talents, and was one of the Justices of Upland Court, until the division of the Province into three counties. He was a man of integrity and influence, a valuable minister of the Society of Friends, and was one of the signers of the celebrated testimony of that Society against George Keith. He frequently visited the settlement at Byberry, and was identified with its early history.

ABEL JAMES.

ABEL, son of George and Susannah James, and grandson of Abel Kingstone, was born at the residence of his grandfather, on the Poquessing Creek, in 1716. He married Rebecca, daughter of Thomas Chalkley, and afterward became a noted merchant of Philadelphia. He was much esteemed for his benevolence, and distinguished himself as an active member of the Friendly Association for regaining and preserving peace with the Indians in 1757.

ANN MOORE.

In 1750, WALTER MOORE and his wife, ANN MOORE, came from Fairfax, and resided at Byberry four years. She was a valuable minister among Friends, and was held in high esteem by all who knew her. Her parents lived in Bucks County, where she was brought up without much, if any, education, and but little care had been ex-

ercised over her in any way. She was unfortunate in her marriage, as her husband was not only
in indigent circumstances, but was intemperate.
She appears, however, to have risen above the
things of time, and looked to a Higher power for
support under those trying circumstances; and, if
we are allowed to judge from her words and actions, the light of truth enlarged her understanding, and, in an eminent degree, qualified her as
a gospel minister. She was indeed a powerful
preacher. Her manners were dignified, her voice
melodious, and when exercised in the ministry, her
words flowed freely; her style was impressive, and
her thoughts were clothed in such beautiful language that she attracted many hearers, and few
preachers in that day were considered her equal.
Of her Dr. John Watson remarks: "That she used
no gestures; her left hand was applied to the side
of her face, while the truths of the gospel flowed
from her tongue in language, accents and periods,
somewhat resembling the style of the poems of
Ossian." They resided in a small tenement belonging to Benjamin Walton, near David Dyer's
present residence. In 1754 they removed to Maryland, and no further account of them has been
found.

NICHOLAS MOORE.

NICHOLAS MOORE, an attorney of London, after
whom Moreland was named, came over from England in company with Penn, in 1682. He took
up a large tract of land, embracing the manor of

Moreland, now Moreland, in Philadelphia, and
Moreland, in Montgomery County. He settled on
this tract at a place called Green Spring, in the
vicinity of the present village of Somerton, where
he erected a dwelling-house near a fine spring of
water. He was a distinguished Judge and Coun-
sellor of William Penn, and was Chairman of the
first Provincial Assembly of Freemen of Pennsylvania, which convened at Chester in 12th mo.,
1682. In 1684 he was elected a member of the
Assembly for Philadelphia, and was chosen its
Speaker, although strongly opposed by a portion
of that body. On the 4th of the 6th mo., in the
same year, Penn granted to him, along with four
others, commissions as Provincial Judges, for two
years from that date, and he was made the Chief
Justice of the number. In 1685 he was again
elected a member of the Assembly, but fell under
its displeasure, and was impeached as a corrupt
and aspiring minister of state. As William Penn
had gone to England, a letter containing the im-
peachment was transmitted to him, but it did not
receive his approbation, and in 1686, when he
changed the Executive Government to a Board of
Five Commissioners, he appointed Judge Moore
and two of his former associates as members of
that board. Moore was retained in this responsible
position until 1687, and during this whole time he
appears to have given satisfaction, as we find no
more said against him. By his course he gained
the good will of most of his contemporaries, and
enjoyed the high confidence of William Penn.

19

While he was Judge, he established a Court at his residence, and erected a jail there for "punishing and reforming culprits;" but it seldom had any occupants. Judge Moore was a man of more than ordinary abilities, and from the high positions he filled, his name has become conspicuously identified with the earliest history of Moreland, and will be remembered by the people of one of the finest agricultural districts in the vicinity. During the latter part of his life he was in a languishing condition, and his pecuniary affairs suffered so much that, at his death, in 1689, his estate was much incumbered, and was afterward disposed of by the sheriff, and was the first sale of the kind ever made in Pennsylvania. He left several children, but we find little said of them in the subsequent history.

JOHN WATTS.

John Watts was a celebrated surveyor, who resided during the greater part of his life in Lower Dublin. He and his brother Silas were both practically acquainted with surveying in all its bearings, and did most if not all of that business in the townships for many years, and were of great use in settling disputed lines. John was a teacher of considerable reputation, and, for some years previous to 1790, taught in Tillyer's school, Moreland. He was very fond of mathematics, and is said to have been among the best in the country.

DR. EDWARDS.

Dr. Edwards was born in Byberry, and was among her most noted sons. During the Revolutionary War he was engaged in the cause of his country, and, for meritorious conduct, was commissioned an officer. After peace was established he returned to his native place, where he filled several public stations with honor and credit. He was commissioned a Justice of the Peace, and in that capacity was of much service in the neighborhood in settling cases to the satisfaction of parties concerned. Dr. Edwards was the first regular physician in Byberry, but he subsequently gave up a good practice, and devoted his attention to politics and agriculture. In 1792 he sold his farm in Byberry and removed to Frankford, after which he was a Judge of the Court of Common Pleas in Philadelphia—a position which it is said he filled creditably. He published some very interesting papers on agricultural subjects; and a charge which he delivered to the Grand Jury, while on the Bench, was published in the "American Museum." He died in 1802, aged 52 years.

PETER YARNALL, M.D.

Dr. Yarnall was born in 1753, and in early life resided in Horsham, where he practised medicine with great success, and was much respected. In 1797 he married Hannah Thornton, of Byberry, and came to the Thornton homestead, where he resided until his death, which occurred after a few days' illness, in 1798, at the age of forty-five years. He was an eminent minister among Friends, and preached the doctrines of peace and good-will to all men, so that the latter part of his life strangely contrasted with his early days, when engaged in the hostile measures of the Revolution.

DR. SWIFT.

DR. SWIFT, an eminent physician, was one of the first who resided in Moreland. His contemporaries represent him as a physician of much skill and prudence, and as having an extensive practice in the vicinity. In him the people placed the greatest confidence, and his success in relieving disease was remarkable. He died in 1780, lamented by all who knew him.

ANDREW OTT.

ANDREW OTT was born at Vartzheim, in Germany, in 1739, and was brought to this country by his parents when about five or six years old. They landed at Philadelphia, where they staid about six weeks, and then moved to a place in the country near the Pennypack Creek. When the Revolutionary War broke out he enlisted in Washington's army, under Captain Douglass. He was in the battles of Long Island and Brandywine, and at Fort Constitution, on the Hudson, where there was some skirmishing. Soon after the war was over he married and settled in Byberry, where he resided for several years. After this he bought a lot of land in Bucks County, where he spent the remainder of his days. He had no school learning, and could neither read nor write, yet he transacted all his business, and seldom made any mistakes. He was a plain, industrious, frugal man, a member of All-Saints' Church, and was much respected by his neighbors. He died in December, 1841, aged 102 years.

THOMAS KNOX.

THOMAS KNOX came from Ireland, and taught school at the Sorrel Horse for several years. After this he taught at Smithfield, and for many years was a tax collector in Moreland. Many of the old people in the vicinity remember old Tommy Knox as their teacher. He had a kind disposition; but when the unruly urchins would try the old man's patience too much he would call them up and lay them over "the bame" (his knee). He would then flourish a ruler over his head, and exclaim at the same time with great earnestness: "Were it not for the bame overhead, oh! how I would whack ye!" He died at Somerton about 1840, aged nearly ninety years. His daughter married Jesse Hawkins.

SAMUEL SCOTT.

SAMUEL SCOTT was an old Friend who had a very remarkable way of whistling through his nose. On one occasion Jeremy Hibbs clothed himself in a skin, with horns projecting from his head, and placed himself in the bushes by a path where he expected Samuel Scott to pass. After Samuel had gone by a few yards, Jeremy came out and hailed him. Samuel gave a whistle through his nose, and exclaimed, "Get thee behind me, Satan!" and walked on as unconcernedly as if nothing had happened. Samuel was a sievemaker by trade, and this seems to have been the usual calling of the family. The old man frequently wore clogs, or wooden shoes, and came very late to meeting one morning. Just as he entered the door he happened to stumble, and fell down, when the rattling of the clogs, and a loud whistle through his nose, made a great noise, and frightened one fellow, who was sound asleep, quite sadly. Samuel got up, however, and without showing any signs of being disconcerted, went to his seat as usual. The stone in Byberry graveyard, marked S. S., indicates the spot where Samuel was buried.

WILLIAM WOOD.

WILLIAM WOOD came from near London, England, in 1772. He married Merab Pennington, and moved to Byberry. He was a baker, but did not follow his trade. Soon after this he removed to Makefield and opened a school. While here he joined the Society of Friends and became a recommended preacher. He continued to teach school for many years, but afterwards led a roving life, and became much reduced before his death.

DR. BENJAMIN RUSH.

DR. RUSH was born in the southern part of Byberry, at the house now occupied by Reuben Parry, on the 24th of December, 1745. He was a descendant of John Rush, who came over with William Penn. His father died while he was young, and his education devolved upon his mother. He was sent to Princeton College, where he graduated with the first honors of the institution, and soon afterward commenced the study of medicine under Dr. John Rodman, of Philadelphia. In 1766, he went to Edinburgh to attend medical lectures, and received his diploma from the institution at that place. In 1769, he returned to Philadelphia, and soon obtained an extensive practice. He was afterward a Professor in the Medical Department of the University of Pennsylvania. It is not our province to write a biography of this distinguished man, for he is known to the whole world as one of the brightest stars in medical science that has yet ornamented the Western World, and his works will live as long as does that science with which he was connected. He died in April, 1813, aged sixty-eight years. Both the Doctor and his brother, the Honorable Judge Rush, frequently visited Byberry in the latter part of their lives; and the township may feel honored in having been the birthplace of two such noble men.

SINIXSON KEEN.

Sinixson Keen was of Swedish descent, and born in 1797. When he was but two years old, he removed to Frankford with his parents, and some years later to Somerton, where he resided for a long time. His parents were not possessed of much

wealth, and from the peculiar circumstances surrounding him he was subject to many temptations;
but bore up against them successfully. He afterward taught school in Somerton, and became
noted in his profession. He shot himself in Byberry in 1819.

JAMES BONNER.

JAMES BONNER, the first of that name in Byberry, emigrated from Ireland, in 1764, at the age
of twenty-six years. He married Martha Worthington, of Byberry, and settled in Buckingham,
Bucks County, but returned to Byberry again in
1813. He was a man of peaceable demeanor, respected for his honesty and uprightness, and by
untiring industry accumulated considerable property. He died in 1818, aged eighty years.

JUDGE SOMMERS.

JUDGE SOMMERS, the collector, owned a large
tract of land in the vicinity of Somerton. He was
a prominent character of that day, and was very
active in behalf of the cause of liberty. His son
Edward, afterward an Associate Judge in Philadelphia, was a lieutenant in the Continental Army
during the Revolution. He was taken prisoner
early in the contest, and confined in a British
prison at Flatbush, Long Island, four or five years.
Although others of the Continental Army were
either released or exchanged, yet the British refused to release Lieutenant Sommers. The attention of the Government was directed to it, when it

was ascertained that Jonathan Walton, a refugee, whose farm adjoined that of Sommers, had represented to the British that young Sommers was a man of great influence, and would hang some neighbors who were suspected of favoring the British cause, if he was released; but the true motive was, probably, that Walton, who had no doubt of the ultimate success of the British cause, and the confiscation of the rebel property, wished to keep Sommers out of the way, so that he might obtain his estate. The authorities sent an order to the British, stating that unless Lieutenant Sommers was released, retaliatory measures would be resorted to, and British prisoners subjected to the same treatment. He was accordingly released, and sent home on parole. While the British were in Philadelphia, Walton went with a party to Sommers's farm, and took horses, cows, and other property to the amount of about four hundred dollars, besides doing much mischief, such as tearing open beds, injuring furniture, &c.

Soon after the war ended Walton found his way to Canada, where he remained for many years. He owned at that time about ten acres of land adjoining Sommers's place, and he and Sommers agreed upon the terms for the property, on which occasion the latter was to have the deed and money ready for Walton at a neighbor's house on a certain evening. They met, when the deed was properly signed, and all the money, except $400, paid over to Walton. This amount was retained to pay for the damage received on the above mentioned

occasion, and in order to get shut of Walton, he
was ordered to leave immediately, or information
would be given, and he be arrested. After the war
was all over Lieutenant Sommers settled on his
paternal estate, where he lived to a good old age.

WILLIAM COOPER.

The earliest account of the Cooper family that
we have met with is, that one WILLIAM COOPER
arrived in this country in 1679, and settled at Burlington, New Jersey. His name appears in the
list of members of the Colonial Legislature for
1681. About the year 1687 he obtained the grant
of a tract of land where Camden now stands, extending for several miles above and below the
mouth of the creek which bears his name. One
branch of this family removed into Pennsylvánia
and finally settled in Smithfield, now Somerton,
where the subject of the present sketch was born,
in the log end of a house afterward occupied by
James Vansant as a tavern. Little is known of
Cooper during his minority, except that he was
apprenticed to a person in Byberry to learn the
wheelwright business. After his majority, he resided with his father in the log house in which he
was born, but the family were exceedingly poor.
This, however, did not damp the ardor of young
Cooper, who began to look about for a wife, and
shortly afterward married the daughter of Richard
Fennimore, of New Jersey, on which occasion the
old man expressed some doubts about Cooper's
being able to provide for his daughter, when Cooper

replied "that he was poor and she must shift for herself."

After their marriage they settled in Byberry, at one time living in a small tenement belonging to William Walmsley, and helping about the business of the farm. After this they lived in a house near Charles Comly's barn, and subsequently in an old house on Edward Parry's, now Charles Martindale's farm, and which was known as the "Potter's Nest." While here he desired to work at his trade, but having no shop, James Thornton gave him permission to work in one belonging to him. This was during the Revolutionary War, when wheelwrights were not in much demand, and Cooper was often without employment. He, however, did not despair, but at such times offered to work for half price at any business, so that he was seldom idle. William Cooper was an eccentric character, and seldom deliberated upon the course to be pursued, but acted entirely from first impressions, which, he said, " were always the best." He possessed a talent for speculation, but with all his exertions remained poor while in Byberry. About the year 1780 they moved to Burlington, New Jersey, where, in partnership with a brother-in-law, Robert Thomas, they opened a small store. Cooper being in want of money at this time, borrowed £5 of William Walton, of Byberry, which he said was the foundation of his fortune. This loan was not paid back until after he was elected a member of Congress, when he paid principal and compound interest for the whole time. Their busi-

ness here was poor, and Cooper turned his attention to speculation in real estate. This was in a
very small way at first, but as he was generally
successful, he was soon able to make heavier purchases, and by 1785 had accumulated considerable
capital. In this year he purchased a large tract of
uncultivated land near Otsego Lake, in New York.
This he divided into small farms, and offered great
inducements to emigrants to settle thereon. In
the spring of 1786 he laid out a town, which he
called Cooperstown, and in that year erected the
first house there. At this time there were no settlements within forty miles of the place, and Cooper left his family at Burlington until 1790, when
they removed to Cooperstown. While residing
at the former place, their son, James Fennimore
Cooper, the celebrated novelist, was born, on the
15th of September, 1789.

From prudent management William Cooper disposed of nearly all his purchase, and realized large
profits, so that he became one of the wealthiest
citizens of the State of New York. Some idea of
his business may be had, when we state that over
forty thousand persons settled on his original tract
within twenty-five years of the time of purchase.
When a Court of Justice was established in Otsego
County, William Cooper was appointed the Presiding Judge, which position he held until 1796,
when he was elected a member of the National
Congress. Judge Cooper was a man of sound
judgment, but of limited education. His character
was very decided, and he was seldom deterred from

carrying out his undertakings by the opinions of others. He was something of a writer, and frequently indulged in poetry, some of which was quite popular in that day. He was of a social nature, and delighted to mingle with congenial companions, on which occasions he would with great pleasure narrate the scenes and adventures of his varied life. He died at Cooperstown about the year 1812, honored and respected by those around him.

JAMES CARTER.

JAMES CARTER was born in a hip-roofed house near Artman's Mill, in Southampton, Bucks county, in 1778. His parents were William and Mary Carter. Mary was a daughter of William Hayhurst, who lived on the farm now owned by the heirs of Mordecai Carter, near Rocksville, where he owned a large tract of land. The name of Hayhurst frequently occurs in the early history of the neighborhood. They belonged to Middletown Friends' Meeting, and the family have generally been interred in the Middletown graveyard. Cuthbert Hayhurst, or "Uncle Cuddy," as he was called, who obtained some notoriety for not being like other men, and who died at James Carter's house some years since, was a son of William Hayhurst. James Carter had two brothers—William, who was a minister in the Society of Friends, and settled near West Philadelphia, and Joseph, who settled near Rocksville—and one sister, Rebecca, who married John Claxton, and settled in Philadelphia.

James Carter learned the blacksmith trade with John Searl, at the Four-lanes-end, now Attleborough, and then removed to Byberry Cross-roads to follow his occupation. He lived in the house now occupied by William Forrest, and had his shop on the opposite side of the road, in what is now Thomas Dyer's field. He married Phebe, daughter of John Tomlinson, and granddaughter of Isaac Carver. He followed his trade until 1819, when he purchased a farm in the northern part of Byberry, on the banks of the Poquessing, where he spent the remainder of his days. His second wife was Annie Harding, who is still living, and is the oldest inhabitant of Byberry. His children were Mordecai, Tacy, Emily, Stephen, Thomas, Mary, James, and William.

James Carter was commissioned a Justice of the Peace by Governor Simon Snyder, in 1813, and from that time to the expiration of his commission by the new Constitution, did most of the business appertaining to the office in the neighborhood. Esquire Carter's integrity and business qualifications won the confidence of the people; and until age and infirmity disqualified him for the service, he was active in whatever appertained to the welfare of the community, either in settling disputes among his neighbors, in which his judgment was rarely called in question, or in whatever was conducive to the public welfare. He died 8th mo. 8th, 1860, and was buried in Byberry graveyard.

JOHN SIMMONS.

JOHN SIMMONS, son of Henry Simmons, was born on his father's farm, near Milford, Bucks County. John became a school teacher, and moved to Horsham, Montgomery County, where he compiled and published the "Pennsylvania Primer," in 1794. In 1795 he removed to Byberry, and in partnership with his brother Thomas opened a store. This was relinquished in 1798, and he again commenced teaching. In 1801 he married a daughter of Henry Atherton, and moved to Philadelphia, where he published "A Treatise on Farriery" and a Reading Book for schools. He died in Philadelphia, in 1843.

JOHN MARSHALL.

JOHN MARSHALL taught school a short time in Byberry, after which he moved to Ancocas, New Jersey, where he died, in 1813.

CHRISTOPHER SMITH.

CHRISTOPHER SMITH was born in England, where he learned the trade of nail-making. He taught school in Byberry from 1784 to 1789, then removed to Horsham, where he died, in 1814.

CHARLES SAYRE.

CHARLES SAYRE spent the greater part of his life in Byberry or Bensalem. He married Hetty, widow of Joseph Croasdale. By trade he was a wheelwright, yet for many years he taught school at

Knightsville, Byberry, and near the Red Lion. He contributed numerous articles, principally poetical, to the various newspapers of the day, thus evincing a creditable talent as a poet. He was of a religious turn, and spent much of his time, when not engaged at his business, in the fields and woods, where he could see and enjoy the works of God. He did not aspire to fame, but was contented with his little circle of friends, by whom he was respected and beloved. He died July 28, 185-, aged 51 years.

GENEALOGIES.

THE BOLTON FAMILY.*

The BOLTON family is of ancient British stock. At the time of the Conquest it was in possession of great landed estates both in Yorkshire and Lancashire. The name of Bolton, or Bodelton (the ancient spelling), is from Boel, a mansion, probably implying that it was the principal residence of some Saxon Thane. Mr. Bolton traces the ancestry of his family to the Lord of Bolton, bow-bearer to the Royal Forests of Bowland and Gilsland, the lineal representative of the Saxon Earls of Murcia, and who was living A.D. 1135. Robert Bolton, his descendant in the fifteenth generation, was born at Wales, in Yorkshire, in 1688, and died in Philadelphia, in 1742. His descendants are now very numerous in the United States. We are, however, unable to trace the relation between him and Everard Bolton, the ancestor of the family whose genealogy is here given, yet they are probably from

* I am indebted to William F. Corbit, of Philadelphia, for the greater part of the genealogy of this family.

20*

the same great family. The name of Everard Bolton occurs only in this branch of the family, and it has been so frequently given to its members that it has become a sort of inheritance. The Boltons were generally followers of George Fox, and numerous instances are recorded where they suffered, while in England, "for conscience' sake and the truth."

(1.) EVERARD BOLTON, his wife ELIZABETH, and their two eldest children, came to Pennsylvania from Ross, in Herefordshire, England, in 1682 or 1683, and settled in Cheltenham, Pennsylvania, on a tract of land a little east of the site of the present village of Milestown. This tract was presented to his eldest son in 1711, but the deed of transfer was not recorded until 1760. Everard Bolton was an active member of the Society of Friends, having been Treasurer of Abington Meeting for nearly forty years. He was much esteemed, and was appointed a Justice of the Peace by a Council held at Philadelphia, May 30, 1715. Elizabeth Bolton died June 5, 1707, and Everard subsequently married Margaret, widow of John Jones, a merchant of Philadelphia. Everard Bolton died in 1727, leaving eleven children, all by his first wife. They were Everard, Elizabeth, Hannah, Mary, Samuel, Abel, Sarah, Lydia, Isaac, Rebecca, and Martha. Margaret died in 1742.

Besides Everard Bolton, we find mention of Edward Bolton, who married Eleanor Jones, of Philadelphia, in 1694, but we have met with no further account of him or his family.

(1.) *Everard and Elizabeth Bolton's Children.*

(2.) EVERARD, born in Ross, England, March 28, 1680, came to America with his parents. He was by trade a glover. In July, 1707, he married Mary, daughter of Robert Naylor, of Plymouth, and settled in Abington, where he followed his occupation. Children : Priscilla, Mary, Elizabeth, and Samuel.

(3.) ELIZABETH, born in Ross, England, June 26, 1681, came to America with her parents. She married Ellis Davis in 1709, and settled in Cheltenham, Montgomery County, Pennsylvania. He died in 1745, and she died in August, 1749. Children : Deborah, born August 3, 1710 ; David, born March 11, 1712 ; Abel, born November 17, 1715 ; Sibel and Hannah, twins, born July 11, 1718 ; Lydia, who married John Hurr.

(4) HANNAH, born in Cheltenham, December 22, 1684, married Richard Carver, of Byberry, in 1708. Children : Mary, born August 15, 1709 ; Ann, born October 15, 1710 ; Sarah, and John. Richard Carver died in 1727.

(5.) MARY, born in Cheltenham, November 4, 1687, married Edmund Roberts in 1714. They removed to the "Great Swamp," near Quakertown, Bucks County, and had children, Abel, John, David, Everard, Martha, Mary, and Jane. Of these, Martha married John Roberts in 1742 ; Mary married J. Foulke, and Jane married Thomas Foulke.

(6.) SAMUEL, born October 31, 1689, married Sarah Dillworth. She died in 1732, leaving a portion of her estate to Janet, wife of Samuel Bolton. He was much esteemed, and Rachel Roberts, who died in 1751, named " her trusty friend, Samuel Bolton, of Cheltenham," as her executor. We find mention of but one daughter, Hannah, who married John Coombs. He being absent for a number of years, she, having first obtained the consent of Friends, married John Clark, in 1746.

(7.) ABEL, born November 9, 1691; died July 19, 1702.

(8.) SARAH, born November 26, 1693, married William Bolton. After his death she married Michael Brown, in 1751. She died in Front Street, above Race, Philadelphia, but left no children.

(9.) LYDIA, born September 3, 1695, married John Biddle, of Philadelphia, in April, 1721. He died June 17, 1750, and she died August 16, 1764, leaving eleven children: Elizabeth, married —— Pearson; Sarah, born October 19, 1723; Hannah, born December 28, 1727, married —— Waterman, and died August 17, 1772; Josiah, born February 16, 1729; John, born April 16, 1730; Abigail, born August 16, 1731; Joseph, born July 4, 1733; Lydia, born March 14, 1735, died June 4, 1773; Mary, born July 4, 1736; John, born November 15, 1738; and Martha, born October 27, 1741.

(10.) ISAAC, born June 27, 1697, married Sarah Jones in 1724. She was born December 6, 1698. In 1722 he removed to Philadelphia, and for several years afterwards resided on the north side of Market Street, below Second. In 1750 he removed to Abington. He subsequently purchased a large tract of land in Bucks County, where he spent the remainder of his days. To this tract he gave the name of the "Bolton Farm," which name it still bears, although it passed from the Bolton family eighty years ago. In addition to farming, he dealt in skins, and was denominated in law papers of that period as "Isaac Bolton, peltsmonger." His possessions continuing to increase, he became one of the wealthiest men in the Province. He was a member of the Society of Friends, yet had no scruples against holding slaves, as is shown by the following inventory of his estate:

"To a negro woman, named Dinah, £00 0 0.
To a negro man, called Berry, £67 10 0.
To a negro woman, named Cate, £35 0 0.
To a negro woman, named Daffane, £45 0 0.
To a negro garle, named Phillis, £22 0 0."

They had eight children: Margaret, Rachel, Sarah, Rebecca, Jemima, Isaac, Joseph, and Everard.

(11.) REBECCA, born May 20, 1701, was married November 4, 1747, to Solomon, son of Dennis Rockford, a noted man in the early days of Pennsylvania. They probably had no children.

(12.) MARTHA, born May 20, 1703, probably died in infancy.

(2.) *Everard and Mary Bolton's Children.*

(13.) PRISCILLA, married Cornelius, son of Matthias Conrad, of Germantown, March 29, 1732. She died November 22, 1765. Children: Matthew, born July 4, 1733; Mary, born June 26, 1735; Ev-

erard, born July 21, 1741; Joseph, born February
23, 1742; Samuel and John, twins, born November
13, 1744; Susannah, born January 7, 1750. Of
these children, *Samuel* married Mary ——, and
had children, Sarah, Samuel, Hannah, Ruth, Samuel, and Cornelius; and *John* married Sarah ——,
and had children, Hannah, Priscilla, Benjamin,
Esther, Sarah, and John.

The Conrad family are of German extraction.
They originally wrote the name *Kunders*, the ancestor of the family being Dennis Kunders, who
settled in Germantown about 1683.

(14.) MARY, is mentioned in her father's will, but
we have no other account of her.

(15.) ELIZABETH, was born June 26, 1708.

(16.) SAMUEL, married Mary Livezey. He lived
first in Abington, and afterwards in Byberry,
where he died September 12, 1757. Children:
Mary, who married John Paul, and died in 1796,
and Martha.

(10.) *Isaac and Sarah Bolton's Children.*

(17.) MARGARET, born April 6, 1726; died, unmarried, May, 1817.

(18.) RACHEL, born September 12, 1727; died,
unmarried, January 1, 1810.

(19.) SARAH, born September 3, 1729, married,
first, —— Massey, of Deer Creek, Maryland, and
had one son, Isaac. She married, second, James
Rigby, and had one daughter, Ann. Sarah Bolton
became a recommended minister in the Society of
Friends at the early age of 23 years, and subse-

quently travelled extensively with Ann Moore and Grace Croasdale, both eminent ministers of that Society. Many of her letters are still extant, and prove her to have been a woman of tender feelings. She died March 29, 1784, and her husband January 6, 1790.

(20.) REBECCA, was born in Philadelphia, June 18, 1731. She removed to Abington in 1750.

(21.) JEMIMA, born January 27, 1733, married Henry Tomlinson November 21, 1753. She died May 2, 1802, leaving three children, Sarah, Jemima, and Jesse.

(22.) ISAAC, born April 27, 1735, married Sarah, daughter of William and Sarah Walmsley, of Byberry. He died February 6, 1783. Children : William, Joseph, Isaac, Mary and Margaret, twins, Jesse, Thomas, and Sarah.

(23.) JOSEPH, born March 13, 1737, married Rhoda, only child of Rebecca Bolton. He died December 18, 1799; she died August 8, 1806.

(24.) EVERARD, born October 1, 1739, married, first, Deborah, granddaughter of Andrew Griscom, a member of the first Provincial Council, in 1683, and noted for having built the first brick house in Philadelphia. She died in 1801, Everard then married Elizabeth Ivins. He died in 1831, leaving seven children, all by his first wife : Isaac, Sarah, Samuel, Rachel, Aquilla, Abel, and Everard.

(22.) Isaac and Sarah Bolton's Children.

(25.) WILLIAM, born September 12, 1767, was by trade a blacksmith, and lived the most of the time in Byberry. He died September 19, 1823, leaving one daughter.

(26.) JOSEPH, born October 28, 1769, married Jane, daughter of Jonathan Knight. He was by trade a tailor, and lived near Knight's Mill, in Byberry, until 1798, when he moved to Frankford. He afterwards went to Black River, New York, where he married a second time. He died there in 1852, leaving several children, among whom were Tacy, born in 1794, and Isaac, born in 1796.

(27.) ISAAC, born October 7, 1771, married Elizabeth, daughter of Evan Townsend. He at first settled on a farm in Byberry, but afterwards moved to Bustleton, and again to Byberry, where he kept a store. Thence he went to Drumore, in Lancaster County, where he died in 1853, beloved and respected by all who knew him. Children: Evan, who died at Pennsgrove, Chester County, in 1840; Jason, Isaac, Sarah, Abi, and Margaret.

(28.) MARY married Nathan Marshall in 1800. He was a blacksmith, and settled in Bustleton, but afterwards moved to Concord, Chester County, and thence to Black River, New York, where he died, leaving several children.

(29.) MARGARET, born September 2, 1773, married James Hayton in 1794. She died in 1795.

(30.) JESSE, born June 30, 1777, studied medicine with Dr. Amos Gregg, of Bristol, and died soon afterwards.

(31.) THOMAS married a sister of Henry Comly, of Frankford, and afterwards moved to Black River, New York.

(32.) SARAH married William Woodward, of Brandywine.

(24.) *Everard and Deborah Bolton's Children.*

(33.) ISAAC, born March 23, 1766, married Phebe Kay. Children: Rebecca, who married Isaac Bartram; Sarah; Deborah, who married Francis Stillman; and Anna Maria, who married James Smith.

(34.) SARAH, born December, 1768, died April 7, 1790.

(35.) SAMUEL, born February 5, 1771, married Rachel Scull, of Cumberland County, New Jersey, who was a descendant of John and Mary Scull, emigrants from England in 1700. Samuel Bolton was a man of inventive genius, and was quite intimate with John Fitch. He took out patents for several inventions, the models of which were destroyed by fire when the British burned the public buildings, at Washington, in 1814. He died April 7, 1812. Children: Aquilla, Gideon, Rachel, Sarah, Joseph R., James Murray, Hannah S., and Samuel.

(36.) RACHEL, born February 15, 1771, died February 25, 1789.

(37.) AQUILLA, born in 1773, married, first, Phebe Yarnall; second, Alice Babitt. He died in 1858, at Dayton, Ohio. Children: Phebe, Denman, Charles, Jane, and Mary.

(38.) ABEL J., born September, 1778, died unmarried in 1858.

(39.) EVERARD, born November, 1784, married Rachel Perkins, and settled in Philadelphia. Children: William P., Everard, and Sarah.

(35.) *Samuel and Rachel Scull's Children.*

(40.) AQUILLA, who married Christiana Aurand, and resides at Port Carbon, Pennsylvania.

(41.) SARAH, born October 11, 1801, married Henry C. Corbit, of Philadelphia, a descendant of Daniel Corbit, who came from Scotland to America in 1700, and settled in Delaware. She died September 7, 1852, leaving children : Caroline R., who married Ellerton Perot; Emma, who married Charles S. Ogden; Henry C., who died aged 14 years ; Everard S., and Charles, who died in infancy ; William F. ; Helen, who died aged 15 years ; and Charles, who married Louisa A. Corbit, of Odessa, Delaware.

(42.) JOSEPH R., born in 1803, married Sarah Jones. Children : Rebecca, who married Edward Bohrek ; Anna, Sarah J., Joseph R., Clifton, who married Jane Whitclock; Henry C., who married Fanny Lippincott; and Samuel, who was killed at the battle of Fair Oaks, Virginia, in 1862.

(43.) JAMES MURRAY, born February 11, 1806, married Mary E. English. Children : Emma, Mary, and Emma Louisa.

(44.) HANNAH S., born September 8, 1807, married Isaac Lloyd. Children : Elizabeth, Bolton, Franklin, William, Edwin, Horace, Clement, and Fanny.

(45.) SAMUEL, born July, 1809, married Hannah Sanders. Children : Anna, Gideon S., Thomas, Alfred, Rachel, and William.

THE CARVER FAMILY.*

(1.) JOHN CARVER, with his brothers, William, Joseph, and Jacob, came to Pennsylvania, from England, in 1682. They were all members of the Society of Friends. Previous to emigrating from England, John married Mary Lane, at the Priory of St. Albans. He took up by patent, from William Penn, 690 acres of land in the northeastern part of Byberry, along the Poquessing Creek. It included the site of the old homestead, which remained in the family for six generations, having descended successively from father to son, all of whom were named John, until 1864. He was a maltster by profession, and the "malt-house" was continued until the fourth generation, when the business became so poor that it was given up. He died in 1714. Children: Mary, John, Ann, James, and Richard.

(1.) *John and Mary Carver's Children.*

(2.) MARY was born in a cave, near Philadelphia, five days after the landing of Penn, and was the first child of English parentage born in Pennsylvania. She married Isaac Knight, of Abington, and was afterwards a noted minister in the Society of Friends. She died 3d mo. 3, 1769, aged 86 years. A memorial concerning her was issued by Abing-

---

* I am indebted to Watson Comly and Mahlon Carver, both of Byberry, for the genealogy of this family.

ton Monthly Meeting, of which she was a member. Some of her descendants still remain in Abington.

(3.) John inherited a part of the paternal estate in Byberry, and like his father, followed the occupation of a maltster in addition to that of farming. The malt-house was about twenty yards south of the present Carver Mansion, and was the only malt-house in that section of the country. He married Isabel Weldon, from the Barony of Kendal, Ireland. He died 5th mo. 14, 1769. Children : John, Ann, and Isaac.

(4.) Ann married John Duncan.

(5.) James built the hip-roofed house now owned by Thomas Townsend. He married, and had one son, Samuel, who moved to Philadelphia. He was a carpenter, and assisted in building Christ Church, in Second Street.

(6.) Richard married a Conrad, and settled at Byberry Cross-roads, where he started the first tavern in Byberry. He afterwards moved to Abington. Children : Mary, Ann, and two sons. His descendants are living near Sumneytown, Chambersburg, and Chester Valley.

(3.) *John and Isabel Carver's Children.*

(7.) John, born 7th mo. 30th, 1717, married Rachel, daughter of Joseph Naylor, of Southampton, and settled on the Carver Homestead. He died 1st mo. 15th, 1791. Children : John, Samuel, Eli, Mahlon, Mary, and Rachel.

(8.) Ann, born 11th mo. 23d, 1719, married Robert Heaton, and settled in Byberry. Children: Isabel, Susannah, and John.

(9.) ISAAC, born 2d mo. 22d, 1722, married Phebe, daughter of Thomas Walmsley, in 1742. He inherited about 200 acres of his father's property, and settled where Richard Cripps now lives. He was somewhat noted as a literary man, and taught school for several years near the Byberry Meeting-house. He was a wit; and, having a poetical turn, was called the "Poet Carver." His verses were shrewd, often sarcastic, and generally had reference to local events transpiring in the neighborhood. He died 12th mo. 25, 1786, aged 64 years. Children: Mary, Nanny, Martha, Phebe, and Isabel.

(7.) *John and Rachel Carver's Children.*

(10.) JOHN, born 10th mo. 26th, 1747, married Mary, daughter of Joseph Buckman, of Wrightstown, and settled on the homestead in Byberry. Children: Martha, Mary, John, Asceuath, Hannah, Sarah, Joseph, and Elizabeth.

(11.) SAMUEL, born 12th mo. 2d, 1749, married Susan Conrad, of Horsham, and settled where Randall Myers now lives. His occupation was that of a carpenter in addition to farming. He died 4th mo. 10th, 1784. Children: Eli, Priscilla, and Rachel.

(12.) MAHLON, born 7th mo. 18th, 1754, married Amy Pickering, of Solebury. He first settled near Byberry Meeting-house, where he followed his trade of blacksmith. He afterwards kept the

Anchor Hotel in Wrightstown, and thence moved
to a hotel at Morrisville, where he died. Children:
Jane, Rachel, and Sarah.

(13.) MARY, born 12th mo. 11th, 1758, married
Thomas Samms, of Byberry. Children: Thomas
and John. Thomas married Mary Hampton ; their
children, John H. and Ann. John married Mercy
Hampton. Children : Mary and Rachel.

(14.) RACHEL, born 1st mo. 24th, 1763; died
single, 4th mo. 4th, 1834.

(9.) *Isaac and Phebe Carver's Children.*

(15.) MARY, married Benjamin Taylor, and had
one daughter, Martha. She married William Tomlinson, of Byberry, and had children, Mary, Aaron,
John, James, Phebe, Silas, Benjamin, William, and
Isaac.

(16.) NANNY, married John Carver, of Buckingham, and afterwards moved to Chester County.
Children : John, Joseph, Isaac, and two daughters.

(17.) MARTHA, died single, in 1771.

(18.) PHEBE, married Thomas Tomlinson in 1773.
They lived back of Smithfield on a farm, which
they rented for forty years. They were quiet and
unassuming in their habits, and although not considered prosperous in business, they were highly
respected for their many virtues. Their children:
Elizabeth, married Benjamin Fields ; Phebe, married James Carter, Esq.; Martha, married John
Praul; Isabel; Joseph ; John, married Martha Worthington ; Amos; Isaac, married Deborah Kline ;
Thomas, married Rebecca Kline ; and Silas.

(19.) ISABEL, married John Davis, and had one daughter, Phebe, who was married first to Miller Duffee, and afterwards to Septimus Tucker.

(10.) *John and Mary Carver's Children.*

(20.) MARTHA, born 4th mo. 27th, 1772; died single, 5th mo. 15, 1818.

(21.) MARY, born 9th mo. 16th, 1773, married William Worthington, of Wrightstown. Children: Ascenath, Margaret, Mahlon, Martha, Sarah, and John.

(22.) JOHN, born 2d mo. 28th, 1776, married Elizabeth Briggs, of Wrightstown. He died 10th mo. 10th, 1849. Children: *John*, Mahlon, Esther, and Eliza.

(23.) ASCENATH, born 3d mo. 23d, 1780, married John Townsend, and moved to Jefferson County, New York. Children: John, Robert, Mary, Ezra, Martha, Evan, and Abi.

(24.) HANNAH, born 2d mo. 16th, 1782, married Benjamin Kirkbride, of Jefferson County, New York. Children: George, Sarah, and Benjamin.

(25.) SARAH, born 8th mo. 29th, 1785, married Josiah D. Banes, M.D. Children: S. Rodman, Rachel, and Mary.

(26.) JOSEPH, born 1st mo. 28th, 1788, married Esther Wiggins, of Newtown. He was a mason by trade, and obtained considerable celebrity on account of his fondness for fun and for playing mischievous pranks on his associates. His children were William, Isaac, Louisa, and James.

(27.) ELIZABETH, born 6th mo. 15th, 1790, mar-

ried Evan Townsend,   Children: Thomas, Jacob,
Abi, Mary, Mahlon, William, Sarah, and Martha.

(11.) *Samuel and Susan Carver's Children.*

(28.) Eli, married Martha Wilson. Children:
George, Samuel, John, Joseph, Mary, Rachel, and
Eli.

(29.) Priscilla, died single.

(30.) Rachel, married James Conrad, of Abington.

(12.) *Mahlon and Amy Carver's Children.*

(31.) Jane, married Philip Sagers. Children:
Stephen, Amy, Rachel, Mahlon, John, Sarah, and
William.

(32.) Rachel, married William Cooper of the
Falls. Children: Mahlon and Erwin.

(33.) Sarah, died single.

(28.) *Eli and Martha Carver's Children.*

(34.) George, married Ann Myers, in 1834.
Children: Mary, Martha, Jane, Jacob M., Charles
R., Agnes, Wilmer, and Edwin.

(35.) Samuel, married Elizabeth Croasdale.
Children: George, Martha, Hannah, Rachel, John,
and Eli.

(36.) John, married Rebecca Whital. Children:
William, Ann, David, Charles, and George.

(37.) Joseph, married Sarah Wood, of Ohio.
Children: Mary, Jane, John, Amos, Phebe Ann,
Emiline, Harvey, Joseph, Eli, and Adra.

(38.) Mary, married Amos Croasdale. Children:
Lydia, Emma, and Martha.

(39.) RACHEL, married William Reed, of Ohio.
Children : Levi, David, Mary Elizabeth, Hannah
Jane, Eli, Amos, Martha, Mary Emma, Wilmer,
and George.

(40.) ELI, married Emiline Rogers. Children:
George, Alexander, and Adra Ann.

THE BROTHERS WILLIAM, JOSEPH, AND JACOB.

(1.) WILLIAM CARVER, brother of (1) John, first
settled where Edwin Tomlinson now lives, but afterwards traded his farm with Silas Walmsley for
land in Buckingham, near the Green Tree, receiving two acres for one. He was married while in
England, but his first wife, Jane, died in 1692,
leaving a daughter, Sarah. William next married
Mary ——. Children: William, Joseph, Rachel,
and Esther.

(1.) William Carver's Children.

(2.) SARAH, married John Rush, in 1707.

(3.) WILLIAM, married Elizabeth, daughter of
Henry Walmsley, and moved to Buckingham.
Children: William, Joseph, John, Jacob, Henry,
and others. Many of William Carver's descendants now reside in Buckingham and Wrightstown,
but we are unable to give any further account of
them.

JOSEPH CARVER, brother of (1) John, moved to
North Carolina, and settled on Carver's Creek,
New Garden, where his descendants still reside.

JACOB CARVER, brother of (1) John, died unmarried, and was buried in the field back of the

barn on the Carver homestead, there being no graveyards in those days.

THE COMLY FAMILY.*

(1.) HENRY and JOAN COMLY, with their son Henry, came to Pennsylvania with William Penn in 1682. A family tradition says that Henry Comly had a brother Walter in England, who possessed a valuable estate, but had no children. It is also said that a person by the name of John Comly came to Pennsylvania from Bristol, England, and that he was a soldier in Braddock's army, but we have no further account of him. We therefore conclude that Henry and Joan Comly were the first of that name who came to America, and that all of the now very extended family of Comlys are descendants from them. They came from Bedminster, near Bristol, England, and were members of the Society of Friends. Persons by the name of Comly are frequently mentioned in the history of the persecutions of Friends in England, as having suffered imprisonment "for attending religious meetings and refusing to swear." Henry Comly was a weaver by trade, and settled in Warminster, Bucks County, on a tract of 500 acres. In the records of Middletown Meeting, then called "Neshaminah," we find that "Henry Comly was buried ye 14th day of ye 3d mo., 1684." " On the 2d day

* I am indebted to Watson Comly, of Byberry, for the genealogy of this family.

of the 12th mo. of the same year, 1684, at a Monthly Meeting of Friends of Tacony and Poetquessink, held at John Hart's house, Joseph English requested a certificate to take* Joan Comly, of the County of Bucks, and John Hart was ordered to write and sign it on behalf of the Meeting."

Joseph and Joan, after having published their intentions of marriage at two successive meetings, " held at Neshaminah Creek, and none appearing to object," were married " at a Publique meeting held at John Otter's, in the presence of twelve witnesses, one of them being a Justice of the Peace," on the 26th day of ye 2d mo., 1685. The witnesses were Mary Eastman, John Otter, Edward Bennit, Robert Hall, John Boyden, Margaret Boyden, Naomi Allen, Henry English, James Spencer, Elizabeth Otter, Rebekah Bennet, John Hust, Elizabeth Lundy, and Robert Rowe.

Joseph English died 8th mo. 10th, 1686, and his widow, Joan, " was buried at the meeting-house at Neshaminah, 10th mo. 20th, 1689." Thus we find that within seven years after the arrival of this family in Pennsylvania, the father, mother, and stepfather of young Henry died, so that Friends were concerned " to extend to him, while yet in his minority, their care and assistance."

HENRY, son of Henry and Joan Comly, married Agnes, daughter of Robert and Alice Heaton, 8th mo. 17th, 1695. Agnes was born 12th mo. 9th, 1677.

---

* The words "in marriage" are wanting in the original document.

The following is a copy of their marriage certificate:

"Whereas, Henry Comley and Agnes Heaton, both of ye County of Bucks and Province of Pennsilvania, having declared their intentions of taking each other as husband and wife before several publick meetings of ye people of God, called Quakers, according to ye good order used among them; whose proceedings therein, after deliberate consideration thereof, and consent of parties and relations concerned being approved by ye said meetings, and publication thereof having been made according to ye law of this Province;

"Now, these are to certifie all whom it may concern, yt for ye full determination of their said intentions, this seventeenth day of ye eighth month, in ye year one thousand six hundred and ninety and five, they, ye said Henry Comley and Agnes Heaton, appeared in a publick and solemn assemblie of ye aforsaid people at ye public meeting-house of Friends in Middletown, near Neshamina, in ye county and province aforesaid, met together for that end and purpose, according to the example of ye holy men of God recorded in ye Scriptures of Truth—he, the said Henry Comly, taking ye said Agnes Heaton by ye hand, did openly declare as follows: 'Friends, in ye presence of ye Lord I desire you to bear me witness, I take Agnes Heaton to be my wife, promising to be to her a loving and faithful husband till it please ye Lord by death to separate us.' And then and there in ye said assemblie, ye said Agnes Heaton did, in like manner, declare as followeth : 'Friends, in ye presence of ye Lord, and before you his people, I take my friend Henry Comly to be my husband, promising to be a loving and faithful wife till ye Lord by death do separate us.'

"And ye said Henry Comly and Agnes, now his wife, as a further confirmation thereof, did then and there to these presents set their hands.

"HENERY COMELY.
"AGNES COMELY.

"And we, whose names are hereunto subscribed as witnesses thereto, have also to these P'snts subscribed our hands ye day and year above written:

"Robert X Heaton, Sr.,
his
mark.

William Paxson, Sr.,
Jonathan Scaife,
Nicholas Walln,
Ezra Croasdill,
Henry Paynter,
James Paxson,
William Paxson, Jr.,
Thomas Stackhouse, Sr.,
Martin Wildman,
Will Darke,
John Croasdill,
Stephen Wilson,
John Scarborough,
John Bunting,
John Cowgill,
John Hough,

John Darke,
Will Hayhurst,
John Cutler,
Peter White,
Peter Worrell,
Jane Paxson,
Mary Paxson, Sr.,
Isabel Cutler,
Rachel Bunting,
Sarah Wilson,
Mary Coat,
Jane Sands,
Rachel Pownall,
Abigail Pownall,
Elizabeth White,
Hannah Hough,
Mary Paxson."

22

On the 11th of September, 1697, Robert Heaton
deeded 300 acres of his estate in the Manor of
Moreland to his son-in-law, Henry Comely, for the
consideration of £72 15s. This place was called
Green Brier Spring, and became the residence of
Henry Comly, in whose family it has since continued.

In the old family Bible brought from England
by the first Henry Comly, and now in the possession of Willet A. Comly, we find the following record of the children of (2) Henry and Agnes Comly : Mary Comly, born 12th mo. 12th, 1699 ; Henry
Comly, born 2d mo. 26th, 1702 ; Robert Comly,
born 4th mo. 12th, 1704 ; John Comly, born 3d mo.
20th, 1706 ; Joseph Comly, born August 8, 1708 ;
Walter Comly, born November 12, 1710 ; Agnes
Comly, born February 20, 1713 ; James Comly,
born June 14, 1715 ; Isaac Comly, born June 4,
1717 ; Grace Comly, born January 24, 1721.

Henry Comly was very active both in civil and
religious matters, and his name frequently appears
on the records of the Meeting and in the civil
affairs of the neighborhood. He died 1st mo.
(March) 16th, 1727, aged 53 years. His will was
dated March (1st mo.) 13th, 1727, and by it he
gave his farm of 292 acres in Warminster to his
sons Robert and James. The Moreland estate was
divided among Henry, Joseph, and Walter, and
the farm adjoining, now owned by Benjamin Tomlinson, was left to John. His personal property
was appraised 2d mo. 13th, 1727, by Bartholomew
Longstreet and Joseph Gilbert, and in it we find

the following items: "A negro girl, £20; a negro
boy, £30."

Agnes (Heaton) Comly was "a woman of small
stature, possessed of a good stock of common
sense, and quite active even in advanced life, so
that she could perform the duties of her household
or ride on horseback with nearly as much ease as
in her youthful days." She died 10th mo. (December) 30th, 1743, aged 66 years. Her will is dated
20th of December (10th mo.), 1743. In the appraisement of her property we find: " One negro,
Phillis, £28; a negro boy, Wallis, £14."

DESCENDANTS OF MARY, DAUGHTER OF HENRY AND
AGNES COMLY.

(1.) MARY COMLY married, first, Thomas Harding, and settled near the Buck, in Bucks County.
Children: Mary, Thomas, Henry, John, Abraham,
and Isaac. She married, second, George Randall,
in 1745. Children: Jacob, George, Sarah, and
Elizabeth.

(2.) MARY, daughter of (1) Mary, married Isaac
Stackhouse, of Middletown, in 1743. She died 3d
mo. 4th, 1782. Children: Thomas, Jonathan, John,
Isaac, Ann, and Martha.

Isaac and (2) Mary Stackhouse's Children.

(3.) THOMAS, married Hannah White. Children:
Thomas, Isaac, Mary, and Ann.

(4.) JONATHAN, married Grace, daughter of Stephen Comfort.

(5.) John, married Sarah, daughter of Jonathan Knight, in 1781.

(6.) Isaac, married Elizabeth, daughter of Thomas Townsend, in 1782.

(7.) Ann, married John Gilbert, in 1768; died January, 1839.

(8.) Martha, died single, 3d mo. 4th, 1782.

DESCENDANTS OF HENRY, SON OF HENRY AND AGNES COMLY.

(1.) Henry Comly, married Phebe, daughter of Joseph Gilbert, of Byberry, 7th mo. 26th, 1728, and settled on the old homestead in Moreland. He died 9th mo. 21st, 1772, aged 71 years, and Phebe died 2d mo. 14th, 1773, aged 72 years. Children: Mary, Rachel, Henry, Phebe, Joseph, Jonathan and Joshua (twins), and Rebecca.

(1.) *Henry and Phebe Comly's Children.*

(2.) Mary, born 7th mo. 23d, 1730; died 5th mo. 8th, 1750.

(3.) Rachel, born 10th mo. 25th, 1732; died single, 8th mo. 6th, 1797.

(4.) Henry, born 3d mo. 7th, 1734, married Rachel Strickland. Children: Jonathan, Mary (who died in infancy), Phebe, Mary, Rachel, and Sarah.

(5.) Phebe, born 2d mo. 15th, 1737, married John Swift, in 1764. She had one son, Edward, who died of typhus fever 12th mo. 28th, 1813, leaving a widow and several children. Phebe died 1st mo. 2d, 1814, aged nearly 76 years.

(6.) JOSEPH, born 3d mo. 10th, 1740, married Eleanor Buzby. In the Revolutionary War he joined the British, and in consequence, had to leave the neighborhood. He went to Long Island, where he died at Thomas Hallet's house, 8th mo. 10th, 1788. It is believed that his estate was confiscated. Children : Jesse, and Henry and Jacob (twins).

(7.) JONATHAN, born 1st mo. 25th, 1741, married Rachel, daughter of Jonathan Thomas, in 1767. They first settled on property now owned by Benjamin Tomlinson, but in 1788 went to Philadelphia. In 1795 they returned to the farm in Moreland, where Rachel died 4th mo. 18th, 1804. Children : Thomas, Grace, Henry (all of whom probably died young), Jonathan, Joshua, and Elizabeth.

(8.) JOSHUA, born 1st mo. 25th, 1741, married Catharine, daughter of Samuel and Elizabeth Willet, in 1766. He was very useful in the affairs of the neighborhood, and was for many years a Justice of the Peace, in which position his correct judgment and honesty of purpose gained him many friends.. He died 4th mo. 20th, 1830, aged 89 years; and Catharine, his wife, died 7th mo. 30th, 1826, aged 76 years. Children : Rebecca, Elizabeth, Mary, Phebe, Hannah, Margaret, Joshua and Samuel (twins), Elizabeth, James, Willet, and Franklin.

(9.) REBECCA, born 8th mo. 6th, 1746; no further account.

(4.) *Henry and Rachel Comly's Children.*

(10.) JONATHAN, was born 12th mo. 3d, 1756. He

22*

was thrown from his horse while a young man, by which his faculties were injured. He remained single, and died at his uncle Joshua Comly's house 9th mo. 26th, 1822.

(11.) PHEBE, born 12th mo. 10th, 1758, married Robert Field. Children : Benjamin and Levi.

(12.) MARY, born 1st mo. 26th, 1761, married Humphrey Waterman. She died 8th mo. 27th, 1817, leaving one son, Gilbert.

(13.) RACHEL, born 11th mo. 29th, 1766, married Eli Shoemaker. She was an authoress, and con-tributed several poetical essays to the " Saturday Evening Post," over the signature of " Ellen." A volume of her essays, called " The Minstrel's Lyre," was published in Philadelphia in 1827.

(14.) SARAH, born 8th mo. 17th, 1768, married James Cooper, uncle of James Fennimore Cooper, in 1792. They removed to the northern part of the State of New York. She died in 1827, aged 59 years. Children : Courtland Comly, William, James, Henry, Sarah Ann, Hamilton, George, and Strickland.

(6.) *Joseph and Eleanor Comly's Children.*

(15.) JESSE, married Tacy Buzby and settled on a part of the old Comly tract in Moreland, where he died 11th mo. 18, 1832. Children: William B., Eleanor, Courtland, Benjamin, Mary Ann, Jackson P., and Robert.

(16.) HENRY, married Rebecca, daughter of Gen-eral Worrell, of Frankford. He died 5th mo. 17th,

1822. Children: James, Elizabeth, Isaac, Eleanor, and Joseph H.

(17.) JACOB, left no children.

(7.) *Jonathan and Rachel Comly's Children.*

(18.) JONATHAN, married Elizabeth Blakey, and had one son, William. They resided for several years where Benjamin Tomlinson now lives, but afterwards settled in Byberry. He was a man of uprightness and integrity, and was respected by all who knew him. He was remarkably even-tempered, and in his latter days never appeared to be discomposed or irritated. He said that he did not meet with anything worth being angry about. The harmony which existed between him and his twin brother Joshua was such, that for many years, seldom a day passed without their being together. He died 4th mo. 16th, 1826, aged 84 years, and was buried at Byberry.

(19.) JOSHUA, married ——. Children: Jonathan, Thomas, George W., and Harriet.

(20.) ELIZABETH, married Dr. John Worthington. Children: Rachel, who married Amos Wilson; Robert; Mary Elizabeth, who married Samuel Williams; and Jonathan, who was drowned at Bridgewater.

(8.) *Joshua and Catharine Comly's Children.*

(21.) REBECCA, born 2d mo. 5th, 1767; died 2d mo. 1st, 1768.

(22.) ELIZABETH, born 12th mo. 28th, 1769; died 6th mo. 21st, 1784.

(23.) MARY, born 1st mo. 13th, 1772; died 9th mo. 12th, 1792.

(24.) PHEBE, born 8th mo. 19th, 1774, married Elijah Thomas. Of their children, Sarah only remains. She married John Walton, who owns the mill at Huntingdon Valley. Phebe was buried at Abington 11th mo. 22d, 1843.

(25.) HANNAH, born 6th mo. 2d, 1777, married Walter Mitchell, of Middletown, in 1799. She was a minister in the Society of Friends, and died in Ohio. Children: Charles, who was a member of Congress; Joshua, James, Walter, Mary, Catharine, and Hannah.

(26.) MARGARET, born 8th mo. 15th, 1780, married Joseph Ogelby, and settled in Lancaster. Children: Charles, Willet Comly, Joseph, Joshua, Samuel, Franklin, Susan, and Mary.

(27.) JOSHUA and SAMUEL (twins), were born 11th mo. 28th, 1783. Joshua died the same day. Samuel married Sarah, daughter of Ryner Lukens. He died 8th mo. 2d, 1835, without children.

(28.) ELIZABETH, born 8th mo. 28th, 1785; died same day.

(29.) JAMES, born 10th mo. 23d, 1787, married Eliza Eyre, and first settled at Walton's Mill, on the Pennypack. This he sold in 1831, and bought a farm near the Fox-chase, where he resided until his death, in 1837. He was a member of the Pennsylvania Legislature, and a Justice of the Peace, and was held in high estimation by those who knew him. Children: Franklin (President of the

North Pennsylvania Railroad Company), Joshua, Samuel, and Sarah.

(30.) WILLET, born 1790 ; died 8th mo. 23d, 1797.

(31.) FRANKLIN, born 7th mo. 18th, 1794, married, first, Mary Austin, in 1825, and settled on the old Comly homestead in Moreland, where he resided during the remainder of his life. Children : Willet, Ellen, and Anna. Mary died 6th mo. 25th, 1834, and in 1836 Franklin married, second, Martha Downing, of Bristol. He was Prothonotary of the District Court in Philadelphia, and for many years a Justice of the Peace and President of the Independent Mutual Fire Insurance Company. Few men occupied a more prominent position in the civil and political affairs of the neighborhood, and none were more highly respected for uprightness and integrity than Franklin Comly.

DESCENDANTS OF ROBERT, SON OF HENRY AND AGNES
COMLY.

(1.) ROBERT COMLY was born in Byberry, in 1706. He married Jane Cadwalader, the preacher, at Horsham, 9th mo., 1727, and settled in Byberry, where he remained until 1730. He then moved to Warminster, and afterwards to Horsham, to a place since owned by Isaac Parry. He was for many years an Overseer in Horsham Meeting, and was a much respected member. He died 3d mo., 1770, aged 66 years. Children : Robert, Agnes, Jane, Grace, Martha, and Mary.

(1.) *Robert and Jane Comly's Children.*

(2.) ROBERT, born 10th mo., 1729, married Sarah Jones. Children: Ezra, John, Robert, Nathan, Clement, Sarah, Agnes, Jane, Rebecca, Charlotte, Hannah, Susan, and Elizabeth.

(3.) AGNES, married Samuel Shoemaker, near the Billet, where they resided 62 years. They were exemplary members of society, and having abundant means, provided for many destitute orphans and others in needy circumstances. Robert died in his 97th year, and Agnes in her 90th year. They left no children.

(4.) JANE, married Nathan Lukens. Children: Lydia, Abraham, Agnes, and Nathan.

(5.) GRACE, married, first, Isaac Parry, of Horsham. Children: Amy, Isaac, Samuel, Robert, Joseph, and Martha. She married, second, Samuel Conard, of Horsham. She died of cancer at Jesse Wilson's, in Byberry, 7th mo. 22d, 1822, aged 75 years.

(6.) MARTHA, married, first, David Parry. They lived at Fair Hill, and had one child, David. She married, second, John Shoemaker, of Shoemakertown; no children. David married Elizabeth, daughter of Mordecai Thomas, of Horsham, leaving five children.

(7.) MARY, married Benjamin Shoemaker, of Cheltenham. She died 3d mo. 17th, 1793. Children: Levi S., Robert, Nathan, Abraham, Benjamin, Amy, Mary, Samuel, Eli, Jane, Jacob, Rebecca, James, and Comly.

(2.) Robert and Sarah Comly's Children.

(8.) EZRA, married Hannah Iredell, in 1779, and had sixteen children: Charles, Sarah, Hannah, Robert, Abraham, Gaynor, Ezra, Thomas, Rachel, Rebecca, Tacy, Ann, Iredell, George, Seth, and Martha. Of the descendants of Ezra Comly we know but little. His son Charles was a merchant in Philadelphia, and afterwards moved to Milton, on the Susquehanna, where he died in 1840, leaving the following children: Lucy, Joshua, Charles, Seth, and Aaron. Ezra died at his son Charles's, in 1832, aged 78 years.

(9.) JOHN, married Martha Shallcross, and settled on the Bristol Road, near Frankford. Children: Samuel, John W., Robert, Thomas, and Joseph.

(10.) ROBERT, went with the refugees to Nova Scotia, where he died in 1837. Children: Robert, John, and Elizabeth.

(11.) NATHAN, married, first, Sarah Kirk, 9th mo., 1782, and lived on the Welsh Road, near Horsham. Children: Elizabeth, Sarah, who married John Tyson, Lydia, Agnes, and Jerusha, who married Jesse Tomlinson. He married, second, Elizabeth Marple, 9th mo., 1795. Children: Elizabeth, who married Benjamin Cadwalader; Abner, who married Margaret Hallowell; Lydia, who married Ezekiel Tyson; Hannah; Nathan; John M., who married Mary Ann Tyson; Daniel, who married Catharine Fitzwater; and Joseph, who married Elizabeth Cadwalader.

(12.) CLEMENT, married Rebecca Jones. Children: Isaac, Henry, Ann, Keziah, Zebedee, Sarah, Clement, Amos, Joseph, and Alfred.

(13.) SARAH, married Isaac Wood.

(14.) AGNES, died single.

(15.) JANE, married Joseph Ratcliff. Children: John, Robert, Seth, Rodolph, William, Sarah, Rebecca, and Susan.

(16.) REBECCA, married Dennis Conard. Children: Martha and George.

(17.) CHARLOTTE, married Thomas Ashton. Children: Sarah, Mary, Joseph, and Elizabeth.

(18.) HANNAH, married, first, John Rush. Children: Elizabeth, Martha, Sarah, Hannah, Louisa, and Mary. She married, second, —— Ashton.

(19.) SUSAN, married Dr. Van Court, but had no children.

(20.) ELIZABETH, married Benjamin Griffith. Children: Benjamin, Samuel, and Comly.

Nathan and (4) *Jane Lukens's Children.*

(21.) LYDIA, married Thomas Livezey, of Spring Mills, Montgomery County, Pennsylvania.

(22.) ABRAHAM, married, and lived in Philadelphia.

(23.) AGNES, married —— Jackson, and lived in Philadelphia.

(24.) NATHAN, married Matilda Bracken, and lived in Horsham.

Isaac and (5) *Grace Parry's Children.*

(25.) AMY, married Jesse Wilson. Children: Rachel, Elizabeth, Amos, Grace, and Jane.

(26.) ISAAC, married Ruth Conard, and lived in Philadelphia.

(27.) SAMUEL, married Martha Thomas, and had one child, Samuel.

(28.) ROBERT, married, first, Sarah Page; second, Sarah Pope.

(29.) JOSEPH, married Sarah, daughter of Naylor Webster. He first settled in Horsham, but afterwards went out West.

Benjamin and (7) *Mary Shoemaker's Children.*

(30.) NATHAN, married Sarah, daughter of Solomon Miller. He was a tanner by trade. They left seven children.

(31.) ROBERT, married Martha Leech, and lived in Philadelphia. He died in early life. Children: Richard M., and two others.

(32.) BENJAMIN, married Jane Allen, of Bucks County, and left four children.

(33.) AMY, married Benjamin Harper. She died young, leaving one child.

(34.) MARY, married Thomas Shoemaker. Children: Dr. N. Shoemaker, and two others.

(35.) ELI, married Rachel Comly, of Byberry. He died young, leaving one child.

(36) REBECCA, married Atkinson Rose, and left three sons, of whom John S. Rose, of Frankford, was one.

(37.) COMLY, married the daughter of Albrick
Bird, and widow of George Shoemaker, Jr., but
had no children. They lived near Shoemakertown.

(38.) JANE, married Anthony, son of William Hallowell, of Abington. Children: Benjamin, Mary
S. (Lippincott), Caleb, James, and Joseph, the latter two deceased.

(9.) *John and Martha Comly's Children.*

(39.) SAMUEL, established the Comlyville Print-
works, near Frankford. He married Elizabeth
Ann Folwell. Children: Nathan Folwell, Samuel,
Rebecca, John, Robert, Thomas, Joseph, William
Folwell, Stephen Girard, Mary Pancoast, and Eliz-
abeth Ann.

(40.) JOHN W., moved to the West.

(41.) ROBERT, married Esther Shallcross, and
lived in Oxford Township, Philadelphia.

(42.) THOMAS and JOSEPH, deceased, without
children.

DESCENDANTS OF JOHN, SON OF HENRY AND AGNES
COMLY.

(1.) JOHN COMLY was born 3d mo. 20th, 1706.
He married Hannah, daughter of Benjamin Mason,
of Fair Hill, 4th mo. 20th, 1728. They first settled on the farm now owned by Benjamin Tomlinson, in Moreland. In 1738 he exchanged with his
brother, James, for a farm on the County Line. In
1754 he obtained a certificate for himself and family to Falls Monthly Meeting. He afterwards lived
on Walter Comly's farm, near Smithfield, and sub-

sequently between Frankford and Germantown,
where he died, 1st mo. 15th, 1761, and was buried
at Frankford. He was not successful in business,
and left but little property behind him. Hannah,
his wife, was born 3d mo. 31st, 1710, and died at the
residence of her son Jacob, in Byberry, 12th mo.
8th, 1782. Children : Abigail, Henry, Abraham,
Isaac, Agnes, Jacob, John, Hannah, Mary, Gaynor,
and Susanna.

(1.) *John and Hannah Comly's Children.*

(2.) ABIGAIL, born 6th mo. 16th, 1730; died at
her brother's residence in York County, 5th mo.
12th, 1812.

(3) HENRY, born 12th mo., 1731; died in 1756.

(4.) ABRAHAM, born 12th mo. 1733, was married
in 1763. He died of yellow fever, in 1793. Children: Benjamin and John. They were both noted
as skilful watermen about Camden and Cooper's
Point, and both left families.

(5.) ISAAC, born 1st mo. 13th, 1735, married Sarah Huston, 10th mo., 1761, and settled near Dar-
by, where he died, in 1812. Children : Timothy,
John, Isaac, Joseph, Isaiah, Israel, Charles, Mary,
and Hannah.

(6.) AGNES, born 3d mo. 13th, 1738; died in 1760.

(7.) JACOB, born 3d mo. 17th, 1740, married Sa-
rah Thornburg, of York County, Pennsylvania.
They first lived in Philadelphia; then at a mill on
the Pennypack, and next on a farm in Byberry.
He subsequently removed to Huntingdon, in York
County, where he died, 6th mo. 21st, 1821, aged 82

years. His wife died a few years previous. Children: Samuel, Jesse, and Susanna.

(8.) JOHN, born 1st mo. 13th, 1743, married Mary ——. They first settled in Byberry, but afterwards moved to Drinker's Alley, in Philadelphia, where he died, in 1792, aged 49 years. Mary died 11th mo. 21st, 1819. Children: David, Richard, Abigail, and Mary.

(9.) HANNAH, born 7th mo. 11th, 1746; died in 1760.

(10) MARY, born 9th mo. 9th, 1747, married —— Robinson, and lived in Brewer's Alley, Philadelphia. She died 12th mo. 1, 1828, aged 81 years, leaving one child, Mary.

(11) GAYNOR, born 7th mo. 15th, 1751; died young.

(12) SUSANNA, born 5th mo. 4th, 1753, married Christopher Smith, a schoolmaster, in 1780, and died the next year.

(5.) *Isaac and Sarah Comly's Children.*

(13.) JOHN, died of small-pox, aged 22 years, leaving one daughter.

(14.) ISAAC, died at Plymouth, in 1812, leaving several children.

(15.) MARY, married —— Perot.

(16.) HANNAH, married Lawrence Lowry.

(7.) *Jacob and Sarah Comly's Children.*

(17.) SAMUEL, married Susanna Wireman. He removed to Washington County, Pennsylvania, in 1837, and remained there until his death. His children were Sarah, Ezra, Hannah, Phebe, Lydia, William, and Isaac.

(18.) JESSE, married Naomi Howell. He removed to Juniata in 1833. Children: Jacob, Joseph, Benjamin, Samuel, Ellen, Jesse, and John.

(19.) SUSANNA married —— Wierman. Children : Thomas, Hannah, and Sarah.

DESCENDANTS OF JOSEPH, SON OF HENRY AND AGNES COMLY.

(1.) JOSEPH COMLY, was born 8th mo. 8th, 1708. He married Elizabeth, daughter of Benjamin Mason, and settled in Moreland, on a farm lately owned by Judge Sommers, about 1730. He was remarkably healthy, and was never sick except it was for a few days previous to his death. He was very fond of strong drink, and frequently drank a quart of rum at one time without becoming intoxicated. This he always called "small beer." He wore stockings without any feet, and went without a coat or upper jacket in winter-time. He removed to Gunpowder, Md., and not asking for a certificate from Byberry Monthly Meeting, of which he was a member, they, in 1759, sent one after him. Previous to this time he had sold his farm, and in old age owned no property. In 1774, he went to Joshua Comly's house apparently in good health, but said he was come to die in his old lodging-room over the kitchen. Shortly afterward he was taken sick, and died in about four weeks from the time of his arrival there, at the age of sixty-six years. During his illness his mind was composed, and he had no

23*

fear of death. He said he never swore an oath in his life, never wronged any man out of a penny, and never told a falsehood to the injury of any person. Some who were well acquainted with him said they had no reason to doubt his assertions. How many who have made far greater pretensions towards possessing religion than he, could with truth adopt the language of Joseph Comly? He was very strong: could put a barrel of cider in a wagon with ease, and take one that was full on his knees and drink out of the bung. His vocal powers were astonishing. On one occasion some of his family started to go to market in the night, but after they had been gone some time the old man recollected he had forgotten to send for a keg of nails by them; he, therefore, called to them and mentioned what he wanted. They heard him, although three miles off, and attended to his request. When going to visit his relations he would, when within about two miles, call to them, that they might know he was coming. He was a great walker, and always went to Gunpowder on foot, which he called an evening's walk. When making the journey he carried his bread, cheese, and a bottle of rum, and ate, drank, and slept by the roadside. His wife died about 1757, and he died 6 mo. 21, 1774, aged 66 years.

(1.) *Joseph and Elizabeth Comly's Children.*

(2.) Agnes, born 4th mo. 2d, 1732, married Evan Roberts.

(3.) ABIGAIL, born 8th mo. 15th, 1733, married David Hallowell.

(4.) JOSEPH, born 1st mo. 9th, 1735, married Rachel Edwards, and had one daughter, "Dumb Becky." He was a soldier in the French and Indian War in 1755, but escaped unhurt. He died in Byberry 2d mo. 19th, 1811. Rachel died 4th mo. 9th, 1815.

(5.) RICHARD, born 4th mo. 1st, 1737, was a soldier in the French and Indian War, and during the famous retreat of Braddock was taken sick. He was left sitting on a log, and was never heard of afterwards.

(6.) SUSANNA, born 5th mo. 15th, 1740, married Samuel Shute. She died in 1802.

(7.) WALTER, born 11th mo. 13th, 1742; no further account.

(8.) BENJAMIN, born 2d mo. 17th, 1744; no further account.

(9.) ELIZABETH, born 1st mo. 8th, 1746, married Benjamin Tomlinson, and moved to Huntingdon, York County, Pa., where she died in 1817, aged 70 years.

(10.) SARAH, born 12th mo. 28th, 1748; died single, 4th mo. 9th, 1810, aged 60 years.

DESCENDANTS OF WALTER, SON OF HENRY AND AGNES
COMLY.

(1.) WALTER COMLY married Susanna, daughter of Benjamin Mason, 1st mo., 1731. He settled on a farm in Moreland, now owned by John Linger-

man, but afterwards purchased the farm back of
Somerton, now belonging to William T. Ervin,
where he died 3d mo. 20th, 1759, aged 49 years.
Susanna, his widow married William Walmsley,
6th mo., 1764. She died 5th mo. 30th, 1795, aged
81 years, having been an Elder in Byberry meeting forty-two years.

(1.) *Walter and Susanna Comly's Children.*

(2.) WALTER; no account.

(3.) SUSANNA; no account.

(4.) THOMAS, who died young.

(5.) MARTHA, born 1st mo. 20th, 1746, married
Silas Walmsley, 6th mo., 1765. Children: William,
Jesse, and Silas.

Silas and (5) Martha Walmsley's Children.

(6.) WILLIAM, born 7th mo. 18th, 1766, married,
first, Phebe, daughter of Giles Knight. She died
8th mo. 18th, 1808. Children: Silas, Ann, and
Martha. William married, second, Margery,
daughter of Evan Townsend. Children: Robert
and Jesse.

(7.) JESSE, married Mary, daughter of James
Paul. Children: Martha, James, Susanna, Elizabeth, Ezra, Hannah, and Mary.

DESCENDANTS OF AGNES, DAUGHTER OF HENRY AND
AGNES COMLY.

(1.) AGNES COMLY, married Nicholas Randall, in
1738. They lived on Duffield's farm in Moreland

for several years. She died, 9th mo. 22d, 1779, and he died in 1783. Children: Comly, Thomas, Jonathan, Nathan, Rachel, Thomas, Mary, and Nicholas.

Nicholas and (1) *Agnes Randall's Children.*

(2.) COMLY, born 12th mo. 9th, 1738; married Mary Phinny, in 1763. Children: Agnes, Martha, and Jonathan.

(3.) THOMAS, born 8th mo. 10th, 1740, died in 1743.

(4.) JONATHAN, born 3d mo. 17th, 1742, died in 1748.

(5.) NATHAN, born 8th mo. 12th, 1743, died in 1748.

(6.) RACHEL, born 11th mo. 21st, 1745, died in 1748.

(7.) THOMAS, born 5th mo. 13th, 1748, died in 1783.

(8.) MARY, born 12th mo. 22d, 1751, married Joshua Gilbert in 1771. They settled on a farm in Byberry, now owned by Thomas James. Mary died 3d mo. 13th, 1812, aged 60 years, and Joshua died 6th mo. 18th, 1833, aged 86 years. Children: Phebe, Benjamin, Tacy, Thomas, Joshua, David, and Beulah.

(9.) NICHOLAS, married Hannah, daughter of Thomas Townsend. Children: Thomas, Jesse, Agnes, who married Jacob Myers, and Mary, who married David Clayton.

(1.) JAMES COMLY, married Mary, daughter of
John Paul, in 1738. Mary was born 1st mo. 28th,
1718. She was an approved minister in the Society of Friends. They first settled in Warminster,
but in 1758 removed to Gunpowder, Maryland.
After the death of James, Mary returned to Byberry, where she frequently preached. Children :
Jacob, James, David, Jonathan, John, Rachel, and
Mary.

(1.) James and Mary Comly's Children.

(2.) JACOB, born 11th mo. 8th, 1738, returned
from Maryland in 1770, and married Rachel, widow
of his cousin, Henry Comly. For many years he
kept a hotel on the turnpike below Somerton, late
the Leedom estate. He afterwards moved to
Philadelphia, and, with the consent of such heirs
as could be found, obtained the city lot granted
to Henry Comly by William Penn. He died near
Abington, 9th mo. 21st, 1825, aged 87 years, leaving no children.

(3.) JAMES, married Charity Hooker of Maryland. Children : John ; Mary, who married Nicholas Merryman, of Jefferson County, Ohio ; Joshua,
who moved to Madison, Indiana ; Charity, who
married Mordecai Price, near Baltimore, Maryland ; David, who died near Baltimore ; Nancy,
who married —— Pettyford, of Baltimore ; Elizabeth and Dobino, both deceased ; Sabret and James,

who married daughters of David Comly, near Lancaster, Kentucky; Sally, married —— Doughty; Rachel, married to Johnson; and Eleanor, who married her cousin Absalom, of Madison, Indiana.

(4.) DAVID, moved to Madison, Indiana. Children : John, Absalom, James, and three daughters.

(5.) JONATHAN, died unmarried.

(6.) JOHN, moved to Ohio. Children : Rachel, Mary, Hannah, Sarah, Eleanor, Rebecca, James, John, Joshua, and David.

DESCENDANTS OF ISAAC, SON OF HENRY AND AGNES
COMLY.

(1.) ISAAC COMLY, was born in Moreland, in 1715. He married Abigail, daughter of Thomas Walmsley, 2d mo., 1738, and settled in the village of Smithfield. He lived in a hip-roofed house, which had, on a stone in the wall near the door, the inscription, " I. C., 1744." This house was removed only a few years since, having stood nearly one hundred years. They afterward moved to a place near the present residence of Silas Vanarsdalen, where Isaac died, in 1748, aged thirty-three years.

He was a blacksmith by trade, and followed that business through life. His children were Agnes; Isaac, born in 1741, died in 1743; Isaac, and William. Abigail, his widow, married Richard Walton, in 1753. Children : Joseph, born in 1754, and Esther, born in 1755.

(1.) *Isaac and Abigail Comly's Children.*

(2.) AGNES, born 11th mo. 2d, 1738, married
John Duncan, in 1759. He died 10th mo. 6th,
1772, aged 51 years. Children: Abigail, Rachel,
Esther, and Phebe. In 1793, Agnes married Andrew Singley, of White Sheet Bay, on the Delaware. He died in 1814, aged 72 years; and Agnes
died in 1821, aged 83 years.

(3.) ISAAC, was born at Smithfield, 9th mo. 25th,
1743. When about five years old he lost his father.
After this event he and his mother went to live
with her father on the farm lately owned by
Charles Walmsley. In 1753, his mother married
Richard Walton, and he resided in that family until 1771, when he married Asenath, daughter of
John and Ann Hampton, of Wrightstown. They
took a farm in the western part of Byberry, where
they resided two years, after which they purchased
of Thomas Knight a farm of about one hundred
and forty acres, near the centre of Byberry, where
they permanently settled. By a regular course of
industry and economy, Isaac and Asenath Comly
accumulated considerable property and brought
up a large family of children, most of whom have
since figured conspicuously in the affairs of the
township of Byberry. Isaac Comly was not ambitious of fame, and never sought after popularity,
his object being to attend to his own business,
leaving to others the cares and responsibilities of
public life. He was a member of the religious Society of Friends, and always bore an unexception-

able character among them. His wife was an Elder in the Meeting, and was much respected. Their children were Martha, John, Joseph, Isaac, Ezra, Ethan, and Jason. He died 8th mo. 3d, 1822, aged seventy-nine; and his wife 3d mo. 3d, 1826, aged seventy-seven years.

(3.) *Isaac and Asenath Comly's Children.*

(4.) MARTHA, born 12th mo. 29th, 1771, married Evan T. Knight. They lived in Bensalem, where he died 2d mo. 6th, 1841; and she died 7th mo. 29th, 1851. Children: Isaac and Phebe.

(5.) JOHN, was born in Byberry, 11th mo. 19th, 1773. He was carefully brought up according to the rules of the Society of Friends, and at an early age, while yet a school-boy, manifested a great interest in the Society, and exhibited those traits of humility and tenderness which so eminently characterized him through life. In 1792 he was placed under Samuel Jones, the Baptist minister at Pennypack, to study the Latin and Greek languages, where he remained until the spring of 1794. He then engaged as a teacher in Byberry School, where he continued until 1801, when he resigned, and from a sense of duty engaged as a teacher in Westtown Boarding School. In 1802 he resigned that situation and returned to his native place, and in the following spring again took charge of Byberry School. In 6th mo. 1803, he married Rebecca, daughter of Dr. Stacy Budd, of Mount Holly, N. J., and settled on a farm lately purchased in Byberry. In 1804 he opened a boarding school for

24

girls at his residence, which was successfully continued until 1810, and was then changed into a
school for boys and young men, and continued till
1815. His literary works are as follows: "English
Grammar," published in 1803; "Spelling Book,"
in 1806; "Primer," in 1807; and "Reader and
Book of Useful Knowledge," in 1840. Some of
these have passed through several editions, and
still have an extensive sale throughout the whole
country. He was also the author of several essays
upon moral subjects, which were published in the
journals of that day. He was subsequently engaged, along with his brother Isaac, in publishing
a periodical called "Friends' Miscellany," which
was continued through a series of years, and has
been the means of preserving many valuable records, biographical sketches, historical notes, and
other matters of peculiar interest. John Comly
appeared as a minister in the Society of Friends
in 1810; and his labors being approved by the
Monthly Meeting, he was recommended in 1813.
Besides his services at home, he frequently made
religious visits, which extended to New England,
New York, Ohio, Maryland, and other places, and
which tended greatly to inculcate the peaceable
principles of Friends. Several of his sermons were
stenographically reported by Marcus T. Gould, and
afterward published. He was also eminently useful as a surveyor, and was often able to satisfac-
torily settle conflicting claims and disputes among
his neighbors. He died at his residence in Byberry, 8th mo. 17th, 1850, after an illness of only a

few days, aged nearly 77 years. His wife died 8th mo. 9th, 1832.

Their children were Stacy, Ann, Charles, Sarah, and Emmor.

(6.) JOSEPH, was born in Byberry, 12th mo. 16th, 1775. He learned the trade of a carpenter, which business he followed for several years, and afterward settled on a part of his father's farm. In 1800 he built a commodious house, the one now occupied by his son, Watson Comly; and in the latter part of the same year was married to Abigail, daughter of Jonathan Parry. She died in 1805. Children, Asenath, Phebe, and James. In 1807 he married Rachel, daughter of Dr. John Watson, of Buckingham. He had a taste for mechanical pursuits, and was the first to introduce several important improvements, in those matters, into the townships. He became quite noted for moving buildings, such as houses, barns, &c.; and, from a record kept by him, he moved one hundred and sixty-five buildings in the course of twenty years. He published several essays in the *Evening Fireside* and other periodicals, wrote several journals of his travels, and collected considerable historical matter of local interest. He was a very useful man, and highly respected by all who knew him. He died in Byberry, 2d mo. 5th, 1854, aged 78 years. His wife, Rachel, died 2d mo. 3d, 1839.

(7.) ISAAC, born in Byberry, 3d mo. 21st, 1779. He was apt at learning while a youth; and, without any other advantages than those afforded by the neighboring school, fitted himself for the duties of a teacher. In 1794 he commenced as an usher under his brother John, at Byberry, and in 1797 engaged as an assistant with Samuel Comfort, of Middletown. He remained here until 3d mo., 1798, when he took charge of the school at Buckingham for one year. He removed to Horsham in 1799, and in the latter part of the same year to Ancocas, New Jersey, where he continued teaching school for two years. During part of 1801 he taught at Mansfield's Neck; and in 1802 took a school at Newton, New Jersey, where he remained until 1809, when he relinquished the business. He then spent some time in travelling; and in 1811 was married to Meribah, daughter of John and Rebecca Barton, of Newton, New Jersey. Soon after his marriage he opened a store in Byberry, which was continued until about 1822, when he moved to the old homestead, where he spent the remainder of his life in tilling the soil. He was a clerk at Byberry Monthly Meeting for many years, and afterward an Elder. As a writer, he ranks second to none who has ever resided in the townships, his information extending to nearly every branch of literature; and his numerous essays, prose and poetical, which were published in several of the best periodicals of the day, and which were extensively copied, exhibit a talent of no ordinary merit. Among those articles we notice many sketches of these townships, and it is to Isaac Comly that we are indebted for much of the present history. Besides these fugitive pieces, he published a reading book for schools, entitled " Easy Lessons for Juvenile Readers," in 1807; the "Philadelphia Primer," in 1808; "A New Assistant," in 1809, and was one of the editors of the "Friends' Miscellany." His great delight, however, seems to have been among the musty records of bygone times; and to hunt up and note down every particular relative to family and local history, was one of the chief employments of his life. He collected much toward a history of his native and surrounding townships, and traced out the genealogy of many of the most prominent families who have resided in the vicinity. He was frequently applied to by those wishing information of this kind, and they were seldom disappointed. Being of an amiable disposition, and just in his dealings, he was honored and respected by all who knew him. The even tenor of his life was rarely disturbed by surrounding circumstances, and he passed through the scenes of this world in peace and contentment. He died at his farm in Byberry, 10th mo. 19th, 1847, aged 69 years. His widow died 11th mo. 8th, 1862. Children : Mary and Robert.

(8.) EZRA, born in Byberry, 9th mo. 3d, 1781. He married Sarah Strickland, in 1804. He resided in Byberry for several years, after which he moved to Black River, in the northern part of New York. In 18— he returned to Byberry, where he spent the rest of his life. He died 8th mo. 27th, 1863; and Sarah died 1st mo. 17th, 1855. Children : Elizabeth and Isaac.

(9.) ETHAN, born 5th mo. 31st, 1784, remained in Byberry until 1804, when he removed to Philadel-

24*

phia and became a merchant. He wrote several
excellent miscellaneous articles for the public papers. On account of an affection of the spine, he
was induced to cultivate his taste for drawing, so
that he acquired very great skill and proficiency
in that art. He was a member of the Academy of
Fine Arts in Philadelphia, and was much respected
by all who knew him. He died 6th mo. 13, 1865.
Children: Allen, Eliza, and Henry.

DESCENDANTS OF GRACE, DAUGHTER OF HENRY AND
AGNES COMLY.

(1.) GRACE COMLY, married, first, Benjamin, son
of John Cadwalader, the preacher, in 1742, and
settled on a farm adjoining Horsham Meeting-
house. Benjamin died 4th mo. 14th, 1753. Children: Rachel, Phebe, Benjamin, and Cyrus. Grace
married, second, Benjamin Powers. She died 1st
mo., 1800, aged 79 years. Children by her last
husband, Mary and Grace.

Benjamin and (1) *Grace Cadwalader's Children.*

(2.) RACHEL, born 6th mo. 9th, 1743; died while
young.

(3.) PHEBE, born 8th mo. 19th, 1747, married
Charles Iredell, and settled in Horsham. Chil-
dren: Rebecca, Grace, Rachel, Robert, Joseph, and
Benjamin.

(4.) BENJAMIN, born 4th mo. 9th, 1749, married
Hannah Bradfield. He lived on the homestead in
Horsham till the decease of his mother, when he

moved to Gill's farm, in Buckingham. During the latter part of his life he resided with his son-in-law, James Bonner, where he died, in 1834, aged 85 years. He was something of a poet, and was a very useful member of society. His children were Ure, who married James Bonner; Betsey, who married John Rich; Benjamin, who married, first, Sarah Townsend, 2d, Sarah Landis; Yarley, who married Christianna Moore; Peter Y., who married Hannah Magill; David, who married Ann Robinson; John, who married Lydia Ann Merrick; and Silas, who married Rebecca Sheppard.

(5.) CYRUS, born 8th mo. 9th, 1752; died while young.

Benjamin and (1) *Grace Powers's Children.*

(6.) MARY, died while young.

(7.) GRACE, married John Carlisle. Children: Phebe and Amos. Phebe married John Burton, and settled at Fallsington, Bucks County; and Amos married —— Kinsey, and settled at Morrisville.

Charles and (3) *Phebe Iredell's Children.*

(8.) REBECCA, married Jacob Kirk, and settled on the Welsh Road, in Abington. Children: Phebe, Ruth, Rebecca, Charles, Aaron, Samuel, Hannah, Elizabeth, Abraham, and Rachel.

(9.) GRACE, married John Conrad, and lived in Horsham.

(10.) RACHEL, died single.

(11.) ROBERT, married Mary Marple. Children:

Oliver, who died young, and Ann, who married Dr. Hunt, of New Jersey.

(12.) JOSEPH, married Hannah Thomas, of Hat-boro'. They resided in Jenkintown, and had one son, Charles, who went to Bristol, Bucks County.

THE DUFFIELD FAMILY.*

(1.) BENJAMIN DUFFIELD, son of Robert and Bridget Duffield, of England, was born September 29, 1661. He married Elizabeth, daughter of Susanna and Arthur Watts, and emigrated to Burlington, New Jersey, in 1679. He purchased a tract of land in the manor of Moreland, in 1685. He died in Philadelphia, May 5, 1741, and his tombstone may be seen at Christ Churchyard, at Fifth and Arch Streets, Philadelphia.

(2.) JOSEPH, eighth child of Benjamin and Eliza-

* I am indebted to Dr. John Neill, of Philadelphia, for the greater part of the genealogy of this family.

beth Duffield, was born in 1692. He owned a few
slaves, which were willed to his wife at his death,
in 1746.

(2.) *Joseph Duffield's Children.*

(3.) BENJAMIN, died young.
(4.) ELIZABETH, married Dr. Samuel Swift.
(5.) MARY, died young.
(6.) SARAH, married Prof. Kinnersley, of the
College of Philadelphia.
(7.) HANNAH, died young.
(8.) JOSEPH, died young.
(9.) JAMES, died young.
(10.) EDWARD, born in 1720, married Mrs. Catharine Parry, daughter of Judge Smyth, of South
Carolina. Sarah Franklin, writing to her father
in Europe, under date of March 23, 1766, says,
"Our dear friend Mrs. Smyth expired yesterday
morning. Poor Mrs. Duffield and poor mamma
are in great distress. It must be hard to lose a
friend of fifty years' standing."

His name appears among the earlier members
of the American Philosophical Society. He was
also a Commissioner to issue colonial paper cur-
rency, a specimen of which, with his autograph, is
on exhibition in Independence Hall. About the
same time he was one of those charged with the
erection of the Walnut Street Prison, and there is
a tradition that when the British occupied Philadelphia, they seized him at his country residence,
and, marching him past his city house, imprisoned

him in the jail, the construction of which he had superintended.

He was a man of considerable talent, and was noted for his scientific acquirements and his skill in agricultural and mechanical pursuits. He is said to have made the first watch, from the raw materials, ever made in Pennsylvania; and some of his clocks, among which is the one on Lower Dublin Academy, are yet to be seen in the vicinity, —monuments of his skill and ingenuity in mechanism. He associated with such men as Kinnersley, Rittenhouse, and Franklin, the latter of whom reposed great confidence in him, often visited him at his residence, and made him one of the executors of his last will.

The only literary production we have met with, emanating from his pen, is "Some Observations on the Application of Plaster of Paris," which was published by Judge Peters, in 1797. He was much interested in educational matters, and was one of the founders of the Lower Dublin Academy; he also was the means of having a schoolhouse erected in his own immediate neighborhood. He died in 1803, aged about seventy-four years, and was buried at All Saints' churchyard. It is traditionally asserted that the first consultation by Jefferson and others, respecting the Declaration of Independence, was held at Edward Duffield's house.

(11.) Uz, eaten by the wolves when three years of age.

(10.) *Edward* and *Catharine Duffield's Children.*

(12.) MARY, JOSEPH, CATHARINE, all died in youth.

(13.) ELIZABETH, married Francis Ingraham.

(14.) BENJAMIN, was born November 3d, 1753. He was educated at the College of Philadelphia, where in 1771, he received the degree of Master of Arts, and delivered on Commencement day, a poem entitled "Science." He became a medical student in the office of Dr. John Redman, and after attending the lectures of Morgan and Shippen, in 1775, he went to Edinburgh and completed his education. On his return from Europe, he married Rebecca, daughter of John Potts, of Pottsgrove, and sister of Dr. Jonathan Potts, Director General of the Hospitals of the Middle and Northern Departments during the Revolutionary War. In 1793, while the yellow fever was raging in Philadelphia, he had charge of the Bush Hill Hospital, and, in 1798, the managers of the Marine and City Hospitals voted him a sum of money, in appreciation of his services. He was the first lecturer on Obstetrics in America, and was a member of the American Philosophical Society. A poem of his inscribed "To the Memory of the late Dr. Rittenhouse, by his sincere admirer," is still extant. In the life of Judge Iredell, one of the first Associate Judges of the Supreme Court of the United States, are several letters from Dr. Duffield, who was the Judge's family physician. Dr. Duffield resided in Front Street, Philadelphia, where his wife died in February, 1797. He died in December, 1799, aged 46 years, and left several children.

(15.) SARAH, married Stacy Hepburn.

(16.) EDWARD, remained a bachelor, and occupied the old Duffield homestead, devoting his time to reading and agricultural pursuits. He is still remembered by some of the inhabitants as a gentleman of the old school. He died in 1836 or 7, and then the old Duffield homestead was purchased by John Murray, who still occupies it.

Francis and (13) Elizabeth Ingraham's Children.

(17.) FRANCIS and CATHARINE, buried at All Saints'.

(18.) EDWARD D., a distinguished lawyer and bibliomaniac, of Philadelphia; married first, Mary Wilson, 'of Snow Hill, Md., and second, Caroline Barney, of Baltimore.

(19.) ALFRED, married Elizabeth, sister of Major-General Meade, and removed to Mississippi, where they have a numerous family.

(14.) Benjamin and Rebecca Duffield's Children.

(20.) CATHARINE, born April 9th, 1779, married Dr. John Church, of Philadelphia. She died in 1804, childless.

(21.) MARTHA R., born August 9th, 1780, married Dr. Henry Neill, of Snow Hill, Md. She died in Philadelphia, June, 1856.

(22.) EDWARD, born December 13th, 1782, married Miss Nolan.

(23.) JOHN POTTS, born November 2d, 1784, married first, Miss Handy, of Snow Hill, Md., and second, Miss Bishop, of the same place. He died at Snow Hill, in 1830.

(24.) REBECCA, born September 7th, 1786, married Dr. John S. Martin, of Snow Hill, Md., where she resided until her death in November, 1843.

(25.) MARY, born 1787, died in infancy.

Stacy and (15) *Sarah Hepburn's Children.*

(26.) JAMES, married in New Orleans, La.

(27.) FANNY, married James Strawbridge and moved to New Orleans, La.

(28.) ELIZA, married John J. Vanderkemp.

THE GILBERT FAMILY.*

The ancestor of this family was (1) JOHN GILBERT, who came over in the ship "Welcome" from England, in 1682. He is supposed to have been the John Gilbert who, during the persecution of the Quakers in England, was taken out of a meeting and sent to Lancaster jail, in 1663. He first settled in Bensalem, but in 1695 he purchased six hundred acres of land in the eastern part of Byberry, of Nicholas Rideout. One-half of this tract he afterwards conveyed to his son Joseph, and the other half he sold to John Carver, after which he

* I am indebted to Gilbert Cope, of West Chester, for a portion of this account.

removed to Philadelphia, where he became a prominent merchant. He remained in the city until his death, on the 13th of 8th mo. (October), 1711. He was married while in England, and his wife's name was Florence. Their children, as far as known, were John, Joseph, Sarah, Mary, Joshua, and Abigail.

(1.) *John and Florence Gilbert's Children.*

(2.) JOHN, came over with his parents, in 1682, and settled in Bucks County, near the Poquessing Creek. Little is known of him except that he was a peace-loving man in the favor of William Penn, and ardently attached to religious worship. He died in Philadelphia 1st mo. 7th, 1701–2, leaving two sons, John and Samuel.

(3.) JOSEPH, married Rachel Livezey, of Abington, in 1699, and settled in Byberry. He was one of the prominent men of his time, being an elder and leading member of Byberry Meeting. This position he filled with great satisfaction; and by his strict integrity, undeviating attention to moral and religious duties, and earnest support of what he believed the testimonies of Truth, he gained the esteem and respect of all who knew him. He was a man of very correct judgment, and had a strong mind, so that he was seldom deterred from doing what he believed to be his duty or led away from a Christian's path. His views were far in advance of those of his contemporaries, and were tempered by justice and moderation. He regularly attended

meetings for religious worship, and encouraged his
family and neighbors to observe the same practice. Although he furnished intoxicating drinks
to his hands in the harvest-field, yet *he* refrained
from its use, and on such occasions drank water
which was taken from a neighboring brook and
kept in a jug in the open sunshine. He was opposed to holding slaves, and united with Benjamin
Lay and other Friends in bearing testimony against
the evil; and in order to make his example correspond with his precept, he liberated several
slaves in his possession. He was opposed to usury,
and being a man of considerable wealth, he put his
views in practice by frequently lending money
without interest to those in necessitous circumstances. On one occasion a travelling Friend held
a meeting at Byberry, when Joseph informed his
hands that they might attend the meeting without
loss to themselves, but that those who refused
should not perform any duty during his absence.
He retained his mental and physical energies un-
impaired to the close of his life, and when fourscore years old led his hands in the harvest-field.
He had such control over his dispositions that for
many years of the latter part of his life he was
rarely, if ever, known to be in a passion. He travelled with Thomas Chalkley on a religious visit to
Friends on Long Island. He died in 1765, at the
advanced age of ninety years, and it may be truly
said that few men of his time were more honored
while living or more lamented when dead. He left
several children, among whom was Benjamin, the

Indian captive. He resided on a place now owned by Thomas James, and built the farm-house, which is still standing, in 1722.

(4.) SARAH, married Henry Elfreth, in 1702. She died in 1728, leaving children.

(5.) MARY, married —— Ballard. Their children were Samuel, William, and probably others.

(6.) JOSHUA, was born 6th mo. 10th, 1684, being the first child of the name of Gilbert born in America. He married Elizabeth Oldham, 8th mo. 19th, 1707. They had one daughter, Elizabeth, who married William Parker. Joshua was a blacksmith in Philadelphia, where he died, 7th mo. 19th, 1711.

(3.) *Joseph and Rachel Gilbert's Children.*

(7.) SARAH, born 4th mo. 21st, 1700, married John Baldwin, in 1725.

(8.) PHEBE, born 12th mo. 7th, 1701, married Henry Comly, of Moreland, 7th mo. 26th, 1728. She died 2d mo. 14th, 1773.

(9.) JOSEPH, born 10th mo. 13th, 1703; died in 1730, unmarried.

(10.) REBECCA, married Patrick Ogilby, of Long Island, in 1735.

(11.) BENJAMIN, was born in Byberry, in 1711. He was one of the most extraordinary characters of his day. In June, 1731, at the age of twenty-one years, he married Sarah, daughter of Benjamin Mason, of Fair Hill. After this event he remained in Byberry several years, and then removed to the great swamp, in Richland, Bucks County, where

he was in 1748. While there he was rather irregular in his life, and was disowned by the Society of
Friends, of which he was a member. Soon after
this he saw proper to change his life, and, from his
general good conduct, Friends reinstated him as a
member of the Society, in 1749. In this year he
removed to a mill in Makefield, Bucks County;
and, in 1755, he returned to his native place to take
charge of his father's farm. Four years later he
purchased one hundred and thirty-six acres of the
Ellis tract, near the centre of Byberry, on the
Byberry Creek, and on which he soon afterward
erected a grist-mill—the one now owned by Charles
B. Comly. In 1759 he lost his wife. Soon after
this his life again became irregular, and he was a
second time disowned. His father, who had died
a short time previous, was very wealthy, and had
left the most of his property to Benjamin, his only
surviving son. It might be supposed that such an
ample fortune would satisfy any one; but Benjamin was of a roving disposition, delighting in
change, and was, therefore, not long contented in
any one place. In 1760, he married Elizabeth, '
widow of Bryan Peart, and daughter of Benjamin
Walton, of Byberry. In 1770, he offered a written
acknowledgment of his offence to the Meeting, but
it was not received; and, in 1776, he made another
to the same Meeting, and was again reinstated.
By this time he was advanced in age, and had seen
several of his numerous family of children comfortably settled around him; but others remained
to be provided for, and he, in 1775, at the age of

sixty-four years, embarked in a new enterprise for
this purpose. He disposed of his mill property in
Byberry, and purchased lands on Mahoning Creek,
in Northampton County, then one of the frontier
settlements of Pennsylvania, whither he removed
with his family in the spring of that year. On
this property was an excellent mill site, where he
erected a saw and grist-mill, and carried on an extensive and prosperous business, and lived at peace
with all his neighbors, both whites and Indians.
At this time the latter were very troublesome, and
Benjamin was frequently warned of the danger;
but being innocent himself, and never having taken any part in the contest, he thought he could
rest in security and peace. In this, however, he
was mistaken, for, on the 25th of April, 1780, a
party of eleven savages came to his house about
sunrise, armed with guns, tomahawks, &c. Benjamin met them at the door, and they shook hands
with him, and called him brother, but immediately
proceeded to tie his arms so that he could not use
them. They then secured the rest of the family,
and proceeded to rob the house, and loaded several
horses with the plunder. Two of the Indians remained behind to set fire to the buildings, while
the remainder marched with their prisoners—fifteen in number—and plunder through the wilderness. After enduring innumerable sufferings and
hardships, they reached Niagara just one month
after they had been taken captives, where Benjamin, his wife, and son Jesse, were surrendered to
Colonel Johnson, but the others were detained

among the Indians. From Niagara they were
sent to Montreal, and at the mouth of Lake Onta-
rio were placed in open boats to descend the St.
Lawrence River to that place. Benjamin was sick
before leaving the fort, and a heavy rain falling
upon him increased the disorder, so that on the
8th of the 6th mo., 1780, his eventful life was ter-
minated at the age of 69 years. On the next day
he was buried under an oak tree on the banks of
the St. Lawrence. The remainder of the family
were, in time, released, and reached Byberry again
on the 28th of 9th mo., 1782. A narrative of their
captivity and sufferings, containing ninety-six
pages, was published by Joseph Cruikshank, in
1784. Benjamin Gilbert was a man of much energy
and determination, and an attentive observer of all
that transpired around him. His mind was of a
religious turn, and he wrote and published several
volumes on theological subjects. They were written in a plain, easy style, and evince considerable
thought and a clear comprehension of the subject
he was considering. Elizabeth, his widow, died
8th mo. 5th, 1810, at the age of 85.

(11.) *Benjamin and Sarah Gilbert's Children.*

(12.) RACHEL, born 11th mo. 14th, 1732, married,
first, Ezekiel Atkinson, in 1754; and second, William Walton. She died 2d mo. 24th, 1791.

(13.) ABIGAIL, born 9th mo. 3d, 1734, married
Benjamin Walton.

(14.) SARAH, born 2d mo. 24th, 1737; died in infancy.

(15.) Joseph, born 12th mo. 10th, 1738; died in 1807, unmarried.

(16.) Benjamin, born 1st mo. 31st, 1741, married, first, Rebecca Watson, in 1771; and second, Margaret Anderson. He died 1st mo. 11th, 1809.

(17.) John, born 5th mo. 23d, 1743, married Ann Stackhouse, in 1768.

(18.) Sarah, born 4th mo. 26th, 1745, married Daniel Walton. She died 7th mo. 25th, 1785.

(19.) Joshua, was born in Richland, Bucks County, 3d mo. 3d, 1748. He came to Byberry with his father in 1755; and being of an active and lively disposition, he was, in the early part of his life, fond of amusements, could dance equal to any of his young companions, and relish a game of cards on every occasion. At the age of twenty-one years he appears to have taken a serious turn, and his mind became impressed with considerations of a more weighty nature, and he was afterward a regular attendant at religious meetings. In 1771 he married Mary, daughter of Nicholas Randall, and purchased the old homestead where Thomas James now lives, with fifty acres of land, and settled thereon. He brought up a large family of children, and was esteemed by all who knew him. Mary died 3d mo. 13th, 1812, aged 60 years, and Joshua died 6th mo. 18th, 1833, aged 86 years. They had children : Phebe, Benjamin, Tacy, Thomas, Joshua, David, and Beulah.

(20.) Caleb, born 9th mo. 19th, 1754, married Martha Stackhouse.

(11.) *Benjamin and Elizabeth Gilbert's Children.*

(21.) JESSE, born 5th mo. 4th, 1761, married Sarah Harding in 1780. He died 3d mo. 10th, 1829, leaving eleven children.

(22.) REBECCA, born in 1763, married Joseph Rakestraw. She died 8th mo. 23d, 1842.

(23.) ABNER, born 3d mo. 2d, 1765, married Ann, daughter of George and Susanna Cooper, 1st mo. 18th, 1799. They settled in Westmoreland County, Pa. Abner died 8th mo. 23d, 1842; his widow died 11th mo. 12th, 1846. They left a daughter Eliza, who married Joseph Cope.

(24.) ELIZABETH, born 9th mo. 14th, 1767, married David Webster. Notwithstanding the sufferings she endured during her captivity, Elizabeth Webster always retained an affection for John Huston, the Indian chief who adopted her in his family, and in 1822, she sent him some mementos of her remembrance, by the noted chiefs Cornplanter and Red Jacket, whom she met in Philadelphia. Of "Aunt Betsy," as she was universally called, it may be said, that few persons filled up the duties of life with more faithfulness, and although she had known trouble, yet she always appeared cheerful and happy. They lived in Byberry, where she died, in 1857. Children : Susan, who married John Matchner; David, who married Sindonia Walton; William; Jesse G., who married Sarah ——, and Nathan, who married Margery Gilbert.

(19.) *Joshua and Mary Gilbert's Children.*

(25.) PHEBE, married Thomas Wilson; she died 4th mo. 12th, 1814, aged 43 years.

(26.) BENJAMIN, went to Black River, where he died unmarried.

(27.) TACY, died single, 5th mo. 2d, 1847, aged 71 years.

(28.) THOMAS, married Martha, daughter of John Knight. He died 10th mo. 2d, 1844, and Martha died 12th mo. 3d, 1822. Children : Mary, Margery, who married Nathan Webster, John, Charles, who married Ellen Renshaw, David, Ezra, Ann P., and Sarah.

(29.) JOSHUA, was a prominent citizen of Byberry, and resided therein the greater part of his life. For many years he was a school teacher, and afterward kept store where Ross Knight now does. He was the author of several essays published in the *Evening Fireside,* and was considered a good writer. He was a man of learning, and took a great interest in scientific and literary studies, and was always one of the principal movers in these matters in the township. He married Mary Ware, and resided during the latter part of his life on property now owned by James Walmsley. He died 5th mo. 7th, 1846, aged 62 years. Children : Frances, who married James Ivins; Emma, who married James Thornton ; and Beulah.

(30.) DAVID, married Joanna, daughter of Jesse James. He died 10th mo. 30th, 1826. Children : Mary, Phebe, Elizabeth, and Abi.

(31.) BEULAH, married Thomas James. He died 5th mo. 16th, 1813; she died 7th mo. 25th, 1850. They had one child, Thomas, who married Elizabeth Knight.

THE KNIGHT FAMILY.

The name of Knight was common in some parts of England more than two hundred years ago. In 1663, Sir John Knight was Mayor of the town of Bristol. A few years after, another John Knight was Vicar of Banbury. We also find notice of many persons named Knight who were among the early converts to the doctrines of George Fox; and in the record of the sufferings of Friends during the reign of Charles II, are the names of Thomas Knight, of Cirencester; William Knight, of Hampshire; George Knight and Mary Knight, of London or Middlesex; Robert Knight, of Oxford, and Giles Knight, of Chesselborough, in Somersetshire. Most of these were apprehended at religious meetings, and, for refusing to take the oath of allegiance, were committed to prison.

Among the emigrants who came to America with William Penn, in 1682, was GILES KNIGHT, of Gloucestershire. While in England, he married Mary, a sister of Henry English; and, at the time of their arrival in America, they had one son, Joseph, who was about two years of age. Their friends endeavored to persuade them to leave Joseph in England, "fearing that he would be devoured by the wolves, bears, or panthers in the wilds of Pennsylvania." During the passage across the Atlantic Mary was very ill, so that her recovery was doubtful; yet she did recover, and lived for many years after their arrival. Her father purchased a tract of five hundred acres in Byberry, and gave one-half of it to his son, Henry English, and the other half to Giles Knight. The latter lived in a cave for six weeks after his arrival, and then constructed a wigwam, in which he resided for several months, and then erected a log house. He was very prosperous in his business, and some time afterward bought the adjoining lands of Tibby and Cross, making altogether a tract of six hundred acres. The house at first erected being too small to accommodate his increasing family, he erected a long log-house, one story high, on the Tibby tract, and opened a store for the sale of dry goods, groceries, &c., which is said to have been the first in either township. From the ancient records we learn that he was one of the leading men in the neighborhood, and that he was highly esteemed for his integrity, good judgment, and correct life. In 1717, he went to England on a visit, when Abington Monthly Meeting of Friends, of which he was a member, gave him the following certificate :

"To our well-beloved friends and brethren in the Truth at Nailsworthe, in Gloucestershire, or elsewhere, greeting: Signifying, that our ancient friend Giles Knight, having occasion to see his native country, and his outward business requiring his personal appearance, doth induce him, as well as affection, to undertake a voyage to see his old friends; now, having made application to our Monthly Meeting in order to have a certificate, and persons appointed to make enquiry how he leaves his family; and, withal, if the ship would not stay until our next Mo. Meeting, he might have a certificate signed by the particular meeting to which he belongs, to wit, Byberry:

"These may certify, that enquiry being made and no objection found, we recommend him as an Elder and one well esteemed by us for many years, having left his family with a great deal of love; he has great comfort in having sober, well-inclined children, and the Lord has blessed him with outward substance, which we hope may be well disposed of to his hopeful offspring.

"We heartily wish the Lord may spare his life to see his friends and family again, having left us in unity and love. We wish and pray for his preservation in the Truth with all the faithful throughout the world. We salute you, and bid you farewell in the Lord Jesus Christ.

"Signed at Byberry, the 8th of the 7th month, 1717, by order of Abington Monthly Meeting:

"William Walton, Thomas Walton, Thomas Knight, Henry English, George James, Everard Bolton, Alexander Mode, Thomas Martin, James Cooper, James Duncan, Henry Comly, John Carver, James Carver, Edward Duncan, John Brock, Joseph Gibbons, Thomas Knight, Daniel Knight, Jonathan Knight."

He possessed considerable literary attainments,

26

302   THE HISTORY OF

and his library contained a number of books re-
lating to civil government. He was repeatedly
elected a member of the Assembly at Philadelphia,
and, in this capacity, was very liberal in his views,
and did much to promote public improvements.
He died 8th mo. 20th, 1726, aged 73 years; and
Mary died 7th mo. 24th, 1732, aged 77 years. They
had twelve children, three of whom died in infancy. Two of these were buried on the farm near
Knight's mill-pond, and the other was the first
person interred in the old grave-yard at Byberry
Meeting. The remainder, so far as known, were
Joseph, Thomas, Daniel, Jonathan, and Ann, from
whom the whole of the family of Knights are
descended. Thomas Knight, mentioned in the
above list, was a half-brother of Giles, and the last
three mentioned were his sons. Joseph, his eldest
son, resided at that time in New Jersey.

JOSEPH KNIGHT, AND HIS DESCENDANTS.

(1.) JOSEPH KNIGHT, was born in England, in
1680, and came to Pennsylvania with his parents,
Giles and Mary Knight, in 1682. He married Abigail Antill, who came from England in 1717. They
were married at a public meeting in Philadelphia,
and their certificate was signed by Thomas Chalkley, David Lloyd, Samuel Preston, Richard Hill,
and other distinguished Friends. They first settled in New Jersey, but returned to Byberry in
1729, and settled on the place now owned by James
Thornton, which contained one hundred and ninety
acres, and was inherited from his father. He was

a man of little or no enterprise, and was content with a very plain way of living. He thought his farm too large, and accordingly sold about one hundred and forty acres of it to Thomas Walmsley, retaining his buildings and only fifty acres of land from which to make a living. They studied and carried out the principles of the most exact economy, and being content with very little, passed through life in a comfortable way and without any longings after those expensive luxuries experienced by many people. He was very careful to attend to all things in season, and suffered nothing to be wasted. He was a kind-hearted man, and a good citizen. His neighbors did not look upon him as a miser; but having been brought up in a new country, where he often suffered many privations, his habits of economy became settled, and continued with him through life. When he was a little boy, the only food they had, often for weeks at a time, was "fish and pumpkins;" and on one occasion, when some of the neighbors paid them a visit and the conversation turned upon the good things left behind them in Old England, Joseph remarked "that he did not know anything about them, but that fish and pumpkins were good enough for him." On one occasion, some one asked him how to make money, when he replied, " Thou knowest how to make it better than I do, but thou dost not know how to keep it." He died 4th mo. 26th, 1762, aged 82 years; and his widow died 11th mo. 19th, 1764, at about the same age. They left two children, Giles and Mary.

(1.) *Joseph and Abigail Knight's Children.*

(2.) GILES was born in Bensalem, Bucks County, 11th mo. 17th, 1719. He married, first, Elizabeth James, in 1737, and settled in Bensalem. They had ten children : Joseph, Susannah, Abigail, Giles, Rebecca, Mary, Elizabeth, Abel, Sarah, and Israel. Elizabeth died in 1766, and Giles married, second, Phebe Thomas. Children : Asa, Evan T., Phebe, Rachel, Jesse, and Ann. Giles Knight was well educated, had a vigorous mind, and conducted his business with energy and success. He early turned his attention to politics; and from being in comfortable circumstances, of known integrity and sound judgment, he soon became prominent as a politician, and was for several successive years a member of the State Legislature, and afterward one of the Commissioners of Bucks County. In 1766 his first wife died, and in 1768 he was married a second time. Of his appearance and manners, Isaac Comly remarks : " I remember the venerable old patriarch in full dress of velvet and broadcloth, with buttons and buckles of silver, a full bottom wig, and first-rate beaver hat, turned up behind and on each side before, all which seemed to belong to a class that did not mix with ordinary characters; and together with an austere, commanding countenance, and dignity of manners and deportment, induced an apprehension and belief that Giles Knight was one of the great men of his day and generation." He died in 1799, and was buried at Byberry.

(3.) MARY, born 2d mo. 22d, 1723, married James Thornton in 1751, and died 4th mo. 20th, 1794. Children: Lydia, Joseph, James, and Asa.

(2) *Giles and Elizabeth Knight's Children.*

(4.) JOSEPH, born 12th mo. 14th, 1738, married, first, Rachel Townsend; second, —— Woolston.

(5.) SUSANNAH, born 9th mo. 11th, 1740, married James Paul. Children: James, Elizabeth, Mary, James and Susannah (twins), and Sarah.

(6.) ABIGAIL, born 8th mo. 11th, 1742, married William Walmsley in 1764, and settled in Byberry. Children: Sarah, Giles, Mary, Joseph, and Israel.

(7.) GILES, born 6th mo. 7th, 1745, married Sarah Townsend. Children: Townsend, Giles, Joseph T., and Thomas.

(8.) REBECCA, born 7th mo. 9th, 1747, married Jonathan Parry. Children: Elizabeth, Martha, Phebe, Susannah, Abigail, and Jonathan.

(9.) MARY, born 5th mo. 25th, 1750, married William Satterthwaite.

(10.) ELIZABETH, born 12th mo. 3d, 1752, married Thomas Samms.

(11.) ABEL was born 3d mo. 19th, 1755.

(12.) SARAH was born 5th mo. 8th, 1757.

(13.) ISRAEL was born in Bensalem, 3d mo. 4th, 1760; he married Sarah, daughter of Isaac and Esther Tyson, of Baltimore, in 1782, and settled in Bensalem, where, in 1799, he built the house now occupied by George Johnson. In 1804 he purchased 440 acres of land at Black River, in the northern part of New York, and with seven of his neighbors visited the place. He concluded, however, to let his children settle there, while he remained at the old homestead in Bensalem, where, in 1805, he built the stone barn still standing. He was a member of the Society of Friends, and was much respected by a large circle of friends. He died 1st mo. 31st, 1810, aged 50 years. Sarah died 4th mo. 8th, 1824, aged 66 years. Their children were: Abel, Isaac, Esther, Giles, George J., John, Nathan T., and Eliza.

(2.) Giles and Phebe Knight's Children.

(14.) ASA, born in 1770, married, first, Elizabeth Paul, and had one child, Joseph P. He married, second, Grace Croasdale. Children: Elizabeth, Mary, and Sarah.

(15.) EVAN T., born 10th mo. 11th, 1771, married Martha, daughter of Isaac Comly, of Byberry. Children: Isaac and Phebe.

(16.) PHEBE, born 1st mo. 31st, 1773, married William Walmsley. Children: Silas, Ann, and Martha.

(17.) RACHEL, born 1775, married Samuel Paul. Children: Robert, Phebe (who married Thomas Stackhouse), McEldery, Ann (who married Aaron Kirk), and Martha, who married Samuel Kirk.

(18.) JESSE, born 12th mo. 9th, 1779, married Mary Stackhouse. Children: Richard, Phebe, Elizabeth, Hannah, and Ann.

(19.) ANN, born in 1781, died in 1786.

(7.) *Giles and Sarah Knight's Children.*

(20.) TOWNSEND, born 11th mo. 2d, 1768; no account.

(21.) GILES, born 1st mo. 4th, 1773; no account.

(22.) JOSEPH T., born 11th mo. 4th, 1775, married Grace ——. Children: Israel, Abi, Rachel, Giles, Townsend, Susannah, Joseph, Stephen, Jane, and Grace.

(23.) THOMAS, born 11th mo. 4th, 1775; no account.

(13.) *Israel and Sarah Knight's Children.*

(24.) ABEL, born 8th mo. 24th, 1783, married Elizabeth Donaldson, daughter of Isaac and Jane Donaldson, of Philadelphia, and granddaughter of John Kaighn, the original proprietor of Kaighn's Point, N. J. Children: Jane, Sarah, Margaret, Israel, Isaac, Tacy, Joseph, Charles, Elizabeth, Martha, and Oliver.

(25.) ISAAC, born 9th mo. 14th, 1785. He removed to Baltimore, and married Julianna Winfield.

(26.) ESTHER, born 4th mo. 19th, 1787, married John Knight. No children.

(27.) GILES, born 4th mo. 16th, 1789, married Mary Yardley. He died in 1866. Children: Thomas, William, Sarah, Susannah, and Edward.

(28.) GEORGE J., born 5th mo. 24th, 1791, married Abi Brown, niece of General Brown. They settled near Brownsville, N. Y.

(29.) JOHN, born 5th mo. 29th, 1793. He was

quite a traveller. He died, and was buried at sea, while returning from a visit to Cadiz, Spain.

(30.) NATHAN T., born 11th mo. 25th, 1796, married Elizabeth, daughter of Jonathan Thomas, of Lower Dublin. Children : Sidney, Sarah T. and Jonathan (twins), Ellen, Elizabeth, Mary Elizabeth, Anna, and Julianna.

(31.) ELIZA, born 4th mo. 24th, 1799, married James Bones, and removed to Iowa. Children : William, Courtland, Sallie, Susan, and Rowland.

(14.) *Asa and Elizabeth Knight's Children.*

(32.) JOSEPH P., born 4th mo. 15th, 1796, married Mary La Rue. Children : Elizabeth and Sallie.

(33.) ELIZABETH, born 12th mo. 16th, 1804; married Jonathan Paxson, of Bensalem. They have no children.

(34.) MARY, born 7th mo. 8th, 1807, married Joshua V. Buckman, of Bristol, Bucks County. Children : Elizabeth, Rebecca, and James.

(35.) SARAH, born 12th mo. 11th, 1811, married James Townsend, of Bensalem. Children : Elizabeth, Margaretta, and Caroline Justice.

(15.) *Evan and Martha Knight's Children.*

(36.) ISAAC, born 9th mo. 8th, 1797, married Lydia Stackhouse. Children : Isaac C., Evan, and Ethan C.

(37.) PHEBE, born 6th mo. 3d, 1802; died single 10th mo. 15th, 1828.

(18.) *Jesse and Mary Knight's Children.*

(38.) RICHARD, born 9th mo. 8th, 1809, married Rachel Kirk, of Horsham. Children: Jesse, Rebecca, Oliver P., and Joseph.

(39.) PHEBE, born 8th mo. 24th, 1811; not married.

(40.) ELIZABETH, born 5th mo. 28th, 1813, married Thomas James, of Byberry. Children: Mary, Tacie, Hannah, Joshua G., Beulah, Edwin, Jesse K., Alvin, and Mary Elizabeth.

(41.) HANNAH, born 1st mo, 13th, 1818; died 4th mo. 22, 1832.

(42.) ANN, born 10th mo. 9th, 1821, married Oliver Parry, of Byberry. Children: Mary S. and Elizabeth.

THOMAS KNIGHT.

THOMAS, son of Giles and Mary Knight, was born in Byberry, in 1685. He married Sarah Clifton, in 1711, and settled on a farm belonging to Titan Leeds, the almanac-maker; but some time afterwards moved to Byberry, and located on the farm now owned by Isaac Tomlinson, where he died in 1774, aged 89 years. They had one child, which died in infancy. Thomas, by prudent management, acquired considerable property. He was at one time an Overseer in Byberry Meeting, but was probably not very remarkable for piety, as he said in an argument on the Conestoga Massacre: "That it was nonsense to talk of such creatures as the Indians having souls or a future being." In

1732 he went on a voyage to Barbadoes with Thomas Chalkley.

DANIEL KNIGHT, AND HIS DESCENDANTS.

(1.) DANIEL, son of Giles and Mary Knight, was born in 1697. He lived in the southern part of Byberry, near the Poquessing Creek. He married, first, Elizabeth Walker, in 1719. Children: Mary, Joseph, and Jonathan. He married, second, Esther, widow of Joseph Walton, in 1728. Children: William, Daniel, Martha, Joseph, Ann, and Thomas. After Esther's death he married, third, Mary Wilson, in 1777. He was a man of good understanding and sound judgment, and much esteemed by those who knew him. He died in 1782, aged 85 years.

(1.) *Daniel and Elizabeth Knight's Children.*

(2.) MARY, born 11th mo. 23d, 1719, married David Buckman, of Wrightstown, in 1742.

(3.) JOSEPH, was born 2d mo. 4th, 1721; no further account.

(4.) JONATHAN, born 8th mo. 5th, 1722, married Grace Croasdale, and settled in Southampton, Bucks County. Children: John, Abraham, Absalom, David, Samuel, and Inglish.

(1.) *Daniel and Esther Knight's Children.*

(5.) WILLIAM, was born 9th mo. 27th, 1729. He was somewhat singular in his habits, and would utter predictions which were afterwards so nearly fulfilled that many persons believed that he had a knowledge of future events, and they looked upon him as more than an ordinary being. He died in 1782, aged 53 years. Children: Daniel, Joseph, Hannah, and Esther.

(6.) DANIEL, born 7th mo. 8th, 1732, married Ann ———.

(7.) MARTHA, born 9th mo., 17th, 1736, married Henry Walmsley, in 1759.

(8.) JOSEPH, born 1st mo. 7th, 1739, married Elizabeth James, in 1765. Children: James, Joseph, Jesse, and Josiah.

(9.) ANN, born 12th mo. 15th, 1741, married Daniel Walton, in 1768. Children: Jane, Mercy, and Daniel.

(10.) THOMAS, born 7th mo. 7th, 1744, married Sarah Walton. Children: Amos, Rebecca, and Esther.

(4.) *Jonathan and Grace Knight's Children.*

(11.) JOHN, born 8th mo. 13th, 1749, married Margery Paxson. Children: Mary, Joshua, Caleb, Martha, and David.

(12.) ABRAHAM, born 3d mo. 28th, 1752, married Anna Croasdale. Children: Asa, Abraham, Sarah, Susanna, Phineas, Jonathan, Ezra, Grace, and Elizabeth.

(13.) ABSALOM, born 9th mo. 17th, 1754, married Ann Winder. Children: Benjamin, Amos, Moses, John, Grace, Abel, and Samuel.

(14.) DAVID, born 5th mo. 27th, 1757; died single.

(15.) SAMUEL, married Mary Paul. Children: Alexander, Hannah, and Julia.

(16.) INGLISH, married Martha Shallcross, and settled in Byberry. Children: Leonard, Seth, Ruth, Owen, Hannah, Samuel, Jonathan, and Anna.

(10.) *Thomas and Sarah Knight's Children.*

(17.) AMOS, born 1st mo. 14th, 1772, married Rebecca Dubre. Children: Dubre, who lives in Wilmington; Julianna, Marmaduke, Beulah, Jacob, and Emmor.

(18.) REBECCA, born 5th mo. 3d, 1774, married Thomas Dubre. Children: Hannah, Sarah, and Martha.

(19.) ESTHER, born 8th mo. 18th, 1776.

(11.) *John and Margery Knight's Children.*

(20.) MARY, married John Wildman, and settled in Bensalem. Children: Charles; Martha; Ann, died single; Elwood, married Mary Thomas; John, married Abigail Thompson; Mary, married Thomas Smedley; Edward, married first, Abi Gilbert, second, Elizabeth Newbold; Joshua K., married Hannah Johnson; Jane, died single; Rachel, married Hughes Warner.

(21.) CALEB, married Mary Stackhouse. Children: Phebe, died single; Jane, married Edward Croasdale; Elizabeth, married Isaac Eyre; Abi; and Mary Ann.

(22.) DAVID, married Sallie Brown. Children: Henry, and Edward.

(12.) *Abraham and Anna Knight's Children.*

(23.) ASA, died single, in 1866.

(24.) ABRAHAM, married Sarah Winder, in 1811, and settled in Moreland, Montgomery County. Children : Anna, married, first, Charles Blake, in 1835 ; second, she married Isaac A. Davis, in 1856, and now resides in Philadelphia; Mary Ann, married Wilkins Hobensack. Child : Anna. Ezra Croasdale, married Catharine Yerkes. Children: Sarah, Chancellor, Susan, Abraham, George, and Laura; Elizabeth, married Alfred Thomas. Children: Anna, Hannah, William, Samuel, Oscar, Martha, Charles, and Abraham ; Susan, married Fitzwater Lukens. Children : Tacie, Sarah, and Charles.

(25.) PHINEAS, married Mary Ridge. Children : Sarah Ann, Hannah, Charles, Ann Eliza, and Julia. Of these, Charles married Rebecca Buckman ; and Ann Eliza married Abraham Hogeland, of Bustleton.

(13.) *Abraham and Ann Knight's Children.*

(26.) BENJAMIN, married Mercy, daughter of Amos Martindale, and lived in Southampton, Bucks County. Children : Paul, Absalom, Ross M., Aaron, Samuel, Rebecca, and Martha Ann.

(27.) AMOS, married Mary Clayton. Children : Mary, Clayton, Ann, Rebecca, Jonathan, and Grace.

(28.) MOSES, married Rhoda Tomlinson. Child ; Sarah Ann.

(29.) JOHN, married Esther Knight. They had no children.

(30.) GRACE, married Joshua Paul. Child: Ann.

(31.) ABEL.

(32.) SAMUEL.

(15.) *Samuel and Mary Knight's Children.*

ALEXANDER, was born in Byberry and received his early education at Byberry school, under the tuition of Watson Atkinson and John Comly. Under the latter teacher he studied Latin, and became well versed in that language. Being of a scientific turn of mind, he studied medicine and graduated at the University of Pennsylvania with honor. He became a physician of skill and respectability, and resided for a short time in Byberry. He then went to Philadelphia, where he obtained a good practice, and was appointed physician of that port. He published several essays on medical subjects, which evinced considerable scientific acumen. His promising life was closed at the early age of thirty-five years. He married Mary Knorr. Children: Elizabeth, Amelia, George.

JULIA, married Charles Stout.

(16.) *Inglish and Martha Knight's Children.*

LEONARD, married Ruth ——, and lived in Byberry. Children: Elizabeth, Hannah, Inglish, and Edward.

SETH, died single.

RUTH, married John Tomlinson, and lives in Byberry. Children: Martha, Samuel, and Julia.

OWEN, married a daughter of Joseph Reese, and
lives near Somerton, Byberry. Children: Mary
Ann, Catharine, and Charles.

HANNAH, married James Walmsley of Byberry.

SAMUEL, married Phebe Tomlinson and had one
son, Aaron.

JONATHAN, married Letitia Leedom, and had one
child, Rachel.

JONATHAN KNIGHT AND HIS DESCENDANTS.

(1.) JONATHAN, son of Giles and Mary Knight,
married Jane Allen, and settled in Byberry on
property lately owned by Ebenezer Knight. " He
was a man of very pleasant and agreeable manners, graceful in his movements, and nice in his
personal appearance. His fine sense of the pro-
prieties of life, combined with his polished manners and a social liberality, made him generally
esteemed, respected, and beloved. He was often
called 'Gentleman Jonathan' to distinguish him
from another of the same name. He took a lively
interest in the support of schools, and in other
matters of benefit to the meeting or the township." He died 5th mo. 1st, 1745, and his wife died
soon afterwards. Children: Jonathan, Mary, and
Thomas.

(1.) *Jonathan and Mary Knight's Children.*

(2.) JONATHAN, born 4th mo. 5th, 1730, married,
first, Ann Paul, in 1748. Children: James, Jonathan, Daniel, Sarah, Tacy, Mary, Jane, Thomas,

Ann, and Paul. He afterwards married, second, Margaret Baldwin, and, third, Martha Lloyd.

(3.) MARY, born 3d mo. 1734, died single in 1759.

(4.) THOMAS, born 9th mo. 1736, married Mary Walmsley in 1759, but had no children. He purchased 240 acres of land, in Byberry, of Benjamin Gilbert, and settled thereon. During the Revolution his barn was burned by the soldiers under General Lacy. He died in 1806.

(2.) Jonathan and Ann Knight's Children.

(5.) JAMES, born 8th mo. 16th, 1753, married Gaynor Lukens. He died in 1784.

(6.) JONATHAN, born 11th mo. 6th, 1755, married Eliza Thomas. He died in 1830. Children: Anna, Jonathan T., Evan, Grace, Hannah, and Edwin.

(7.) DANIEL, born 4th mo. 8th, 1757, married Rachel Walton. He died in 1821. Children: Sarah, Ann, Margaret, James, Charles, Ebenezer, Lydia, Hannah, Thomas, Mary, Paul, Allen, and Robert B.

(8.) SARAH, married John Stackhouse. She died in 1838.

(9.) TACY, married Robert Croasdale.

(10.) MARY, married Josiah Costill.

(11.) JANE, married Joseph Bolton. Children: Tacy and Isaac.

(12.) THOMAS, born 9th mo. 1st, 1769, married Mary Worrell. He died in 1824. Children: Jonathan, Elizabeth, Ann, Rebecca, Isaiah, William, and Stephen.

(13.) ANN, married Benjamin Albertson. She died in 1828.

(14.) PAUL, married Eliza Boucher.

(6.) *Jonathan and Eliza Knight's Children.*

(15.) ANNA, born 6th mo. 6th, 1789; died 9th mo. 9th, 1801.

(16.) JONATHAN T., born 11th mo. 21st, 1791, married Elizabeth, daughter of Jesse Wilson, and settled in Byberry. He was a prominent politician, and served several terms in the Pennsylvania Legislature. He was afterwards an Associate Judge in Philadelphia. During the latter part of his life he was of full habit, and took but little part in public affairs. He died in Philadelphia in 1858, aged 67 years. Their children were Amy, Ann Eliza, Edwin, Jesse W., Grace, Wilson, Amos W., and Paulina Jane.

(17.) EVAN, born 5th mo. 8th, 1793, married Martha James, and settled in the southern part of Byberry. Children: Elizabeth T., Phebe Ann, Mary Ann, Jonathan, and Tacy. After his death, Martha married Ebenezer, son of (7) Daniel Knight. Children: Evan and Samuel.

(18.) GRACE, born 6th mo. 3d, 1795, married Samuel Smedley, but had no children.

(19.) HANNAH, was born 1st mo. 5th, 1798.

(20.) EDWIN, born 9th mo. 3d, 1800; died 8th mo. 19th, 1803.

(7.) Daniel and Rachel Knight's Children.

(21.) SARAH, born 2d mo. 8th, 1783, remained single.

(22.) ANN, born 10th mo. 5th, 1784, married Samuel Smedley, but had no children.

(23.) MARGARET, born 8th mo. 22d, 1786, remained single.

(24.) JAMES, born 5th mo. 23d, 1788, married Edith Plumly and had one child, Rachel, who died of cholera in 1849.

(25.) CHARLES, born 3d mo. 13th, 1790, married Jane Hillborn, and settled in Byberry. Children: Daniel, Hillborn, Charles, Ruth Ann, Emily, Margaret, and Jane.

(26.) EBENEZER, born 11th mo. 14th, 1791, married Martha, widow of (17) Evan Knight. Children: Evan and Samuel.

(27.) LYDIA, born 1st mo. 4th, 1794, married Stephenson Croasdale, and settled in Byberry. Children: Rachel, Anne B., Margaret, Joseph S., Jane, Willis, and Sarah.

(28.) HANNAH, born 3d mo. 7th, 1796: died 8th mo. 5th, 1796.

(29.) THOMAS, born 5th mo. 3d, 1798; died 8th mo. 10th, 1798.

(30.) MARY, born 11th mo. 28th, 1799; died 3d mo. 10th, 1800.

(31.) PAUL, was born 4th mo. 25th, 1801.

(32.) ALLEN, born 8th mo. 30th, 1805, married Elizabeth Parry, and had one child, Edward.

(33.) ROBERT B., born 1st mo. 22d, 1809; died unmarried.

Of (12) Thomas and Mary Knight's children we have no account.

Three half brothers of the ancient Giles Knight came over to Pennsylvania probably about 1683. Their names were Benjamin, Abel, and John. Benjamin settled in Bensalem, but we have no further account of him. Abel went to North Carolina, where his descendants still reside. John went to Massachusetts. His descendants are quite numerous, and may be found scattered all over the New England States and in Canada. Some of them were quite noted, among these was Jeremiah R. Knight, a Senator in Congress from Rhode Island. In the list of pensioners on account of services in the Revolution are more than twenty of the name of Knight.

THE MARTINDALE FAMILY.*

(1.) JOHN MARTINDELL,† the ancestor of the family in America, was born 8th mo. 24th, 1676. He married Mary Bridgman, daughter of Walter Bridgman and Blanche Constable, who came from England in 1684, and located near Newtown, Bucks County. Mary died 12th mo. 7th, 1726. Children : William, Thomas, Ann, Mary, Alabrethe, and John.

---

* I am indebted to Thomas Warner, of Wrightstown, for much of this account.

† Usually so spelled in the old records.

(1.) *John and Mary Martindale's Children.*

(2.) WILLIAM went to South Carolina.

(3.) JOHN, born 6th mo. 22d, 1719, married Mary Strickland, 2d mo. 9th, 1746. Children: Joseph, John, William, Rachel, Sarah, Miles, Strickland, Amos, Jonathan, Thomas, Isaac, and Mary.

(3.) *John and Mary Martindale's Children.*

(4.) JOSEPH, born 6th mo. 20th, 1747, married, first, Hannah Buckman, and had one daughter, Hannah; he married, second, Sarah Merrick. Children: Joseph, Martha, Thomas, and Isaac.

(5.) JOHN, born 12th mo. 15th, 1749, married Ann Lambert. Children: John, Amos, Ann, Jesse, Richard, Mary, Mahlon, and Phineas.

(6.) WILLIAM, born 6th mo. 2d, 1751, married Esther Buckman. Children: Jacob, Mary, Esther, William, Amos, Samuel, Sarah, Rachel, and Hannah.

(7.) RACHEL, born 10th mo. 1st, 1752, married Charles Reeder. Children: Joseph, Mary, and Amos.

(8.) SARAH, born 10th mo. 13th, 1754, married Matthias Harvey, but had no children.

(9.) MILES, born 6th mo. 2d, 1757, married Susannah Harvey. Children: John, Margaret, Mary, Susannah, Lucy, Thomas, Jane, Robert H., Sarah, Isaiah, and two others.

(10.) STRICKLAND, born 6th mo. 19th, 1759, married Sarah Sands. Children: Mary, Rachel, Sarah, Jane, William, Hannah, Ann, and Beulah.

(11.) Amos, born 8th mo. 10th, 1761, married Martha, daughter of Thomas Merrick, of Upper Wakefield, in 1789. Children: Hannah, Tacy, Abner, Amos, Charles, Thomas R., Mercy, Martha, Lucy Ann, and Mary.

(12.) Jonathan, born 7th mo. 10th, 1763, married Rachel Morgan. Children : Isaac, Jonathan, Charity, Samuel, John, Rachel, Elizabeth, Mary, Phineas, and Frances.

(13.) Thomas, born 1765, married, first, Mary Boothe. Children : William, Sarah, Rebecca, Thomas, and Mary. His wife died, and at the age of 82 he married, second, Sarah Ann Conrad, aged 22, by whom he had two or three children.

(14.) Isaac, born 12th mo. 2d, 1767, married Rachel Bonham. Children : Esther, Elijah, Mary, and Sarah.

(15.) Mary, born 1st mo. 16th, 1769, married Isaiah Morgan. Children : Samuel, Isaiah, Mary, Sarah, Amos, Joshua, Miles, Rachel, Charity, and William.

(4.) Joseph Martindale's Children.

(16.) Hannah married Robert Jolly. Children : Hannah, Robert, Joseph, Rachel, Martha, Sarah, Jane, Phebe, Eliza, and Samuel.

(17.) Joseph married Jemima Ingham. Children : Cyrus, Martha, Sarah, Joseph, John, Lydia Ann, Lewis, and Charles.

(18.) Martha married Amos Corson. Children : Sarah, Benjamin, and Richard.

(19.) Isaac married Sarah Hagerman, and had two children.

(4.) *John and Ann Martindale's Children.*

(20.) John married Charity Wilson. Children: Wilson, Wakefield, and Ann.

(21.) Amos married Susannah Lambert. Children: Lander, John, Lambert, Amos, Alfred, Mahlon, and Charles.

(22.) Ann married Peter Wilson. Children: John, Samuel, Wakefield, Sarah, and Ann.

(23.) Richard married Ann Wallace. Children: Mahlon, Charlotte, Mary Ann, Harriet, John, Maranda, Martha, David, Ann, Richard, Franklin, Charles, Louisa, James, and one other.

(24.) Mary married John Carver. Children: Keziah Maria, Amos, Yardley, Caroline, Mary, Jesse, Oliver, John, Aden, Rebecca, Wilson, Margery Ann, Cynthia, and two others.

(25.) Mahlon married and had five children.

(26.) Phineas married and had children: Sarah Ann, Martha, Hannah, Francis, Nelson, and Henry.

(6.) *William and Esther Martindale's Children.*

(27.) Jacob married Ann Bonham. Children: Levi, Ivy, Abraham, William, Hannah, Frances, and Ann.

(28.) Mary married Benjamin Leedom. Children: Elizabeth, Ann, William, Alice, Elijah, Benjamin, Amos, Sarah, Hannah, John, and Samuel.

(29.) Esther married Thomas Harvey. Chil-

dren: Harriet, Belinda, Joseph, William, Sarah
Ann, Elizabeth, Rebecca, Mary Ellen, Susan, and
Letitia.

(30.) WILLIAM married Sarah Morgan. Children:
Garret, Newkirk, William Elwell, and Abigail Ann.

(31.) AMOS married Sarah Kinsey, but had no
children.

(32.) SAMUEL married, first, Hannah Briggs.
Children: Albert G., Elizabeth, and Lucilla. He
married, second, Martha Landis. Children: Samuel, William George, and Amanda Melvinia B.

(33.) SARAH married Thomas Betts. Children:
William, Matilda, Cyrus, Tamar, Hannah, and Rebecca.

(34.) HANNAH married Amos Wilkinson. Children: Esther, Rachel, Ross, William Ryan, Ellen,
and Gertrude.

(9.) *Miles and Susannah Martindale's Children.*

(35.) MARGARET married Richard Neal. Children: Susannah, Priscilla, Miles, Hannah, Mary,
Elizabeth, and John.

(36.) SUSANNAH married John Tomlinson. Children: Miles, Asher, Cynthia, Lucy, John, Susannah, Alfred, Eliza, Mary, and Harvey.

(37.) THOMAS married Mary Warner. Children:
Warner, Adaline, Anne, Susannah, and Eliza.

(38.) ROBERT H. married Elizabeth Doan: Children: Jane, Jesse, and George.

(10.) *Strickland and Sarah Martindale's Children.*

(39.) MARY married Cornelius Carver. Children:
Rebecca and Sarah Ann.

(40.) SARAH married Isaac Carver, and had one child, George W.

(41.) JANE married Thomas Goslin, and had one child, Sarah.

(42.) WILLIAM married Hannah Holcomb,

(43.) HANNAH married Charles Watson.

(44.) RACHEL married David Carver.

(45.) ANN married Miles Carver.

(11.) *Amos and Martha Martindale's Children.*

(46.) HANNAH, born 4th mo. 19th, 1790, died single, 1st mo. 7th, 1841.

(47.) TACY, born 2d mo. 21st, 1792, married Joseph Jenkins, of Abington. She died 8th mo. 10th, 1857. Children : John, Martha, and Mahala.

(48.) ABNER, born 9th mo. 3d, 1794, married, first, Ann Dubre. Children : Amos, Rachel, Angeline, and Martha. He married, second, Eliza Boucher, and moved to Indiana in 1838.

(49.) AMOS, born 3d mo. 27th, 1797, died 9th mo. 2d, 1821.

(50.) DAVID, born 8th mo. 3d, 1799, died 7th mo. 7th, 1801.

(51.) CHARLES, born 10th mo. 24th, 1801, married Phebe, daughter of Joseph Comly, and lives in Byberry. Children : Watson C., Martha K., Joseph C., Elizabeth C., Annie L., Tacie, Isaac C., and Charles P.

(52.) THOMAS R., born 2d mo. 13th, 1804, married Ellen, daughter of Andrew Singley. Children : Samuel, Mary, Ellen, Amos, Rebecca, Alice, and Hannah Ann. They reside in Maryland.

(53.) MERCY B. married Benjamin Knight. Children: Joshua Paul, Absalom, Ross M., Aaron, Samuel, Rebecca, and Martha Ann.

(54.) LUCY ANN, born 8th mo. 13th, 1808, died single, 12th mo. 5th, 1857.

(55.) MARTHA, born 12th mo. 13th, 1810, married James Walmsley, in 1839, and lives in Byberry.

(12.) *Jonathan and Rachel Martindale's Children.*

(56.) SAMUEL, married Ann Yard. Children: Samuel, Elizabeth, and Rachel.

(57.) JOHN, married, first, Beulah Hagerman. Children: Beulah and Martha. Second, he married Jane Hogeland. Children: Mary Ann, Jonathan, Rachel, Jacob, and John.

(58.) RACHEL, married John Chambers. Children: Mary, Elizabeth, Rachel, Phebe, and Fanny.

(59.) ELIZABETH, married Peter Rozel, and had one child, Jonathan.

(60.) MARY, married James Girton. Children: Rachel, Samuel, James, Sarah Ann, Garret B., and Hutchinson.

(61.) PHINEAS, married, first, Elizabeth Yerkes. Children: William, Rachel, Elizabeth, Ann, and Jonathan. Second, he married Elizabeth Rutherford, by whom he had one child.

(62.) FRANCES, married Charles McNeal. Children: Rebecca, James, Charles, Amos, Elizabeth, and Ann.

(13.) *Thomas and Mary Martindale's Children.*

(63.) SARAH, married John Vanhorn.   Children:
Thomas and one other.

(64.) REBECCA, married William Pearson.

(14.) *Isaac and Rachel Martindale's Children.*

(65.) ESTHER, married Garret D. Percy.   Children: Watson, Isaac, and Mary Jane.

(66.) ELIJAH, married Sarah Ann Harvey.

(67.) MARY, married William Hellyer, and had
one child, Isaac.

(68.) SARAH, married Joseph Martindale, and
had three children.

THE SAURMAN FAMILY.

The primitive ancestor of this family in America
was (1) PHILIP SAURMAN, by trade a shoemaker,
who came over from Germany about 1743.   During the Revolutionary struggle he was a soldier
in Washington's army, and fell a martyr to his
country.   He left four children, Peter, Jacob, Philip,
and Martin.

(1.) *Philip Saurman's Children.*

(2.) PETER, was born in Germany, and at the
time of immigration to America was about three
years old.   He learned the trade of shoemaking
from his father, but having a taste for military

life, he entered the British army during the latter part of the French and Indian War, and served therein about one year. He then returned to Philadelphia, where he followed his occupation until the Revolutionary War, when he entered the army under Washington. He remained with it until it was disbanded in 1783, and although he was in all the battles fought by it, yet he was never wounded nor taken prisoner, and never sick during the whole time. On the evening preceding the battle of the Billet he obtained leave of absence to visit the young lady afterwards his wife, who was then residing at Thomas Wood's house, near Hatboro'. He remained here all night, and early the following morning he saw an English soldier, armed with a musket, coming up the lane. He immediately secreted himself behind a large cherry tree, and waited until the soldier walked past, when he stepped out and ordered him to surrender, at the same time presenting a pistol. The summons was obeyed, and the English soldier became a prisoner. Upon examining the captive's gun, it was found to be filled with mud and water. Upon the principle that "to the victors belong the spoils," Peter cleaned the gun and loaded it with three buckshot and a bullet, after which he started towards Hart's (William Hallowell's) Mill, where he saw five English soldiers along the roadside dividing their booty. He attempted to shoot them, but the gun missed fire, and he was forced to run for his life. As he leaped over a fence the British fired at him, one ball passing through his coat pocket, and two others striking the fence near him, but he escaped unhurt. After serving his country faithfully during the war, he returned to his trade, and located on the Pennypack, near what is now John Shelmire's Mill, in Moreland, Montgomery County. In 1788, he moved to Hatboro', and in 1795 to Bucks County, where he commenced farming. In 1804, he purchased a farm of ninety-four acres, near the Sorrel Horse, for $46.62 per acre, where he remained until 1812, when he sold out and went to the West. He died there in 1830, aged about 90 years. He married Margery, daughter of Josiah Yerkes, of Moreland. She died in 1835. Their children were, Ann, Josiah, Mary, Rebecca, Jacob, Yerkes, and Jonathan.

(3.) JACOB and (4) PHILIP, resided in Philadelphia until the Revolutionary War, when they entered the Continental Army, and were both slain during the struggle.

(5.) MARTIN, was born in Philadelphia. He was a hatter by trade, his place of business being in Second Street, between Race and Vine. He married Rosanna Essler, of Philadelphia. Children: Maria, John, Jacob, Martin, William, Sophia, and Thomas.

(2.) *Peter and Margery Saurman's Children.*

(6.) ANN, married James Vansant, of Somerton, Twenty-third Ward, Philadelphia. He was a carpenter, and some time after his marriage moved to Trenton, and still later to Philadelphia. Ann died in 1845. Children: Thomas Jefferson, Julia Ann, Cornelius, Austin, and Alfred.

(7.) JOSIAH, learned the shoemaker trade, and went to West Virginia, where he married. In 1840 he removed to Sandusky County, Ohio. Children : Mary Ann, Elizabeth, Archibald, Ebenezer, and two or three others.

(8.) MARY, remained single; still living.

(9.) REBECCA, remained single. She died in 1859, aged 75 years.

(10.) JACOB, was born in Moreland, Montgomery County, April 14, 1789. He married Sarah, daughter of Daniel Hallowell, in 1819, and settled in Cheltenham. In 1823, he moved to a farm in Moreland, Philadelphia, which he afterwards purchased. He remained on this farm until within a short period of his death. During his entire life he was an ardent Democrat, and much attached to the principles of that party. He took an active part in the local affairs of the township in which he lived, and was frequently called upon to fill the various local offices. He was a warm friend to public education, and was one of the first Directors under the Public School system in Moreland. He favored every work of public improvement, and fully kept pace with the age in which he lived. In 1853, he was elected a member of Common Council, in Philadelphia, and served one term. In 1864, he removed to Philadelphia, where he died, July 27, 1865, aged 76 years, much respected by a large circle of friends. His children are, George W., Charles E., Mary L., Caroline W., Ellen L., Norris S., John W., and Benjamin F.

(11.) YERKES, was born in Moreland, January

28*

20, 1791. He went to Philadelphia, where he learned the trade of copper-plate printer, which he followed for several years, after which he became a real estate agent. He married Mrs. Martha Brown, who had two children, Susanna and Joseph. By her he had the following children : Maria, Angeline, Rebecca, Abner, Amanda, and Madison.

(12.) JONATHAN, married Sarah McChan, and settled in Chester County, where he resided for several years, after which he moved to Abington, and thence to Philadelphia. While in Philadelphia he was occupied as a pump-maker, and was killed in 1850, while blowing the rocks in a well which he was digging. Children : Sarah Ann, Mary, Caroline, Augustus, George, and William.

(5.) *Martin and Rosanna Saurman's Children.*

(13.) MARIA, died of yellow fever in 1794; unmarried.

THE TOWNSEND FAMILY.*

(1.) THOMAS TOWNSEND, and SARAH, his wife, came from Westbury, Long Island, and settled in Chester County, Pennsylvania, previous to 1734. They had seven children : Hannah, Thomas, Nathaniel, Sarah, Phebe, Thomas, and John. After the death of (1) Thomas, Sarah, with her children,

* Furnished by Watson Comly, of Byberry.

Sarah, Thomas, and John, removed to Byberry, in 1735. She subsequently married George James, but had no children. She died 1st mo. 25th, 1773, aged 82 years.

(1.) *Thomas and Sarah Townsend's Children.*

Of HANNAH, NATHANIEL, and PHEBE, we have no account.

(2.) SARAH, born 12th mo. 26th, 1713, married Silas Titus, from Long Island, and settled in Byberry. Children: Nathaniel and Silas, both of whom died of small-pox, in 1757; and Phebe, who married Edward Parry, who for many years kept the hotel at Bell's Corner.

(3.) THOMAS, born 8th mo. 5th, 1720, settled on lands adjoining the Poquessing Creek, where he built a saw-mill. He married Elizabeth, daughter of Evan and Rachel Thomas. Children: Rachel, Sarah, Martha, Evan, Ann, Hannah, Thomas, Jesse, Phebe, Elizabeth, and Samuel. He died 12th mo. 28th, 1794; and Elizabeth died 8th mo. 21st, 1769, aged 49 years.

(4.) JOHN, born 1st mo. 7th, 1724, purchased a property on the Poquessing, adjoining that belonging to Thomas, on which he erected a flour-mill. Here he spent his life. He married Grace, daughter of Jeremiah Croasdale, of Bucks County, and settled on the Poquessing Creek, in Byberry. He was remarkable for the regularity of his temper and conduct through'the whole course of his life, which was consistent with his high professions, he being a member of Byberry Monthly Meeting, and occupying the station of Elder for nearly forty years. In 1768 he was appointed Clerk of the Meeting, which station he filled with more than ordinary ability. In all the concerns of civil and social duty he supported the character of a sincere and well-meaning man, and was universally respected and beloved. He was greatly interested in the education of youth, and much of the efficiency of Friends' school at Byberry was owing to his care and attention. As an author, he possessed more than ordinary ability, and two excellent essays of his were published in " Friends' Miscellany." He died 4th mo. 5th, 1800, aged 76 years. She died 6th mo. 23d, 1803. Children : Phebe, Sarah, Ezra, and John.

(3.) *Thomas and Elizabeth Townsend's Children.*

(5.) RACHEL, born 11th mo. 26th, 1742, married Joseph Knight. She died in 1769.

(6.) SARAH, born 6th mo. 4th, 1744, married Giles Knight. She died 11th mo. 27th, 1775. Children : Townsend, Giles, Joseph T., and Thomas.

(7.) MARTHA, born 6th mo. 10th, 1746; died 8th mo. 28th, 1769.

(8.) EVAN, born 8th mo. 14th, 1748, married Abi James. He died 12th mo. 24th, 1824. She died in June, 1819. Children : Thomas, Margery, John, Elizabeth, Rachel, Robert, Evan, Abi, and Martha.

(9.) THOMAS, born 1st mo. 10th, 1756; died 9th mo. 8th, 1769.

(10.) JESSE, born 2d mo. 15th, 1758; died in 1769.

(11.) PHEBE, born 12th mo. 20th, 1760, married

Jesse James. She died 9th mo. 25th, 1832. Children : Samuel, Thomas, Elizabeth, Mary, Joanna, Jesse, Phebe, and Abi.

(4.) *John and Grace Townsend's Children.*

(12.) PHEBE, born 5th mo. 7th, 1746; died, unmarried, 10th mo. 8th, 1783.

(13.) SARAH, born 8th mo. 29th, 1748; died, unmarried, 3d mo. 2d, 1770.

(14.) EZRA, born 4th mo. 14th, 1760, married Elizabeth, daughter of James and Susannah Paul, and settled on the old homestead. Few men stood higher in the estimation of the community than Ezra Townsend. His children were, John P., James, Grace, Susan, Sarah, Elizabeth, Tacy, and Ezra.

(8.) *Evan and Abi Townsend's Children.*

(15.) THOMAS, born 9th mo. 3d, 1773, married Elizabeth Strickland. They removed to Black River, New York. Children : Jesse, Sarah, Ann, Thomas, and Abi.

(16.) MARGERY, born 6th mo. 24th, 1775, married William Walmsley. She died 2d mo. 1st, 1832. Children : Robert and Jesse.

(17.) JOHN, born 3d mo. 1st, 1777, married Asenath Strickland, and went to Black River. Children : Robert, Mary, Martha, Ezra, John, Evan, and Abi.

(18.) ELIZABETH, born 6th mo. 3d, 1779, married Isaac Bolton, and went to Lancaster County, Pennsylvania. Children: Evan, Sarah, Abi, Jason, and Elizabeth.

(19.) Evan, born 4th mo. 25th, 1788, married Elizabeth Carver. He died in 1846. Children: Thomas, Abi, Mary, Mahlon, William, and Sarah.

(14.) *Ezra and Elizabeth Townsend's Children.*

(20.) John P., born 6th mo. 10th, 1787, married Rachel Wilson. Children: Ezra, Wilson and Paul, twins, Jesse, Grace and Sallie Ann, twins, and Rachel.

(21.) James, born 1st mo. 12th, 1789, married, first, Eliza Raison, and had one child, Tacie. He married, second, Sarah Knight. Children: Elizabeth, Maggie, and Carrie.

(22.) Susan, married Israel Walton.

(23.) Sarah, married Benjamin Cadwalader. Children: Hannah, who married Jonathan Gillam; and Elizabeth, who married Joseph Comly.

(24.) Grace, married James Thornton.

(25.) Elizabeth, married Warder Cresson. Children: Ezra, John, Jacob, Clement, and Anna Bella.

(26.) Tacy, married Charles Walmsley. Children: Elizabeth, Agnes, Susan, and Beulah.

THE THORNTON FAMILY.

James, son of James Thornton, was born at Stony-Stratford, Buckinghamshire, England, in 1727, and came over to America in 1750. In 1752 he took up his residence in Byberry, having purchased the farm still in the possession of the family, where he lived the remaining part of his life. He was a man of superior abilities and of rare qualifications as a minister of the gospel. There was a dignity about his personal appearance, and a forcibleness in his declamation, vouchsafed to but few. Upon rising to speak he always remained silent for a few moments, then slowly uttered a few words, but as he proceeded in his discourse his whole being seemed to be fired with the thoughts which he was uttering, and his voice and manner on such occasions became solemnly impressive. He was considered eminent in the ministry, and travelled extensively, both in America and England, in that capacity. In social conversation he was pleasant and cheerful, but never light or trifling; and he always clothed his thoughts in such plain language that his meaning was clearly understood by all. James Thornton was not perfection, but the errors he made were of the head rather than of the heart, and his contemporaries all unite in considering him an honorable and highly useful member of society. He was the principal minister at Byberry for forty years, and during that time he made several religious visits to different parts of the country,—the first to Delaware and the Eastern Shore of Maryland in 1780; and afterwards to New Jersey in 1781, and to New York in 1793. Mary, his wife, was also a paragon of excellence, both in domestic and other matters, so that from a very moderate beginning they soon attained a competence. She was also of a literary turn, and among other articles composed

an essay on the death of her son, Asa, which was
a production of considerable merit. James died
in 8th mo., 1794, leaving a son, James, who succeeded to the estate.

MARY, died in 1793. Children : Lydia, Joseph,
James, and Asa. Of these Asa died while a youth ;
James died unmarried in 1794, aged 33 years.
Horsham Monthly Meeting issued a testimony concerning him, in which " he was stated to be a pious
young man, and a bright example for the young
men of his day." He was of a literary turn, and
a manuscript volume of his poems is still extant.
Lydia married William Walton ; Joseph married
Hannah Warrington, of New Jersey, and settled in
Byberry, where he died in 1790, leaving one son,
James, who married, first, Grace, daughter of Ezra
and Elizabeth Townsend, and settled on the old
homestead. They had one daughter, Elizabeth,
who married Dr. Isaac Comly. After his wife's
death, James married Rebecca Stokes, of Moorestown, New Jersey. Children : James, John, and
Edmund.

THE WALMSLEY FAMILY.*

THE earliest mention of the Walmsley family
that we have seen, is a certificate from Settle
Monthly Meeting of Friends, near Bristol, England, containing a list of the names of Friends who

* I am indebted to Watson Comly, of Byberry, for the greater
part of the genealogy of this family.

were about to remove to Pennsylvania, in which there is mention of Thomas Walmsley, Elizabeth, his wife, and six minor children. This was about the time of Penn's first visit to Pennsylvania. According to Watson's Annals, some of the earlier emigrant ships were nearly three months on the passage, during which time the small-pox broke out among the immigrants, and about forty of them died. As there is no account of more than three of Thomas Walmsley's children in this country, to wit, Thomas, Henry, and Elizabeth, it is probable that the rest died while coming over.

Thomas before leaving England bought a tract of land on the Neshaminy Creek, in Bucks County, probably near Hulmeville. As he designed building a mill on that stream he brought from England the irons and several other articles for its construction, from which we infer that he was a man of property. They landed at Burlington, New Jersey, and within two weeks of the time of landing he was attacked with the dysentery, from which he died. His three children were thus left under the care of their mother, who was a very estimable woman. She, however, married John Paisley about two years subsequently.

THOMAS WALMSLEY AND HIS DESCENDANTS.

THOMAS, the elder son of Thomas, married Mary, daughter of John Paxson, in 1698, and settled first in Bensalem, probably on his father's farm, but not being satisfied he sold that place and bought

fifty acres of Cross's patent in Byberry, recently
owned by Charles Walmsley, one of his descendants. He removed to this place in 1703, and resided there the remainder of his life. He soon
afterwards purchased fifty acres of the Tibby tract
adjoining, one hundred and twenty-five acres of
Henry English, and eight acres of Joseph Knight,
where Robert Purvis now lives. He also owned
two hundred and twenty-five acres in Middletown,
Bucks County, fifty acres where Spencer Worthington now lives, a farm at the foot of Edge Hill,
now William F. Ervin's, also four hundred acres in
Buckingham. The latter farm was so far back
in the woods that he traded with one of the Carvers for the lands lately belonging to Jesse Walmsley and William Walmsley, giving two acres for
one. He was a farmer and dealer in horses, and
was very successful in both. He is represented as
a quiet, peaceable man, attending to his private
business, and doing but little in the affairs of either
Church or State. He had good natural abilities,
and although successful in accumulating property
was not at all parsimonious. As a proof of this,
having a number of daughters, most of whom were
married in meeting, he made provision to enter-
tain large companies of wedding guests, sometimes
amounting to more than a hundred; and on one
occasion, after meeting broke up, he invited the
whole congregation to dine with him. He was
considered a wealthy man, and his property consisted principally of lands and horses. His house
contained three rooms, which were built at differ-

ent times ; it was one story high, and was covered
with oak shingles. He died in 1754, aged about
80 years. His widow died in 1755, aged 79 years.
Children : Thomas, William, Elizabeth, Agnes,
Mary, Abigail, Phebe, Esther, and Martha. In
his will Thomas Walmsley left fifty acres to his
daughter Mary, the Edge Hill property to Abigail,
and the remainder of his real estate to his son
William.

(2.) *Thomas and Mary Walmsley's Children.*

(3.) THOMAS, married Hannah, daughter of William Walton, the preacher, in 1728. They settled
on the Edge Hill farm, and within a year from
their marriage, as he was returning from Horsham
meeting, he was thrown from his horse and so
badly injured that he died shortly afterwards.

(4.) WILLIAM, was born in Byberry, in 1709.
In 1735 he married Sarah Titus, of Long Island,
and settled where Edwin Tomlinson now lives.

On the occasion of his marriage, Friends gave
him a certificate, stating that " he was of a sober
and orderly behavior, and in good unity with
them." He seems to have sustained this good
character, and to have advanced in the good opinion of his contemporaries, as we find him filling
several important positions in the Meeting, such as
clerk, overseer, and elder, all of which were to the
satisfaction of his friends. He wrote a good plain
hand, and kept the Meeting records, as well as his
own private accounts, in excellent order ; and in
all business transactions he was very correct and

methodical. He inherited considerable real estate in Byberry from his father; also, a number of slaves, which he afterwards emancipated. He was justly esteemed as an honest and upright man. His wife died in 1763, and in 1764 he married Susanna, widow of Walter Comly. He died in 1773, aged 64 years, leaving five children by his first wife: Thomas, William, Silas, Mary, and Sarah. Susanna, his widow, died in 1795, aged 81 years.

(5.) ELIZABETH, married Jeremiah Walton, in 1718.

(6.) AGNES, married Job Walton, in 1728.

(7.) MARY, married John Worthington.

(8.) ABIGAIL, married Isaac Comly, in 1738.

(9.) PHEBE, married Isaac Carver, in 1742.

(10.) ESTHER, married Stephen Parry, in 1755.

(11.) MARTHA, married David Parry, in 1761. Children: Martha and David.

(4.) *William and Sarah Walmsley's Children.*

(12.) THOMAS, married Agnes Mason, of Fair Hill, in 1768. He inherited from his father the homestead, with 168 acres of land, also one-third of the Middletown tract, and a lot of land in Smithfield. He afterwards sold the Middletown and Smithfield tracts. He was a man of more than ordinary abilities, and was noted for his industry and honesty. He was so peaceable that his neighbors said they did not recollect that he ever had a quarrel with any one. He held a respectable position in Meeting affairs, being Overseer for many years, and an Elder during the last 30 years of his life. In person he was rather above middle size; strong-built, though not fleshy, and possessed of great strength. His health was remarkably good until a short time previous to his decease. In 1792 he buried his first wife, and in 1794 married Ruth Kirk, of Little York, an eminent minister in the Society of Friends. He died in 1819, aged 82 years. Ruth died in 1798. His children by the first wife were Benjamin, Mary, Asa, Richard, Thomas, and William.

(13.) WILLIAM, married Abigail, daughter of Giles Knight, in 1764. They settled first in Middletown, but afterwards removed to Byberry, and built the house where Robert Purvis now resides. He inherited considerable property from his father, but, like many others, he preferred an easy life to one of toil, hence his estate did not increase. He was possessed of good natural abilities, yet he took but little interest in the affairs of the neighborhood. He died in 1819, aged 79 years. Abigail, his widow, died 11th mo. 8th, 1820. Children: Sarah, Giles, Mary, Joseph, and Israel.

(14.) SILAS, married Martha, daughter of Walter Comly, in 1765. Children: William, Jesse, and Silas.

(15.) MARY, married Thomas Knight, in 1759. She died in 1802, aged 60 years, leaving no children.

(16.) SARAH, married Isaac Bolton, in 1766, and settled near the county line in Southampton. Isaac died in 1783, and his widow and children moved to the house now occupied by William Forrest, in Byberry. She died in 1795. Children : William, Joseph, Isaac, Mary and Margaret (twins), Jesse, Thomas, and Sarah.

David and (11) *Martha Parry's Children.*

(17.) MARTHA, married David Cummings, of Philadelphia.

(18.) DAVID, married Elizabeth, daughter of Mordecai Thomas. Children : Joseph, Samuel, and Martha.

(12.) *Thomas and Agnes Walmsley's Children.*

(19.) BENJAMIN, married Beulah Newbold, of Springfield, N. J., and settled on the homestead in Byberry. He was a Justice of the Peace for several years, and occupied a prominent position in the affairs both of the church and the neighborhood. He died at about the age of 70 years. Children : Charles, who married Tacy, daughter of Ezra Townsend ; Agnes (deceased), and Ann.

(20.) MARY, died young.

(21.) ASA, married Mary Paxson, of Bensalem. He erected the buildings now occupied by Ross M. Knight, and afterwards kept a store there for eleven years. He then sold the property, and removed to the farm now owned by Horace Smyth, where he spent the remainder of his days. He was for several years a clerk, overseer, or elder, in the meetings, and was highly respected. His wife died in 1838. Children : Sarah ; Thomas, who married

Elizabeth, daughter of Ephraim Haines; Anna; Mary; Morton, who married Eliza Moon; Richard, who married Rebecca Smith, and Margaret.

(22.) RICHARD, died young.

(23.) THOMAS, was born in Byberry, 3d mo. 25th, 1781. In the early part of his life, while yet a schoolboy, he gave evidence of more than ordinary talent, and acquired a knowledge of all the branches then taught in the school at Byberry Meeting with unusual facility. After having mastered all these, he commenced the study of Latin under a ripe scholar and an excellent teacher, the late John Comly; and by close application, along with a retentive memory, soon gained a good knowledge of that language. He had a great love for books, and generally carried one with him, which he studied whenever opportunity offered. He became particularly interested in scientific subjects, and resolved upon becoming a physician. He accordingly entered as a student of medicine under Dr. Gregg, of Attleboro', Bucks County, where he remained closely pursuing his studies for three or four years. While thus engaged, his active mind led him into other channels of learning, and we find him the ardent promoter of several literary societies. He then went to Philadelphia, in order to become more proficient in the various branches of medicine, and attended lectures in the University of Pennsylvania. While here he made the acquaintance of many of the most eminent literary men of that day, from whom he derived much profit, as they assisted him in his studies. He was elected a member of the Philadelphia Medical Society, and was among the original founders of the American Linnæan Society, of which he became Vice-President. While attending lectures he made several experiments in regard to the absorption of medicines; and these experiments, together with some other observations, formed the basis of his inaugural thesis for the degree of Doctor of Medicine, which was conferred upon him by the University in the spring of 1803. Soon after graduating he removed to Chambersburg, Pennsylvania, where he obtained considerable practice in his profession. In 1805 he was solicited by Dr. Young to settle in Hagerstown, Maryland, where a physician was badly needed, and he concluded to remove thither. In the 8th mo. 1806, he was seized with bilious fever, and, after twelve weeks' sickness, died, in the twenty-sixth year of his age. He was the author of a number of original essays, political and scientific, the former of which was published in the newspapers of Maryland, and the latter in Barton's Journal. A eulogium on him was published, but has probably been lost.

(24.) WILLIAM, went to Philadelphia, where he was at first unsuccessful in business, but becoming a broker he was more fortunate, and amassed considerable property. He died single, 3d mo. 27th, 1839.

(13.) *William and Abigail Walmsley's Children.*

(25.) SARAH, married Thomas Phipps, of Abington. Children: Abigail, who married, first, Thomas Stackhouse; second, Robert Eames; Drusilla, who married John Rowlett.

(26.) GILES, was subject to convulsions, and died at the age of forty.

(27.) MARY, married, first, Joseph Stackhouse. He died in 1806, and she married, second, John Lester, of Richland, but left no children.

(28.) JOSEPH, married Ann, daughter of John Barton, near Camden, New Jersey. He settled where Robert Purvis now resides. He was very successful in business, and was very active in the affairs of the Meeting, as well as the neighborhood. He afterwards moved to Frankford, and subsequently to Philadelphia, where he died. Children: Abigail, Rebecca, Morgan, and William.

(29.) ISRAEL, married Rebecca, daughter of William Walton, and settled in Byberry, where John Comly now lives. He died in 1822, from a fall down the cellar steps, leaving one child, Delilah.

HENRY WALMSLEY, AND HIS DESCENDANTS.

(1.) HENRY, the younger son of Thomas, married Mary Scarl, in 1699. They settled in the lower end of Southampton, Bucks County, on or near the Lead Mine Farm. He was above the middle size of men, and was a jovial, comical sort of person. He did not inherit much property from his father, and never became so wealthy as his brother Thomas. He died in 1760. Children: Thomas, Francis, Elizabeth, Joan, and Rebecca.

(1.) *Henry and Mary Walmsley's Children.*

(2.) THOMAS, married and settled on the homestead, where he died, in 1786. Children: Henry, Ralph, Mary, Sarah, and Elizabeth.

(3.) ELIZABETH, married William, son of William and Mary Carver, in 1719, and settled at Buckingham.

(4.) JOAN, married Thomas Tomlinson, in 1719. She died in 1772.

(2.) *Thomas Walmsley's Children.*

(5.) HENRY, married, first, Martha, daughter of Daniel Knight, and settled on the Lead Mine Farm. Children : Daniel T. and Sarah. After Martha's death Henry married Esther Duncan, but had no children. He died in 1792.

(6.) RALPH, settled on part of the homestead. He married, and had two sons, Thomas and William.

(7.) SARAH, married John Terry, and had one son, James, and probably other children.

(8.) ELIZABETH, married Joseph, son of Thomas Worthington.

(5.) *Henry and Martha Walmsley's Children.*

(9.) DANIEL T., married Mary, daughter of General Augustin Willet. He inherited a large portion of his father's estate, but lost the greater part of it. Afterwards he kept tavern at Smithfield, where he died, leaving children, Elizabeth, Martha, Sarah, Mary, Grace, and James Madison.

(10.) SARAH, married William Ridge, and settled in the northern part of Bensalem. They were highly respected in the community, and by industry acquired a competent estate. They had children, Isaac, Daniel, Martha, William H., Walmsley, Rachel, Effie, Anna, and Samuel.

(9.) *Daniel T. and Mary Walmsley's Children.*

(11.) ELIZABETH, died unmarried.

(12.) MARTHA, married Mahlon Atkinson, and moved to Drumore.

(13.) SARAH, married Dr. Benjamin Rush Banes.

(14.) MARY, married Isaac J. Rush.

(15.) GRACE, married, first, Bernard Walton; second, James M. Boileau.

(16.) JAMES MADISON, died young.

THE WALTON FAMILY.*

The name of Walton frequently occurs in Besse's Account of the Sufferings of Friends in England, published about 1751. The first of that name who came to America were four brothers, NATHANIEL, THOMAS, DANIEL, and WILLIAM, who arrived at Newcastle early in 1675. They ascended the Delaware River and settled in Byberry, on land now owned by George Dehaven.

* I am indebted to Watson Comly, of Byberry, for the greater part of the genealogy of this family.

In the records of the Monthly Meeting of Friends, held alternately at Tacony and Poquessing, we find that NATHANIEL WALTON had their approbation to accomplish his marriage with Martha Bownall, of Philadelphia, which was accordingly done 11th mo. 26th, 1685. When the Keithian controversy divided the Society of Friends, Nathaniel and his family joined the Keithian Church, of which John Hart was the minister. When Hart joined the Baptists, Nathaniel joined the "Church at All-Saints." In a letter found some years since, written by Nathaniel to his brother William, dated 7th of October, 1713, he reminds him "that he paid five pounds for his passage from England, which had not been repaid, and makes a demand for the money." We have no other account of him, except that he lived on property now belonging to George Dehaven, and left two sons, Nathaniel and Benjamin.

(1.) *Nathaniel and Martha Walton's Children.*

(2.) NATHANIEL, was a schoolmaster as early as 1727, and Thomas Chalkley speaks in his Journal of having sent his children to Nathaniel's school. He died in Moreland, back of Edge Hill, in 1784, aged about 80 years, and left two sons, Boaz and Joseph.

(3.) BENJAMIN, we have no account of, except that he left a son, Benjamin.

(4.) JOSEPH, son of (2) Nathaniel, lived on property now owned by William Wenzell. He taught the school at Byberry for fifteen years, after which he moved to the Falls, in Bucks County, to follow his profession. It is said he was a teacher for sixty years. He died 10th mo. 4th, 1759.

(5.) BENJAMIN, son of (3) Benjamin, was a rigid Whig in the time of the Revolution, and very active in his distraints upon Friends on account of military requisitions, exorbitant in his seizures, and of imperious disposition. He was commonly called " Black Ben," on account of his dark complexion, and to distinguish him from another of the same name.

(1.) THOMAS WALTON, AND HIS DESCENDANTS.

(1.) THOMAS WALTON, the second of the four brothers, settled back of Smithfield (Somerton), on the Horsham Road, in the Manor of Moreland. Nothing is known of his history, except that he married Priscilla Hunn, of Philadelphia, 12th mo. 24th, 1689 (O. S.), and that he died in 1758, at a very advanced age, probably near one hundred years. He left several children.

(2.) THOMAS, son of (1) Thomas, lived with his father, and was a preacher in the Society of Friends. He usually walked to meeting at Byberry, a distance of five miles, and officiated when no other minister was present. He was afterwards disowned for not paying his debts. He was commonly designated as the " Old Bishop." He died 1st mo. 31st, 1777, aged 84 years, unmarried.

(1.) DANIEL WALTON, AND HIS DESCENDANTS.

(1.) DANIEL WALTON, one of the four brothers, settled on his tract of land near the present residence of Linford Tomlinson. He married Mary Lamb, 6th mo. 21st, 1688 (O. S.). Throughout his long life he was much respected, and was considered among the faithful Friends of that day. He died in 1719, leaving seven children : Samuel, Daniel, Joshua, Joseph, Benjamin, Nathan, and Mary. Nearly all the Waltons at present residing in the vicinity of Byberry are descendants of the ancient Daniel.

(1.) *Daniel and Mary Walton's Children.*

(2.) SAMUEL, was disinherited by his father, for "disobedience to his mother," but inherited the estate belonging to his brother Nathan, who died intestate. He left the neighborhood and settled near Quakertown, in Bucks County. He had four sons, Samuel, Benjamin, Abraham, and Jacob, most of whom emigrated to the Western country.

(3.) DANIEL, married —— Clifton, and settled where English Knight now lives. His farm extended eastward to John Samms's Corner. He left three children, Daniel, Jane, and Massy.

(4.) JOSHUA, took the western part of his father's farm, and settled where Watson Tomlinson now lives. He married Catharine Albertson, usually called " Case Walton." In the domestic history of the family many unpleasant traits are apparent. Joshua committed suicide by hanging himself to a tree in front of his house, and was buried in one of his back fields. His widow died 12th mo. 18th, 1759. For many years after the death of Joshua the premises were believed by the superstitious to be haunted, and "marvellous tales were told of sights, sounds, and presentations, terrific in their nature." Men were actually frightened from the "Timber Swamp" in the daytime, but the ghosts have since departed. Joshua left three sons: Joshua, who died in 1779; Albertson, and Jonathan.

(5.) Joseph, married Esther, daughter of John Carver, of Buckingham. Children: Richard and Rachel.

(6.) Benjamin, was born in Byberry about 1693. He married Rebecca Homer, in 1724, by whom he had nine children. He settled on his father's farm in Byberry, and was prosperous in business. He was a member with Friends, and much respected by his contemporaries. He died in 11th mo. 1753; and his widow in 8th mo., 1783, aged 79 years. Rebecca was much esteemed, and her virtues are handed down to us in some verses made by James Thornton, Jr., shortly after her decease. Their children were, Elizabeth, Mary, Daniel, Hannah, Rebecca, Sarah, Benjamin, Esther, and William.

(7.) Mary, married William Homer, and settled where William Carter now lives. She died in 1788. Her sons, "Taff, Joe, and Jake, were bachelors, lounging about home and drinking a great deal of whiskey." They were called "The young Homers," being from their father's second wife.

(3.) *Daniel Walton's Children.*

(8.) DANIEL, married Ann, daughter of Daniel Knight, and settled on the homestead, where he died 10th mo. 29th, 1776. Children: Daniel, Aaron, and Ann.

(9.) JANE, married Isaiah Walton.

(10.) MASSY, married (9) William, grandson of (1) William Walton, the preacher. Child: Jacob.

(4.) *Joshua and Catharine Walton's Children.*

(11.) ALBERTSON, lived where George Weiss now owns. During the Revolutionary War his attachment to the British led him to secrete his title-papers in a hollow tree, and join the English army in New York. He returned to Byberry after the war, but was taken and tried for treason. He was acquitted, but lost his title-papers, and had to apply to the Legislature to make his title good. He died in 1821, aged 90 years. Children: Jesse, William, and Jonathan.

(12.) JONATHAN, was born in Byberry, where Watson Tomlinson now lives, about 1733. He never married; but in early life was very anxious to accumulate property, and frequently plowed all night. He removed to a farm on the Old York road, near Hartsville, where he spent the most of his life, and where he died in 1790. He is particularly noted for the legacy left to Byberry Meeting, called "Walton's Donation," for schooling poor children. This amounted to $886.46, the income of which has been judiciously applied to the bene-

fit of many children who would most probably
have otherwise grown up without any school learning. The other two-thirds of the estate were bequeathed, for similar purposes, to Friends of Richland and Horsham.

(5.) *Joseph and Esther Walton's Children.*

(13.) RICHARD, married Abigail, widow of Isaac
Comly and daughter of Thomas Walmsley. He
died 10th mo. 6th, 1776. Children: Joseph, Benjamin, and Esther.

(6.) *Benjamin and Rebecca Walton's Children.*

(14.) ELIZABETH, born 3d mo. 27th, 1725, married Bryan Peart. Children: Benjamin, who moved
to Salem, Ohio, Rebecca and Thomas. Bryan Peart
died in 1757, and Elizabeth married Benjamin Gilbert, the Indian captive, in 1760. Children: Jesse,
Abner, Rebecca, and Elizabeth. On account of
her captivity, she became well known to the public.
She lived about thirty years after her return, and
was universally respected by her numerous friends
and connections, and peacefully closed her earthly
career, at her residence near Fallowfield, Chester
County, in the eighty-sixth year of her age.

(15.) MARY, born 12th mo. 17th, 1726, married
David Thomas. She died in 1804, aged 78 years.

(16.) DANIEL, born 12th mo. 1st, 1728, married
Sarah, daughter of Benjamin Gilbert, and settled
near the Red Lion. During the Revolutionary
War he suffered much from the depredations of

the Continentals, and had his barn burnt by General Lacy's men. He died near Fallowfield, Chester County, in 1798, aged 70 years. Sarah died in 1785. Children: Rachel, Rebecca, Sarah, Lydia, Asa, Jesse, and Gilbert.

(17.) HANNAH, born 12th mo. 28th, 1730, remained unmarried; died at the age of 86. She was a poet, and wrote several articles which were circulated in MS.

(18.) REBECCA, born 9th mo. 24th, 1723, married Joseph Warrington, of Moorestown, N. J. She was highly esteemed as a worthy member of society, and "was probably as near perfection as mortals ever are." She sometimes wrote poetry, and several of her effusions are still extant. She died 7th mo. 8th, 1812.

(19.) SARAH, twin sister of Rebecca, married Thomas Knight in 1771. She died 1st mo. 4th, 1807. Children: Amos, Rebecca, and Esther.

(20.) BENJAMIN, born 12th mo. 1st, 1735, married Abigail, daughter of Benjamin Gilbert. After living a few years in Byberry they moved to Fallowfield, Chester County. Children: Benjamin, Nathan, Joseph, and Rebecca.

(21.) ESTHER, born 3d mo. 17th, 1738, married (21) Thomas Walton, descendant of William.

(22.) WILLIAM, born 5th mo. 29th, 1740, married Lydia, daughter of James Thornton, in 1771, and spent his life at the homestead now owned by Linford Tomlinson. He inherited a small estate from his father, to which he made large additions by the industrious and prudent course he pursued. For many years previous to his death, he was regarded as the largest landholder and the most wealthy man in either township. He, however, seems not to have been elated by his wealth, but scrupulously adhered to his plain old-fashioned way of living, and made no ostentatious display. He carefully maintained a concern for the institutions and principles of the Society of Friends, of which he was a member; and was for several years a clerk of the Monthly Meeting; afterward an overseer, and for twenty-five years an elder; he was the author of the original " Narrative of the Captivity of Benjamin Gilbert and Family by the Indians." He died the 14th of 5th mo. 1824, aged eighty-four years, and Lydia, his widow, died 2d mo. 23d, 1827. Children : Beulah, James, Martha, Phebe, Jabez, Josiah, Jason, Rebecca, Israel, Mary, Joseph Thornton, and Edmund.

(23.) REBECCA, daughter of (20) Benjamin, married Benjamin Kite. She died 12th mo. 20th, 1840.

(8.) *Daniel and Ann Walton's Children.*

(24.) DANIEL, married Elizabeth ——, and settled at Sandyford. Some of his descendants now live in Philadelphia.

(25) AARON, married Ann Thomas, and lived on the lower end of the old homestead, next to Samms's Corner. He died 12th mo. 19th, 1834. Children : Brazilla, Clifton, Maria, and Sindonia.

(26.) ANN, married John Cornell.

(13.) *Richard and Abigail Walton's Children.*

(27.) JOSEPH, married Deborah Lee. Children: Sarah, Abigail, Deborah, Asenath, Agnes, Ann, and John. He died 3d mo. 19th, 1821, aged 67; Deborah died in 1840.

(28.) BENJAMIN, died young.

(29.) ESTHER, married Ephraim Howell. Children: Joseph, Rebecca, Richard, Abigail, Mary, Ephraim, Elizabeth, and Deborah.

(25.) *Aaron and Ann Walton's Children.*

(30.) BRAZILLA, married Jane Feaster; died 12th mo. 27th, 1836.

(31.) CLIFTON, died 9th mo. 30th, 1838; unmarried.

(32.) MARIA, married Giles, son of Joseph T. Knight. Children: Abby Ann, and Grace.

(33.) SINDONIA, married David, son of David and Elizabeth Webster. Children: Aaron, Mary, Thomas, Byron, and Warren.

(1.) WILLIAM WALTON AND HIS DESCENDANTS.

(1.) WILLIAM, one of the four brothers, married Sarah Howell, 4th mo. 20th, 1689 (O. S.), and located near the present residence of Josiah Walton. He was the first preacher of Byberry Meeting after the Keithian separation, and continued the principal, if not the only one, for the next forty years. But little account of his religious labors has been preserved; but his ministry met with the approval of the Meeting, and he was recommended as a minister. In 1717, he visited all the families belonging to Byberry Meeting; and, in 1721, in company with Richard Busby, paid a religious visit to Maryland, Virginia, and Carolina. This gave great satisfaction to those visited, and on his return he produced several certificates from meetings visited, stating that they "felt great unity with his visit of love." He again visited the families of Byberry in 1723, and was then accompanied by Henry Comly. He died 12th mo. 9th, 1736-7 (O. S.), and left ten children: Rachel, Isaac, Jeremiah, Jacob, Sarah, William, Abel, Job, Hannah, and Mary. Although this family was so large, and many of their descendants still reside in Horsham, yet very few are now living within the vicinity of Byberry.

The name of William Walton has been so frequently adopted that it is amusing, without intending any disrespect, to note how the different men were designated. The first was William Walton, the preacher; besides him we have "William, Jr.; William Walton, Benjamin's son; William Walton, Isaac's son; William Walton, Job's son; William Walton, Abel's son; Billy Thornton Walton; Jersey Billy; Shoemaker Billy; Duke Billy; Pony Billy; Hector Billy; Billy Duke; Soldier Billy; Shoe. Billy's son Bill; Pony Billy's son Bill; and Hector Billy's son Bill."

(1.) *William and Sarah Walton's Children.*

(2.) ISAAC, left three children, William (Jersey Billy), Jacob, and Isaac.

(3.) JEREMIAH, married Elizabeth, daughter of Thomas Walmsley, and settled near Horsham. He died in 1741. Children: William, Thomas, Rachel, Jeremiah, Jacob, James, Mary, Sarah, Elizabeth, and Phebe. Most of the Waltons about Horsham are of this family.

(4.) WILLIAM, died unmarried.

(5.) ABEL, married Rebecca, daughter of Henry Walmsley, and lived near Somerton, where he died 12th mo. 25th, 1771. Children: Abel, Henry, and William.

(6.) JOB, married Agnes, daughter of Thomas Walmsley, and settled where Nathaniel Richardson now lives. He had a strong constitution and performed a great deal of hard work, yet did not get rich. He sometimes preached at Byberry. He died 4th mo. 16th, 1784. Children: Isaac, Sarah, Job, Isaiah, Thomas, Mary, William, and Elijah.

(7.) HANNAH, married, first, Thomas Walmsley, Jr., who was killed by being thrown from his horse, in 1728; second, Thomas Mardon, a tailor, "who had been purchased from off shipboard" by George James. As his time of servitude had not expired, his wife bought the remainder of his time. She died in 1741. Children: Rachel, Mary, Jacob, and Sarah.

(8.) MARY, married William Homer, and settled

near Willow Grove, where her descendants still reside.

(2.) *Isaac Walton's Children.*

(9.) WILLIAM (Jersey Billy), married (10) Massy Walton, descendant of (1) Daniel, by whom he had one son, Jacob. After her decease he married Rachel Atkinson, formerly Gilbert. He lived at one time in New Jersey, hence the name of "Jersey Billy." He was a strong man, and considered himself in his prime at 65. He probably had more enjoyment in catching "coons and wild pigeons," and sports of a similar character, than any other man in the township. He loved to converse upon his hunting adventures, and knew every place frequented by game in the vicinity. He shot the last bear killed in either township, in a large tree back of where George E. Weiss now lives. He died in 1807, aged 82 years. Child by last wife, William (Billy Broady).

(10.) ISAAC, married and settled in Buckingham, and was the father of Jacob and Benjamin of that place.

(3.) *Jeremiah and Elizabeth Walton's Children.*

(11.) WILLIAM, married and had seven children, all of whom, except one, died before they were seven years old.

(12.) THOMAS, married and settled at Horsham. Children: Jeremiah, Silas, Thomas, Phebe, and Elizabeth.

(13.) JEREMIAH, was a short fleshy man, and was

called "Chunky Jerry." He married and settled
in Upper Moreland. Children: Jesse, Jeremiah,
Elizabeth, Isaac, Joseph, and Jonathan.

(14.) JACOB, married and settled at Horsham.
Children: Isaiah and Charles.

(5.) *Abel and Rebecca Walton's Children.*

(15.) ABEL had eight children: Rebecca, Mary,
William, Abel, Jonathan, Elizabeth, Henry, and
Silas.

(16.) WILLIAM (Old Duke), married Mary Davis,
and settled in Byberry. Children: William (Young
Duke), Reese, Abel, and Job.

(6.) *Job and Agnes Walton's Children.*

(17.) ISAAC, married and settled on the York
Road, near the county line. He had one son, Jonathan, who married Hannah, daughter of Benjamin
Worthington, and had children: Josiah, Hannah,
and Agnes.

(18.) SARAH, married Jacob Tompkins, of Philadelphia.

(19.) JOB, married Margaret Powel, in 1763, and
settled in Middletown. They afterwards moved to
a farm on the York Road, near Hartsville, where
they ended their days. Children: Job and Isaac.

(20.) ISAIAH, married Sarah Pennington, and
resided in Bensalem, near the river. Children:
Isaiah, Mary, Jane, and Agnes.

(21.) THOMAS, married (21) Esther Walton, descendant of (1) Daniel, and resided on a farm now
owned by Isaac Tomlinson. He afterwards traded

this farm to Jacob Comly for a mill on the Pennypack Creek. Children : Solomon, Mary, Amelia,
Thomas, Rebecca, Keziah, Abiathar, and Asher.

(22.) MARY, married —— Lloyd. Children :
Martha and Samuel.

(23.) WILLIAM (Shoemaker Billy), married Mary
Search, and lived in Byberry. Children : William
(Old Boy), Elijah, Mary, Agnes, Amos, Christo-
pher, and Job.

(24.) ELIJAH, married and lived in Horsham.

(7.) *Hannah (Walton) Walmsley's Children.*

(25.) RACHEL, MARY, and JACOB died single.

(26.) SARAH, married Jonathan Wilson. Children :
Jacob, Rachel, and Sarah. Of these Jacob married
Rebecca Thomas, and inherited the homestead of
(1) William. Children : Ann, Mardon, Jonathan,
David, Robert, Ethan, Jabez, and Jehu T. Jacob
Wilson died 9th mo. 30th, 1814, and Rebecca, his
widow, 11th mo. 25th, 1842.

Sarah, daughter of Jonathan Wilson, married
Jesse Tomlinson, of Bensalem. She died 11th mo.
3d, 1849. Children : Jesse, Rhoda, and Charles.

(12.) *Thomas Walton's Children.*

(27.) SILAS, married Phebe, daughter of John
Parry. Children : Thomas, Margaret, and David.
Silas died 9th mo. 19th, 1824.

(28.) PHEBE, married Daniel Shoemaker, and
had three daughters, who severally married Joseph
Foulke, Salathiel Cleaver, and Nathan Cleaver.

(15.) *Abel Walton's Children.*

(29.) WILLIAM (Pony Billy), married Mary, daughter of Henry Ridge, and settled near the Cross-roads, in Byberry.

(30.) MARY, married John Sickel, and settled in Bensalem.

THE WORTHINGTON FAMILY.*

The WORTHINGTONS came originally from Lancashire, England. The first of them that emigrated to America were three brothers, John, Samuel, and Thomas, who reached Byberry in 1705. Two others, Daniel and Richard, are mentioned about the same period, but they were probably of a different family.

In the records of Abington Meeting, we find that "Daniel Worthington brought a certificate there for himself and wife from Philadelphia, 10th mo. 30th, 1728."

An old family record of Wrightstown states that Richard Worthington and wife were living there previous to 1750. They had children : Mahlon, born 12th mo. 19th, 1750, married Mary Paxson; John, born 9th mo. 21st, 1753, died in infancy; Joseph, born 9th mo. 19th, 1754, married Rebecca Willet; Mary, born 2d mo. 5th, 1756, married Matthew Wood; Thomas, born 7th mo. 4th, 1758, mar-

* I am indebted to Thomas Warner, of Wrightstown, for the greater part of the genealogy of this family.

ried Amy Paxson; Sarah, born 5th mo. 1st, 1760,
married John Wetherill; Elizabeth, born 1st mo.
4th, 1762, married Edmund Plumly; Tamor, born
10th mo. 20th, 1763, married Jesse Lacey; John,
born 8th mo. 1st, 1765; Hannah, born 5th mo. 18th,
1767, married Francis Hood; Letitia, born 4th mo.
18th, 1769, married Joseph Collins; William, born
4th mo. 8th, 1771, married —— Thorn; and Isaac,
born 1st mo. 20th, 1773, married Elizabeth Mar-
celius.

Besides Daniel and Richard, the record of Abington mentions the children of Thomas and Hannah Worthington as follows: Rebecca, born 1st
mo. 17th, 1752; John, born 9th mo. 1st, 1753; William, born 6th mo. 4th, 1755; Joseph, born 10th
mo. 28th, 1757; but no further account of them
has been found.

Thomas, one of the three brothers, was received
as a member by the Monthly Meeting of Friends,
at Buckingham and Wrightstown, in 1732. About
two years subsequently he obtained a certificate
to Abington Monthly Meeting. From 1733 to 1759
he was at Byberry. In the latter year he had a
difficulty with one Dunkin, but nothing further is
known of him.

Samuel, one of the three brothers, took a certificate for himself and wife to Abington, 10th mo.
28th, 1724. They had been lately married. They
settled in Byberry, where they remained until
1732. Some time after that they removed to the
Eastern Shore of Maryland, where they spent the
remainder of their days. It is said their descend-

ants have very much increased, and that one of
them was a member of Congress, and another a
Governor of ~~the~~ Ohio ~~Territory~~.

(1.) JOHN, the eldest of the three brothers, was
a weaver. He married Mary, daughter of Thomas
Walmsley, about 1720, and settled on property
since occupied by Joshua Worthington, in the
northern end of Byberry. He was an active member of Byberry Meeting, and was much respected.
His wife died 4th mo. 18th, 1754, and he died 1st
mo. 14th, 1777, aged about 80 years. Children :
Elizabeth, Mary, Thomas, Hannah, John, William,
Isaac, Joseph, Martha, Benjamin, and Esther.

(1.) *John and Mary Worthington's Children.*

(2.) ELIZABETH, born 1st mo. 15th, 1721, married
Joseph Tomlinson, in 1740. Children: Rebecca,
John, Thomas, Joseph, Francis, Mary, and Ben-
jamin.

(3.) MARY, born 12th mo. 9th, 1723–4; died
single.

(4.) THOMAS, born 2d mo, 2d, 1726, married Hannah Pritchet, and settled at Churchville, Southampton, Bucks County. He died 6th mo. 4th,
1798. Children: Joseph, Isaac, John, Thomas,
Amos, Nathan, Benjamin, William, Rebecca, and
one daughter.

(5.) HANNAH, born 12th mo. 7th, 1727–8.

(6.) JOHN, born 2d mo. 17th, 1730; died 6th mo.
20th, 1744.

(7.) WILLIAM, born 7th mo. 20th, 1732, married
Esther Homer, and settled near the forks of Nesh-

aminy, Bucks County. Children : Mary, William, Jesse, John, Esther, Benjamin, and Hiram.

(8.) Isaac, born 6th mo. 13th, 1735, married Martha, daughter of John Carver, of Buckingham. They settled near West Chester in 1783, and continued to reside there until his death, in 1800. Children : Mary, William, John, Amos, Elizabeth, Eber, and Joseph.

(9.) Joseph, born 6th mo. 12th, 1737, married, first, Esther Carver, in 1767, and settled in Warwick, Bucks County. Children : Joseph, who went to Virginia; and John, who went to Ohio. After Esther's death, he married Sarah Malone. Children : Abner and Sarah. After Sarah's death, he married Esther Kimble. Children : Anthony, William, Joel, Elisha, Amy, Jesse, and Isaac.

(10.) Martha, born 1st mo. 19th, 1740.

(11.) Benjamin, born 12th mo. 19th, 1742–3, married Sarah, daughter of Patrick Malone, and settled in Byberry. Children : Asa, John, James, Benjamin, Hannah, Mahlon, Joshua, Elizabeth, Enos, and Martha.

(12.) Esther, born 12th mo. 2d, 1749–50.

(7.) *William and Esther Worthington's Children.*

(13.) Mary, married Benjamin Smith. Children : Esther, who married Jonathan Atkinson ; and Mary, who married Henry Woodman.

(14.) William, married, first, —— Spencer. Children : William, Spencer, Asenath, and Margaret. He married, second, Mary Carver, and had one son, John C., who married Mary, daughter of William Yonker.

(15.) JESSE, married Martha Walton. Children : Jacob, William, Mary, Jesse, Chalkley, and Martha.

(16.) ESTHER, married a Spencer.

(17.) BENJAMIN, married Mary Welding. Children : Esther, who married Jonathan K. Bonham; Amasa, who married Amy Spencer; and Benjamin, who married Patience Heston.

(18.) HIRAM, married Agnes Walton. Children : Hiram, Susan, and Sarah.

(8.) *Isaac and Martha Worthington's Children.*

(19.) MARY, married Francis Tomlinson. Children : Tacy, who married John Roberts; and Martha, who married —— Twining.

(20.) WILLIAM, married Amy Underwood. Children : Martha, who married William Given ; John, who married Phebe Moore, and had children, William, Mary, Charles, Phebe, and Oliver; Eber, who married and resided in Philadelphia; and Charlotte, who married George W. Norris, and moved West.

(21.) JOHN, was a physician. He married Elizabeth Comly. Children : Lydia; Rachel, who married Amos Wilson, of Philadelphia; Robert; Jonathan; and Mary, who married Samuel Williams, of Philadelphia.

(22.) AMOS, born 9th mo. 2d, 1773, married Jane Taylor. Children : Isaac, who married Rebecca Newlin, and had children, John S., William N., and Harriet; John Taylor, who married Rachel

Watson, and had one son, Wilmer; Dr. Wilmer, who married Elizabeth Hemphill, and had children, William H., Ann Jane, Amos Edward, Emily E., Antoinette B., Malinda M., Kate D., and Caspar W.; Carver, who married Ruth Reed, and had children, Mary, Jane, Elizabeth, Henrietta M., and Antoinette B.; Malinda, who married John Marshall, and had children, Amos W., Thomas W., and Sarah Jane; Amos, who died young; and Lewis, who married Caroline Wilson, and had children, David W., Amos E., and Jane T. Amos died 1st mo. 3d, 1834, aged 61.

(23.) ELIZABETH, married, first, Jesse Roberts; second, Thomas Temple, but left no children.

(24.) EBER, married Lucy Patton. Children: Emily, who married William Siter, and had children, Wilmer W., Lucy W., John, Adam T., Eber W., Mary A., Harriet S., William, Emily, and Malinda; Harriet, who married Jesse Conard, and had children, Eber W., Sarah Ann, and Caroline; Francina, who married Daniel Buckwalter, and had children, Isaac B., William Siter, Eber W., and Francina.

(25.) JOSEPH, married Emeline Evans, of Norristown. Children: Sarah, who married Robert Chalfant, and had children, Emily S., William S., Lucy W., Mary Ann, Harriet S., Eliza R., Margaret C., and Jefferson W.; Jefferson, who married Ann Hernan, and had five children, Mary Ann, Charles M., Emily M., Rachel K., and William; Evans; Adaline; Eliza; and Joseph.

(9.) *Joseph and Sarah Worthington's Children.*

(26.) ABNER, married Abigail Walton. Children: Eber; Joseph; and Sarah, who married Ezra Walmsley.

(27.) SARAH, married John Tomlinson.

(9.) *Joseph and Esther Worthington's Children.*

(28.) ANTHONY, married Deborah Walton. Children: Joel, Anthony, Robert, Esther, and Ann.

(29.) JOEL, married Agnes Walton. Children: Abner, John, and two daughters.

(30.) AMY, married Evan Thomas, and had two daughters, one of whom married Eleazer Doan, and the other William Kirk.

(11.) *Benjamin and Sarah Worthington's Children.*

(31.) ASA, married Rebecca Subers. Children: Amos S., Adin, Ann, Chalkley, Asa, and Rebecca.

(32.) JOHN, married Sarah Walton. Children: Edward, who married Susan Singley; George, who married Harriet Comly; Melvina, who married Thomas Carter; Benjamin; Asenath; and Walton.

(33.) JAMES, married Ann Maclay, and had one son, Franklin.

(34.) BENJAMIN, married Ann Walton. Children: Amanda, Rebecca, Alfred, Abner, and Mary.

(35.) MAHLON, married Matilda Edwards. Children: Charles, Benjamin, and others.

(36.) HANNAH, married Jonathan Walton, and had several children.

(37.) JOSHUA, married Mary, daughter of John Tomlinson, and lived on the homestead in Byberry. Children : John, Spencer, Comly.

(38.) ENOS, married Sarah Heaton. Children : Thomas, Benjamin, Joshua, and one daughter.

(39.) MARTHA, married John Tomlinson.

THE TOMLINSON FAMILY.*

The earliest account of this family in Byberry is the record of the marriage of Thomas Tomlinson and Joan, daughter of Henry Walmsley, in 1719. They first settled on a farm back of Edge Hill, but afterwards sold the property and purchased a large farm in Bensalem, where he resided the remainder of his life. He died in 1764, and his widow Joan in 1772. Children: Henry, Elizabeth, Joseph, Thomas, Francis, Mary, and Rebecca.

(1.) *Thomas and Joan Tomlinson's Children.*

(2.) HENRY, born 11th mo. 16th, 1720, married Jemima Bolton, in 1753. At the death of his father, who died intestate, he being the eldest son secured all the real estate, thus leaving the rest of the children poor. He was a carpenter by trade, and frequently made plows, grain-cradles, &c. He died in 1800 much respected by his contemporaries. Jemima died in 1802. Children : Sarah, Jemima, and Jesse.

* The account of this family was furnished by Watson Comly of Byberry.

(3.) JOSEPH, born 10th mo. 13th, 1724, married Elizabeth, daughter of John and Mary Worthington, in 1740. Children: Rebecca, John, Thomas, Joseph, Francis, Mary, and Benjamin. Elizabeth died in 1761, and Joseph married Peggy McCann. The union being an unhappy one, they finally parted. Joseph died in 1793. Children: Keziah, Benjamin, Naomi, Phebe Ann, and Issachar. Of these, Benjamin married Betsy Carlisle, and moved to Delaware County.

(2.) *Henry and Jemima Tomlinson's Children.*

(4.) SARAH and JEMIMA died single.

(5.) JESSE, born 3d mo. 1st, 1766, married Sarah, daughter of Jonathan Wilson, in 1794, and settled on the homestead in Bensalem. He was a man of great physical endurance and was much respected. He died 10th mo. 27th, 1821. Children: Jesse, Rhoda, and Charles.

(3.) *Joseph and Elizabeth Tomlinson's Children.*

(6.) REBECCA, born 3d mo. 2d, 1745, married Andrew Singley, of White Sheet Bay, on the Delaware River. Andrew started a lumber yard, and although unacquainted with figures, was very successful in his business, and amassed a considerable estate. Rebecca died in 1791. Children: Elizabeth, Catharine, Mary, John, Joseph, Andrew, Rebecca, Phebe, and Jemima.

(7) JOHN, born 1st mo. 26th, 1748, married Phebe, daughter of Patrick Malone, in 1773. Several

years afterwards he purchased a farm of Amos Simpson, near Bustleton, where he resided the remainder of his life. He was a very quiet man, and by industry and good management acquired a large estate. Their children: William, John, Sarah, Elizabeth, Benjamin, James, Mary, and Thomas.

(8.) THOMAS, born 2d mo. 21st, 1747, married Phebe, daughter of Isaac Carver, in 1775. They lived for forty years on a farm back of Smithfield, which belonged to Silas Walmsley, but they never accumulated much property. Their children: Elizabeth, Phebe, Martha, Isabel, Joseph, John, Amos, Isaac, Francis, Thomas, and Silas.

(9.) JOSEPH, married Mary, widow of Benjamin Taylor, and daughter of Isaac Carver. He died in 1792, leaving no issue.

(10.) FRANCIS, born 8th mo. 8th, 1753, lived near the Forks of Neshaminy. He married, and had children,—Tacy, who married John Roberts, and Elizabeth, who married William Tomlinson.

(11.) MARY, born 6th mo. 22d, 1755, married James Malone, and settled near West Chester.

(12.) BENJAMIN, born 4th mo. 25th, 1758, died 3d mo. 22d, 1775.

Andrew and (6) Rebecca Singley's Children.

(13.) ELIZABETH, married Daniel Osmond. Children: Rebecca, who married John Osmond; Mary, who married Daniel Stevenson; and Sarah, who married Elisha Newbold.

(14.) CATHARINE, married John Hill, and lived near the Red Lion. They had one daughter.

(15.) MARY, married Abraham Vansant. Children : John and Alonzo.

(16.) JOHN, married Sarah, daughter of William Walton (Jersey Billy). They had one child, Hannah, who married John Lippincott.

(17.) JOSEPH, married Esther, daughter of Thomas Knight. They had two daughters.

(18.) ANDREW, married Mary, daughter of John Edwards. They had children : Amos, Ellen, Susan, Edward, Joseph, Andrew, and Mary.

(19.) REBECCA, married Joseph Rees. Children : William, Mary, Phebe, John, Catharine, Charles, and George.

(20.) PHEBE, married, first, Robert Ervin, and had two sons, Andrew and William. She married, second, John Price, and had one daughter.

(21.) JEMIMA, married Moses Davis. Children : William, and others.

(7.) *John and Phebe Tomlinson's Children.*

(22.) WILLIAM, married Martha, daughter of Benjamin Taylor and granddaughter of Isaac Carver, and settled in Byberry. They had children : Mary, Aaron, John, James, Silas, Benjamin, Phebe, William, and Isaac.

(23.) JOHN, married Sarah, daughter of Joseph Worthington. Children : William, Mary, Sarah, Joseph, and Jason. John died 1st mo. 21st, 1841.

(24.) SARAH and ELIZABETH died single.

(25.) BENJAMIN, married Asenath, daughter of Joseph Walton, but had no children.

(26.) JAMES, married Tacy, daughter of James Carter.

(27.) MARY, married Joshua Worthington, and settled on the old Worthington homestead, in Byberry. Children : John, Comly, and Spencer.

(28.) THOMAS, married Ann, daughter of Joseph Walton. They have children : Watson, Spencer, John, Isaac, and Lydia Ann.

(8.) *Thomas and Phebe Tomlinson's Children.*

(29.) ELIZABETH, married Benjamin Field. Children : Robert, Phebe, Thomas, Tomlinson, Isaac, Mary, Benjamin, and James.

(30.) PHEBE, married James Carter. Children : Mordecai, Tacy, Emily, Stephen, Thomas, Mary, James, and William.

(31.) JOSEPH, married Elizabeth Twining. Children : James, Caroline, Hannah. Thomas, and Joseph.

(32.) ISABELLA, died single.

(33.) THOMAS, married Rebecca Twining. Children : Elizabeth, Emmor, Mordecai, Abner, Hannah, Phebe, Thomas, James, and Rebecca.

(34.) ISAAC, married Mary Dewees. Children : Samuel, Aaron, Rebecca, Carver, Susannah, Comly, Chalkley, Thomas, and Sarah.

(35.) JOHN, married Martha Worthington. Children : Ezra, Hannah, Wilmer, Francis, and Stephen. He died 4th mo. 5th, 1846.

(36.) FRANCIS, married Deborah Twining. Children : Edward, Hannah, Phebe, Deborah, and Francis. He died 5th mo. 2d, 1825.

(37.) MARTHA, married John Praul. Children: Isaac, Thomas, William, Francis, Elias, and Philip.

(38.) AMOS, married Caroline Praul. Children: Rebecca, Charles, Francis, Edward, and Amanda. He died 1st mo. 31st, 1841.

(39.) SILAS, unmarried.

THE SHEARER FAMILY.*

JACOB SHEARER emigrated to America from Berne, Switzerland. He died prior to the Revolution, and left seven children: Jacob, known as Jacob Shearer, Sr., Jonathan, Henry, William, Catharine, Mary, and Elizabeth.

JACOB SHEARER, SR., was born in Moreland, in the year 1755. At the commencement of the Revolution he entered the Continental Army as a private, but was afterwards made a captain, in which capacity he served until the close of the war. He was in several minor engagements, also in the Battle of Germantown. Throughout the whole struggle, he steadily relied on the success of the American army, even amid its most discouraging reverses, and his sword, now in the possession of his grandson, Jacob Shearer, bears this motto on its blade, "The Got whome we serve is able to deliver us." During the war he casually formed the acquaint-

* I am indebted to Charles S. Keyser, Esq., of Philadelphia, for the account of this family.

ance of Lafayette, by whom he was pleasantly remembered on the return of "the nation's guest" to this country in 1824. He was accustomed to relate to his children many anecdotes in connection with this acquaintance. Jacob Shearer was elected a member of the Pennsylvania House of Representatives, in 1805, and continued in that office until 1811. In 1814 he was elected to the Pennsylvania Senate, where he served until 1817. He held several other offices, among which was that of County Commissioner. He resided during the greater part of his life on his farm above Bustleton, where he died in 1837, aged 82 years.

He was three times married. His first wife was Mary, daughter of Jeremiah Northrop; she died soon after her marriage without issue. He then married her sister, Sarah Northrop, by whom he had three children, Elizabeth, John, and Jacob. His third wife was Rachel, daughter of John de Nyce, by whom he had three children, Jane, Susan, and Ann.

ELIZABETH, married Jesse Randall, and died soon after her marriage, leaving one child, Comly Randall, still living.

JOHN, married Mary Jane Wright, of Philadelphia, and emigrated to Illinois, where he now resides. Children: Jacob, deceased; John, Edward, Sarah, deceased; Mary, deceased; and Ann, deceased.

JONATHAN, the second son, resided also in Moreland, and left children: Sarah, Elizabeth, Rebecca, Mary Ann, Catharine, Amanda, and Emeline.

HENRY, left three daughters and one son, Joseph, who emigrated with John Shearer to Illinois, and died at Kaskaskia.

WILLIAM, married Eliza Maris, niece of Rachel de Nyce, and left five children : Caroline, deceased; Anna, Catharine, deceased; William, deceased; and Eliza.

CATHARINE, died unmarried.

MARY, married —— Scates, and had three children : Alexander, Sarah, deceased; and the third, who died young.

ELIZABETH, married —— Schock, and had four children.

JACOB SHEARER, JR., inherited the qualities of his father, and became prominent early in life as a politician. Few things indeed transpired in the townships without being more or less influenced by him. After serving in all the township offices, such as supervisor, assessor, school director, &c., he was elected to the Pennsylvania Legislature, where he acquired considerable reputation for his sound judgment. On the rise of the Native American party he was by them nominated as a candidate for Congress, but was defeated by Charles J. Ingersoll. After this he withdrew from the active field of politics. He married Margaret Pitman, of the Baldwin family, and settled on the old homestead in Moreland, where he spent his whole life. He died in 1854, leaving five children : Josephine, Martha, Susan, Jacob, and Margaret.

JANE, married Jesse Dungan, and resided in Bustleton. She had children : Joseph, Jacob S., Caroline, deceased; Alfred; Charles, deceased; and Edward, deceased.

SUSAN, married Joseph Keyser, of the Germantown family. She has children: Charles S., William F., Caroline, Martha Jane, deceased, and Joseph, deceased.

ANN, married John Vansant. She has children: Ann, deceased, Edward, Joseph, William Henry, Robert, and John.

CONCLUSION.

THE history of Byberry and Moreland is now completed. It would be folly for us to expect it to be free from errors, for it has been obtained almost entirely from old manuscripts, some of which were not easily deciphered; yet nothing has been inserted unless there was a strong probability of its truth; and we think it will be found as reliable as any similar production heretofore published.

The preparation of this history was commenced many months since, but the difficulties attending its compilation were so great that we often despaired of ever completing it.

The cares and perplexities of business were so manifold, that nothing but an ardent attachment to our native place, its people, and its institutions, could have induced us to deny ourselves the many hours of needed recreation and even of sleep that were necessary to work the matter into its present condition. But this has been done; and now that the toil is over, we can revert with satisfaction to the many pleasant hours which we have thus spent in looking over the records of bygone times, and tracing the pages written by hands long since mingled with the dust. From these we have learned some of the many difficulties attending the early settlement, and can picture to ourselves the destitute condition of those primitive settlers who left comfortable homes in Old England and came over here to reclaim the uncultivated wilds of America. We have traced their history as generation succeeded generation, carefully noting the improvements which from time to time were introduced, the rise and progress of their religious institutions, and the introduction of schools and societies for the diffusion of learning,—that talisman which so effectually dispels the dark and dangerous clouds of error and superstition. We have viewed them almost in a state of semi-barbarism, living the lives of the savages around them, and we have watched them emerging from this condition as each succeeding generation became better and better acquainted with the teachings of science and reason, until now they stand confessedly in the first ranks of an enlightened people, with institutions in their midst which, we trust, will forever dispel all dreams of witchcraft and similar follies, and leave the human mind to be guided by the light of truth and religion. It has been under a government—the best the world ever saw—that our forefathers of Byberry and Moreland have been so prosperous and happy; and that that government may continue in all its glory and efficiency, so that the sons and daughters of these lovely districts may, for all time to come, bask in the sunshine of peace and prosperity, under the benign influence of this republic, is the earnest wish of the author.

www.ingramcontent.com/pod-product-compliance
Lightning Source LLC
Chambersburg PA
CBHW030904270326
41929CB00008B/576